T0327979

"In this important new update to the debate on power and the Christian life, a generous but sharp-minded dialogue between top scholars will help the confused and the curious understand what's at stake in the means and the aims of just and unjust peace. For both the initiate and the expert, here is a model in tone and a rigor in content that will leave you wishing for more."

Robert J. Joustra, associate professor of politics and international studies at Redeemer University

"Key to understanding one's own views on a subject is the requirement that one charitably considers legitimate alternatives. These four authors reliably map the terrain on war, peace, and violence in a way that will help readers sort out their own views on these perennial topics. Alas, given the tragic state of our fallen world, this is a much-needed volume."

C. Ben Mitchell, Graves Professor of Moral Philosophy at Union University

"Like a thorn in the flesh of our conscience, war demands our attention. Reflection on war reveals the inadequacy of simplistic thinking and unsettles easy assumptions about the correspondence between theology and moral life. Thinking particularly of our nation's warfighters and especially in light of our deepening understanding of moral injury—crippling degrees of shame or remorse born of believing you have done evil—it is critical that Christians think rightly about war. The four viewpoints in this book—sometimes overlapping yet distinct in essential ways—offer a crucial overview of the best of Christian thought on war and peace."

Marc LiVecche, McDonald Distinguished Scholar in Ethics, War, and Public Life at Christ Church, Oxford University, and executive editor of *Providence: A Journal of Christianity & American Foreign Policy*

"In *War, Peace, and Violence,* Paul Copan assembles a sample of scholars committed to robust defenses of divergent views on the believer's right response to a fallen and violent world. Remarkably, in an age of polarized vitriol, the four authors—representing not only competing Christian traditions but also quite distinct disciplines—demonstrate in their arguments rigor and charity in equal measure. What results is an excellent primer on the current state of a long intrafaith debate over how to hold together our faith and the competing interests shaping the interstate system."

Joshua Hastey, assistant professor in the Robertson School of Government at Regent University and fleet professor of strategy for the US Naval War College

"*War, Peace and Violence: Four Christian Views* is a very helpful survey of the key positions in this still very relevant subject. The contributors represent their views clearly and well, and the counterarguments are done with respect for the positions with which each disagrees. I highly recommend this for anyone interested in how to think well about war and peace from within a distinctively Christian worldview."

Scott Rae, professor of Christian ethics at Talbot School of Theology, Biola University

SPECTRUM MULTIVIEW BOOKS

WAR, PEACE, AND VIOLENCE

FOUR CHRISTIAN VIEWS

EDITED BY PAUL COPAN

WITH CONTRIBUTIONS FROM
Eric Patterson, Myles Werntz,
A. J. Nolte, *and* Meic Pearse

Academic
An imprint of InterVarsity Press
Downers Grove, Illinois

InterVarsity Press
P.O. Box 1400 | Downers Grove, IL 60515-1426
ivpress.com | email@ivpress.com

InterVarsity Press® is the publishing division of InterVarsity Christian Fellowship/USA®. For more information, visit intervarsity.org.

All Scripture quotations, unless otherwise indicated, are taken from the New American Standard Bible®, copyright 1960, 1962, 1963, 1968, 1971, 1972, 1973, 1975, 1977, 1995, 2020 by The Lockman Foundation. Used by permission.

The publisher cannot verify the accuracy or functionality of website URLs used in this book beyond the date of publication.

Cover design and image composite: Kate Irwin
Interior design: Daniel van Loon

ISBN 978-1-5140-0234-6 (print) | ISBN 978-1-5140-0235-3 (digital)

Printed in the United States of America ♾

Library of Congress Cataloging-in-Publication Data
Names: Copan, Paul, editor.
Title: War, peace, and violence: four Christian views / edited by Paul
    Copan.
Description: Downers Grove, IL : IVP Academic , [2022] | Includes
    bibliographical references and index.
Identifiers: LCCN 2022019828 (print) | LCCN 2022019829 (ebook) | ISBN
    9781514002346 (print) | ISBN 9781514002353 (digital)
Subjects: LCSH: War–Religious aspects–Christianity. | Just war doctrine.
    | Violence–Religious aspects–Christianity. | Peace–Religious
    aspects–Christianity.
Classification: LCC BT736.2 .W3465 2022 (print) | LCC BT736.2 (ebook) |
    DDC 261.8/73–dc23/eng/20220608
LC record available at https://lccn.loc.gov/2022019828
LC ebook record available at https://lccn.loc.gov/2022019829

28   27   26   25   24   23   22 | 8   7   6   5   4   3   2   1

To Vic Copan,

who is my dear brother by birth and by faith,

and who served as an excellent colleague

at Palm Beach Atlantic University for eighteen years.

Psalm 133:1

Contents

Preface

About forty years ago, InterVarsity Press published Robert G. Clouse's edited book *War: Four Christian Views* (1981). The evangelical Protestant contributors included Herman Hoyt, Myron Augsburger, Arthur Holmes, and Harold Brown. They represented, respectively, the positions of nonresistance, pacifistic, just war, and preventive war. I picked up this book in seminary. I found the multiple-views format a useful, thought-provoking exchange on the complexities and challenges Christians must contemplate concerning war.

The book was published during the Cold War, and the book's content seemed all the more relevant to me. My mother was born in Latvia and my father in "the Ukraine," as we called it back then. Along with relatives on both sides of my family, my parents endured the travails, ravages, and losses of World War II Europe and the scourge of Soviet communism. My paternal grandfather died in February 1932 as a result of starvation in a Soviet labor camp during the Ukrainian Holodomor. Because of the war, my father would be torn away from his remaining family—his mother and brother—whom he would not see again. To avoid the advancing Soviet army, he would eventually make his way to Germany on foot—a harrowing journey. My mother survived the bombing of Berlin, and my maternal grandmother ("Oma") narrowly escaped death in Bitterfeld, Germany: during a trip to the outhouse, an Allied plane dropped a bomb on the vacated house in which my grandmother was temporarily staying. Two of my great-aunts and one of my great-uncles endured the Allied bombing of Dresden.

My parents were ever grateful for the United States not only as a land of opportunity but also as a haven of political freedom and general tranquility. My parents would express their gratitude to the United States for its military involvement in the war that helped free Western Europe from Nazi tyranny, and they rejoiced to see day the Soviet Union collapsed along with its Eastern Bloc satellite states, symbolized by the fall of the Berlin Wall.

Though the Cold War ended, new threats have emerged. We all have been horrified by the emerging phenomenon of terrorist attacks and the dangers they posed, given their asymmetrical, indiscriminate, and destabilizing nature—that is, unauthorized individuals or groups engaging in "unconventional" actions against nation-states; making no combatant-civilian distinctions; and creating a sense of terror that leaves citizens feeling vulnerable and helpless while disrupting civic order, commerce, and even leisure activities.[1]

Some of these attacks include the first World Trade Center attack (1993), the Khobar Towers (1996), September 11 (2001), and the Paris attacks (2015). Also, in addition to Russia's takeover of eastern Ukraine (2014) and China's military buildup and its ongoing threat against Taiwan and in the South China Sea, war has come to Kuwait, the Balkans, Rwanda, Iraq, and Afghanistan—and this is just a sampling. Terrorist groups like al-Qaeda, Boko Haram, ISIS, Hezbollah, and Iran's Quds Force continue as pernicious threats and regularly make news headlines. And more recently (August 2021), with the United States' precipitous withdrawal from Afghanistan, the Taliban have reasserted their brutal reign of terror there. Half a year later, Russia invaded Ukraine, and—like my father—some of my Ukrainian relatives have had to flee to the West for safety.

We could add further developments such as surveillance capacities, competition over satellites in space, drone warfare, "enhanced interrogation techniques" (e.g., waterboarding), and more.

In light of the four decades since InterVarsity Press published Clouse's four-views book, it seemed good to IVP Academic and to me that an updated multiple-views book on war and peace be published.

---

[1]Thanks to Daryl Charles for this summary on the essence of terrorism. Michael Walzer lays out the purpose of terrorism: "to destroy the morale of a nation or a class, to undercut its solidarity; [terrorism's] method is the random murder of innocent people. Randomness is the crucial feature of terrorist activity. If one wishes fear to spread and intensify over time, it is not desirable to kill specific people identified in some particular way with a regime, a party, or a policy. Death must come by chance." *Just and Unjust Wars* (New York: Basic Books, 1977), 197.

I am grateful to my longtime friend and previous publisher at IVP, Jeff Crosby, for his enthusiasm about this project, and to IVP editor Jon Boyd and his wise guidance and encouragement as this book proceeded from proposal to publication. Thanks to Rebecca Carhart for her editorial involvement in this process as well. I am grateful for Jonathan Cooper, who worked on the indexes.

I dedicate this book to my beloved brother, both by birth and rebirth, Vic Copan—a lifelong friend and, for eighteen years, a dedicated and faithful colleague at Palm Beach Atlantic University. Though I am a just war proponent and he is a pacifist, "behold, how good and how pleasant it is for brothers to live together in unity!" (Ps 133:1).

Introduction

Dirty Hands?

PAUL COPAN

In keeping with other movies in the Bourne series, *The Bourne Legacy* (2012) is not only fast-paced and intense but also features a collection of various corrupt government-agency officials in the CIA and the US Senate desperate to shut down various "black ops"—covert operations. They do so in response to information leaks that threaten to expose both these officials and their dubious methods, including their claims to "plausible deniability." The cut-throat Colonel Eric Byer (played by Edward Norton) heads this clean-up operation and demands not only shutting down ops like Treadstone or Blackbriar but also eliminating any agents involved, including this particular movie's hero, Aaron Cross.

Partway through the film, a subordinate questions Byer's ruthless methods. Byer defends his methods by issuing this stern lecture in response:

> Do you know what a sin-eater is? That's what we are. We are the sin-eaters. It means that we take the moral excrement that we find in this equation, and we bury it down deep inside of us so that the rest of our cause can stay pure. That is the job. We are morally indefensible and absolutely necessary.[1]

This brings us to important questions for Christians. Without endorsing Byer's brutal order to assassinate agents on the field as part of the shutdown

---

[1] *The Bourne Legacy*, directed by Tony Gilroy (Universal City, CA: Universal Pictures, 2012). For the sake of readability, I have slightly modified the transcript's formatting, though without word alteration. Subslikescript, "The Bourne Legacy (2012)—Full Transcript," https://subslikescript.com /movie/The_Bourne_Legacy-1194173.

operation, we can acknowledge inevitable tensions and perhaps no-win situations in warfare and policing situations. No matter how just sounding the reasons for killing might be, some Christians will insist it is merely doing evil that good may come (Rom 3:8). The killing of any person—even in self-defense—does not leave one guiltless.

This brings us to the notion of "dirty hands"—a tradition that can be traced back to the sixteenth century, with the publication of Niccolò Machiavelli's book *The Prince* (*Il Principe*). Most people interpret Machiavelli as advocating the politician's compromise of moral standards—that doing evil is justifiable in order to achieve "the greater good" for society. Contrary to popular belief, however, Machiavelli was not denying objective moral standards or the reality of evil. However, in cases of supreme emergency, those in power may need to dirty their hands because there simply is no way out of their tragic dilemma. Guilt is simply unavoidable.[2]

So what about killing a home intruder in self-defense to prevent him from raping or kidnapping or murdering household members? Wouldn't a Christian who kills the intruder be exonerated in God's sight? After all, many human judges would rule in favor of the homeowner in such an attack. And doesn't the Old Testament law permit it (Ex 22:2-3)?

Noted New Testament scholar (and my former professor) Scot McKnight rightly insists that "Jesus is the one to whom we listen."[3] The point of Jesus' countercultural teaching in the Sermon on the Mount is "to *avoid violence, absorb injustice*, and *live in light of what the kingdom is like* in spite of what the world is like now."[4] What does he think about "just" killing? He says this: "I've been asked time and time again these two questions: Do you think the entire country should demilitarize? (What the country does is the country's *business*. As a citizen I advocate following Jesus.) What about a person who invades your home? (I'd use force to the point of not murdering him.)"[5] McKnight rejects the distinction of the just war theorist that, while

---

[2]See Giovanni Giorgini, "Machiavelli on Good and Evil: The Problem of Dirty Hands Revisited," in *Machiavelli on Liberty and Conflict*, ed. David Johnston, Nadia Urbinati, and Camila Vergara (Chicago: University of Chicago Press, 2017), 58-86.

[3]Scot McKnight, *The Sermon on the Mount*, Story of God Commentary (Grand Rapids, MI: Zondervan, 2013), 131.

[4]McKnight, *Sermon on the Mount*, 131.

[5]McKnight, *Sermon on the Mount*, 131.

all murder is killing, not all killing is murder. The British philosopher Elizabeth Anscombe argued that a pacifist is unable to distinguish between the shedding of *innocent* blood and the shedding of *any* blood.[6] But for Mc-Knight, *all* killing is murder, even if one might allow for degrees of culpability in cases of self-defense or killing to protect innocent victims.

The famed theologian of the cross Jürgen Moltmann takes a slightly different view. He gives the example of a bus driver who suddenly goes mad and drives toward the precipice. What to do? Moltmann claims that it may be "unavoidable" to not only disable but perhaps to kill the bus driver. After all, "doing nothing would have meant being responsible for the deaths of many people." However, in itself, "such an act of violence cannot be approved [guilt is still incurred], but it can be answered for. Responsible action in such cases demands a love that is ready to incur guilt in order to save."[7]

He goes beyond this. He states that in the case of violent people who have exhausted all options and steadfastly refused attempts at mutual respect, shared power, and so on, then "counterviolence is often the only remedy."[8] Yet Moltmann insists that the "spilling of innocent blood should never be tolerated if it can be avoided."[9] Even in such extreme circumstances, however, those engaging in this virtuous "counterviolence" nevertheless incur guilt.[10]

FOUR VIEWS

As Christ's appointed peacemakers and messengers of reconciliation, what does the Lord require of us? How should we respond to violence—including terrorism—that threatens communities, countries, and large regions of the world? What does it mean for Christians to live as citizens of heaven, citizens within our own respective earthly countries, and members of an international community? When it comes to war or policing, can one truly love

---

[6]G. E. M. Anscombe, "War and Murder," in *War, Morality, and the Military Profession*, ed. Malham M. Wakin (Boulder, CO: Westview, 1979), 294.

[7]Jürgen Moltmann, *The Experiment Hope* (1975; repr., Eugene, OR: Wipf & Stock, 2003), 142.

[8]Moltmann, *The Experiment Hope*, 135.

[9]Moltmann, *The Experiment Hope*, 97.

[10]See Paul Parker, "An Evangelical Assessment of Jürgen Moltmann's Ethics," in *Jürgen Moltmann and Evangelical Theology: A Critical Engagement*, ed. Sung Wook Chung (Eugene, OR: Wipf & Stock, 2012), 232-33.

one's enemies when resorting to (potentially) lethal force to take their lives, even if the intent is to protect innocents? Should enhanced interrogation techniques such as waterboarding be utilized to extract information from those threatening large-scale violence? Does the use of lethal force actually reflect the spirit of our self-sacrificing, life-surrendering Savior? And what were the disciples doing with swords in their possession if Jesus was so clear about nonviolence (Lk 22:35-38)? These are important questions worthy of a discussion in a book such as this.

N. T. Wright observes that the desire that the state protect innocent citizens and punish criminals is a "basic, and correct, human instinct."[11] But what view should Christians take on these issues? This book presents four positions, which do have some overlapping concerns and approaches.

Just war. Just war thinking in the Christian tradition began to take shape in the fourth century—namely, with Ambrose of Milan and his pupil Augustine. Though many Christians throughout the century have believed that just war is compatible with the Christian faith, its principles are more basic, being rooted in "natural law" or the world's basic moral framework. Christians have typically maintained that these principles are rooted in the character and commands of God, who has made human beings in his image. Thus, the Roman statesman Cicero (106–43 BC) articulated key themes of just war in his *De officiis* (*On Moral Duties*), in which he said that the rights of war should be strictly observed—including noncombatant immunity, using proportional means, and so forth.

Just war scholar Eric Patterson defends the Christian articulation of the classic just war principles, leading off with reflections and illustrations from C. S. Lewis, who had himself fought in World War I. Patterson distinguishes between *just* and *unjust* coercive force—similar to the difference between shedding *any* blood and shedding *innocent* blood.

Just war criteria divide into three categories: *jus ad bellum* (the justice of war), *jus in bello* (justice during war), and *jus post bellum* (justice after war). Patterson categorizes these criteria as follows:[12]

---

[11]N. T. Wright, *Romans Part 2: Chapters 9–16*, Paul for Everyone (Louisville, KY: Westminster John Knox, 2004), 85.

[12]Eric Patterson, "Just War Theory and Terrorism," *Providence*, November 30, 2016, 38-44. Available at https://providencemag.com/2016/11/just-war-theory-terrorism/.

Jus ad bellum

- *Legitimate authority:* Supreme political authorities are morally responsible for the security of their constituents and therefore are obligated to make decisions about war and peace.

- *Just cause:* Self-defense of citizens' lives, livelihoods, and way of life are typically *just causes*; more generally speaking, the cause is likely *just* if it rights a past wrong, punishes wrongdoers, or prevents further wrong.

- *Right intent:* Political motivations are subject to ethical scrutiny; violence intended for the purpose of order, justice, and ultimate conciliation is just, whereas violence for the sake of hatred, revenge, and destruction is not just.

- *Likelihood of success:* Political leaders should consider whether their action will make a difference in real-world outcomes. This principle is subject to context and judgment, because it may be appropriate to act despite a low likelihood of success (e.g., against local genocide). Conversely, it may be inappropriate to act due to low efficacy despite the compelling nature of the case.

- *Proportionality of ends:* Does the preferred outcome justify, in terms of the cost in lives and material resources, this course of action?

- *Last resort:* Have traditional diplomatic and other peaceable efforts been reasonably employed in order to avoid outright bloodshed?

Jus in bello

- *Proportionality:* Are the battlefield tools and tactics employed proportionate to battlefield objectives?

- *Discrimination:* Has care been taken to reasonably protect the lives and property of legitimate noncombatants?

Jus post bellum

- *Order:* After war, establishing and ensuring domestic and international security as well as proper governance is critical.

- *Justice:* What just punishments and restitution are called for?

- *Conciliation:* How can both parties imagine and move together toward a shared future?

Again, the aim of a just war is cessation of hostilities, pursuing a fair peace, and helping establish a stable government. This postwar state involves conciliation and healing. Patterson argues that Christians can have a role not only in this final stage but *throughout* the entire process of contemplating war and engaging in it.

Nonviolence. The Christian nonviolence view (which has also been called "pacifism") is actually a cluster of variegated positions, but they all assume that the killing of humans conflicts with the gospel of Jesus Christ. The particular position defended by theologian Myles Werntz further argues that a properly Christian response to international conflict depends on the prior groundwork of Christian nonviolence.

Werntz lays out four central principles that set forth a robust vision for his position:

1. *The taking of life in war is incompatible with the Christian life.* Although certain Old Testament passages may be a challenge for Christian pacifists to navigate, they focus on the peacemaking message and example of Jesus. Pacifism is intrinsic to the Christian faith, they argue, and we are to read those challenging biblical texts according to Christ, in whose new economy killing is a contradiction.

2. *The refusal to take life in war does not mean abandoning the good of the world.* Some Anabaptists have emphasized how preserving societal order and some uses of force need not conflict with the refusal to take life. Pursuit of peacemaking through nonviolent means has a track record of resolving conflict without larger-scale military action. The call to suffering, praying for enemies, and trusting in God are included in seeking the good of the world.

3. *The commitment to pacifism is not solely about fulfilling a command but also about entering into a life of discipleship and virtue.* A person may refuse to fight another person in battle, but this may be due simply to lack of courage rather than principle or conviction. Christian discipleship requires courage and brings with it its own share of burdens— peacemaking and reconciliation included. As Jesus himself illustrates, the virtuous path is no guarantee to living an enemy-free life.

4. *Christian pacifism refuses an ultimate divide between the private and public.* If a Christian ends up serving in some official capacity, this does

not create a new or different measure for Christian discipleship. To be a Christian in the military in particular entails a logical disaster; it makes for a bifurcated morality that undermines the believer's pursuit of integrity.

This position of pacifism cannot be called "quietism." It is a matter of Christian nonviolent peacemaking—a position that can be grounded in the biblical text, theological considerations such as the doctrine of creation, and ethnographic study. Faithfulness to Christ rather than to earthbound criteria of success is to be the believer's ultimate concern.

Nonviolence can speak to the issue of terrorism by focusing on avenues of interpersonal peacemaking and proactive addressing of the conditions that foster conflict. Using techniques of interreligious dialogue, coalition building, capacity-building for different constituencies within a country, and international aid, nonviolence seeks to address the roots of political violence in a multifaceted way.

Christian realist. A standard, third alternative to just war and nonviolence has been the political realist position. This realpolitik position is commonly associated with the thinking of theologian Reinhold Niebuhr (1892–1971), whose view emerged in strong opposition to Nazism as well as America's position of isolationism in light of the danger that Nazism posed.

He took a pragmatic or consequentialist view on the use of force, attempting to steer between pacifism and the "rules" guiding just war theory. This realist school of thinking concerns international relations as well as domestic policies. Formative thinkers in this movement were Hans Morganthau and E. H. Carr—and in our day, Stephen Walt, Daniel Byman, and John Mearsheimer. This school of post–World War II thought is another key voice in the discussion because of the significance and influence of its ideas, because of its examination of how realism and just war thinking interact, and because of the great failure of liberal "idealism" to realistically address international affairs in the 1920s, 1930s, and 1940s.[13]

A. J. Nolte, a professor of politics and international relations, articulates a view that comes as close to this political realist position as possible while remaining true to an authentically Christian tradition. After all, thinkers

---

[13]Thanks to J. Daryl Charles for his input on this point.

like Waltz, Walt, and Mearsheimer ("neorealists") make clear that their position *cannot* be harmonized with the Christian faith at all. They fundamentally reject the notion that determinations of war and peace are moral in any sense. Rather, they see it as similar to solving a mathematical equation or testing an economic-scientific model.

By contrast, earlier thinkers in this tradition—Reinhold Niebuhr and Morgenthau, for example—took a different view. Yes, they argued, war is indeed a dirty business—the dirty-hands concept mentioned above—but it still needs to be undertaken. And unlike more recent neorealist realpolitik thinkers, both Niebuhr and Morgenthau understood their project quite explicitly as having moral content—meaning you can actually meaningfully engage their thought on the basis of Christian theology and moral reasoning. Nolte's essay reflects this essentially Niebuhrian view, though it overlaps with Morgenthau's. And though an Anglican, Nolte draws on the resources of Eastern Orthodox thought on the subject of war and peace.

Church historical. Church historian Meic Pearse argued in his 2007 book *The Gods of War* (also with InterVarsity Press) that both the just war and pacifist views—however well-intentioned—are untenable. Drawing on his perspective as a church historian, he follows three main theses.

First, the Christianized just war position assumes a view about how society as a whole should be run, but such a view is wholly contrary to the Christianity of the first three centuries prior to Constantine's rise to power (AD 312). And across history, *both* sides in most wars have claimed that their cause is just (just cause, just intent, and lawful declaration—*jus ad bellum*), which leads to skepticism of the worth of such criteria. And, historically, virtually no purported "just war" has actually been fought according to the *jus in bello* criteria of proportionality and noncombatant immunity.

Second, although Christian pacifism ("nonviolence") has much to commend it, this position comes to grief when fearful violence threatens, say, women and children and it is within the pacifist's power to stop violent attacks. Such pacifist principles look like moral narcissism, as pacifism apparently hands the world over to those evil persons and nations most prone to inflict violence on the innocent.

Third, war is a radical, inescapable evil that pulls all of its participants into the vortex of ever-deepening wickedness. Those hoping to avoid participation invariably get sucked in as well. Despite attempts to constrain evil or, according to the utopian vision, utterly expunge it from the world, all such peaceable efforts will have intermittent success. What's more, for the Christian to sign up for military service essentially subordinates conscience to military high command. But when war is unavoidable, it must be fought to win, although every effort should be made to prevent such occurrences from arising in the first place.[14]

Having reviewed the various Christian positions concerning war, peace, and violence, we now embark on the contributors' articulation and defense of their respective positions and their engagement with the alternatives. The issues are complex and the stakes momentous. The ensuing discussion invites our careful attention and thoughtful reflection as we seek to live faithfully before God amid the complexities of a fallen, violent world.

---

[14]Thanks to Meic Pearse's helpful corrections on certain infelicities in the introduction.

1

A JUST WAR VIEW

A Just War View

Christian Approaches to War, Peace, and Security

ERIC PATTERSON

C. S. Lewis (1898–1963) was a survivor. Like so many who scraped through the Great War, he suffered trench fever, fought in bloody battles, endured a miserable winter in the trenches, and then was seriously wounded with shrapnel in three different parts of his body. He left the hospital, and the war, on Christmas Eve 1918, a confirmed atheist like so many others.

But he was no pacifist, not then, and not later when his Christian worldview had fully matured. He volunteered to serve a second time, at age forty, in World War II, perhaps as an instructor (he was denied), and subsequently joined the Local Defence Forces (Home Guard). He traveled the country speaking at Royal Air Force bases. One air marshal said that Lewis helped the pilots and aircrews understand what they were fighting *for*.

Lewis famously responded to the notion that "turn the other cheek" required pacifism in the face of the Nazis with this response: "Does anyone suppose that our Lord's hearers understood him to mean that if a homicidal maniac, attempting to murder a third party, tried to knock me out of the way, I must stand aside and let him get his victim?"[1] Lewis was speaking common sense: we know in our hearts that we have a duty to protect the vulnerable. Lewis was also speaking from within the mainstream tradition of biblical and Christian thinking on issues of protection, the use of force, justice, and neighbor love. We often call that tradition "just war thinking" or "just war theory," but it is really a much larger tradition that would better be termed "just war statecraft" or "just statecraft" because the tradition begins

---

[1] C. S. Lewis, "Why I Am Not a Pacifist," in *The Weight of Glory and Other Addresses*, ed. Walter Hooper (1949; repr., San Francisco: HarperOne, 2006), 86.

with broad issues of legitimate political authority, political order, and justice. All of our major Christian traditions accept applied just war reasoning in one form or another: Catholic, Orthodox, Lutheran, Anglican, Reformed, Wesleyan (and thus its Holiness and Pentecostal descendants), and Baptist.[2] The only tradition that entirely rejects just war thinking, because it denies the notion that Christians have a responsibility to public service, is the Anabaptist tradition, an anomaly that began in the sixteenth century and makes up less than 1 percent of Christendom.

Lewis wrote a great deal on issues of war, peace, and security. His academic work on medieval literature, which he taught at Oxford and Cambridge, steeped him in the ideas of chivalry, *noblesse oblige*, responsibility, and sacrifice. World War I forced him to consider mortality and the meaning of life, which he did in a short book of poems published in 1919. His fiction, written after he became a Christian, gives us scenes of heroes battling injustice, motivated by righteous indignation. Two of his most famous characters demonstrate the difference between the moral use of force and immoral violence. Dr. Weston, the evil mastermind of Lewis's Space Trilogy, justifies a rapacious conquest of other worlds in language that the Nazis or imperial Japan would have understood. Weston argues for a Nietzschean approach: he sees humanity (Earth) as superior and therefore justified in invading and using for our own purposes, other, inferior civilizations.

In contrast, Narnia's Reepicheep, a valiant mouse knight, leads his community to serve their country and Aslan. Reepicheep is particularly important as a role model: his love of Narnia, rightful patriotism, gives him a spiritual intuition that there is something bigger and better than his comrades or even his country. That *love* leads him to search out Aslan's Country. This is a portrait, according to Lewis in his discussion of patriotism in *The Four Loves*, of how love of one's home can point one to wider circles of neighbor love (e.g., love of country) and ultimately point us to love of God and his creation.

We live in an era when there is tremendous social confusion with regard to morality, ethics, patriotism, and the use of force. We hear moral

---

[2]For details of these denominational positions and the nuanced differences among them, see Eric Patterson and J. Daryl Charles, *Just War and Christian Tradition: Denominational Perspectives* (Notre Dame, IN: University of Notre Dame Press, 2022).

equivocations all the time, such as "one man's terrorist is another man's freedom fighter." We have seen the loss of respect for any sort of shared moral code and any form of authority, whether in the home, our churches, or in civic life. Many have—even in the church—lost the ability, or the will, to make right distinctions.

Getting back to Lewis's remark, "Does anyone suppose that our Lord's hearers understood him to mean . . . ?" we are faced with a challenge: Should you and I let evil go unopposed? Did anyone listening to Jesus think that he was preaching anarchy or revolution? Did they think he was preaching unqualified nonresistance to evil? Of course not. The God of the Bible is the God of love and justice. We live in a fallen world, a world that God has nonetheless assigned to us—despite our fallenness—to steward as his co-regents. We have responsibilities to him and to one another. That is the foundation of the great commandments, to love God and to love our neighbor.

How does one love one's neighbor in one's calling and in social life?

This book looks at these responsibilities from the perspective of just state-craft with a focus on issues of justice, order, authority, and the goal of peace. I will use the terminology just war "thinking," "tradition," and "statecraft" interchangeably to indicate a long-standing tradition in Christianity that focuses on the responsibility that people serving in government have for order, justice, and peace. Too often analyses of just war principles start with a narrow checklist, without examining broader foundations of biblical teaching. Thus, we will start with key biblical doctrines that inform how we are to see people living in society, such as the fact that a healthy society has people living out different *vocations* (callings) for the common good, just as there are a variety of gifts, symbolized by Paul as hands and eyes and feet, in the church. Some people are called to public service, where they serve as stewards of public order and justice. We see the principle of *stewardship* throughout the Bible, in the lives of leaders such as Joseph, Moses, Nehemiah, and David as well as in the Wisdom literature and parables, where wise kings count the cost of action and seek wise counsel.

The Bible says a considerable amount about the need for *political order* (i.e., a framework for the rule of law that protects the vulnerable, deters wrongdoing, and punishes violators). *Justice*, in its narrowest form, means getting what we deserve, and therefore should make Christians particularly humble when it comes to civic life, because we know that "all have sinned and fall short of the glory of God" and "the wages of sin is death" (Rom 3:23; 6:23).[3] What we truly deserve is the full weight of God's wrath. This should make us humble in dealing with our neighbors and vigilant toward unchecked evil. Unfortunately, the spirit of our age is the exact opposite, a haughtiness that demands the gratification of our rights and our desires. This becomes a form of idolatry, as Lewis noted in *The Screwtape Letters* and *The Four Loves*, whether in the form of radical personal autonomy (individual) or forms of collective chauvinism that makes my group superior to all others (nationalism, antisemitism, violent populism, racialism, etc.).

This chapter begins with the presuppositions, rooted in Christian doctrine, that are the foundation of just war statecraft. Then I will look at how Christians, from the first centuries of Christianity to today, have worked out a framework for responsible action in a competitive, sinful world. Classic just war reasoning argues that *political authorities* are authorized to utilize force when they are acting on a *just cause* and with *right intention*. Just as we can tell the difference between child abuse and loving but firm parental discipline, so too can we tell the difference between police or military brutality in contrast to limited, restrained, lawful use of force. This is the distinction between *force* (lawful, restrained) and *violence* (vengeful, unrestrained).

I will look at the just causes for employing force and the importance of right motivations. I will look at secondary, stewardship criteria that call for counting the cost, such as accounting the *likelihood of success* and taking all reasonable diplomatic measures before employing force (*last resort*). I will then go a step further and consider how force is used: it should be used in ways that are *proportionate* to the injustice, injury, or threat and should be used in ways that distinguish (*distinction*) between lawful targets, such as foreign military personnel, and unlawful and immoral targets (e.g., houses of worship, hospitals, innocent bystanders). I will then look at definitions of peace and the practical steps that must be taken to establish a just and enduring peace at war's end (*jus post bellum*), a peace based first on a secure

---

[3]Unless otherwise indicated, Scripture quotations in this chapter are from the New American Standard Bible.

political order, that seeks justice, and that promotes conciliation. I will conclude with a look at how Christians are desperately needed to serve their
fellow men and women in all phases of war and insecurity, from humanitarian assistance to diplomacy to healing and conciliation.

Why did Reepicheep carry a sword? Because he, as a knight of Narnia,
lived in a dangerous world, he went to dangerous places, and he wanted to
protect his family, countrymen, and his leaders. Although Reepicheep was
easily offended, he was not an aggressor. He did not bully his fellow citizens.
He did not seek to conquer or enslave foreigners. He was a protector, a
defender, a champion. He was motivated by love: love of home, love of
family, love of country, and, ultimately, in Lewis's rendition, love of God.
That is the essence of just war statecraft.

THE DOCTRINAL UNDERPINNINGS OF
JUST STATECRAFT

Christian ethicist Paul Ramsey (1913–1988) helps us understand the call of
neighbor love (charity) in his retelling of the story of the good Samaritan.

> It was a work of charity for the Good Samaritan to give help to the man
> who fell among thieves. But one step more, it may have been a work of
> charity for the inn-keeper to hold himself ready to receive beaten and
> wounded men, and for him to conduct his business so that he was solvent
> enough to extend credit to the Good Samaritan. By another step it would
> have been a work of charity, and not of justice alone, to maintain and serve
> in a police patrol on the Jericho road to prevent such things from happening.
> By yet another step, it might well be a work of charity to resist, by force of
> arms, any external aggression against the social order that maintains the
> police patrol along the road to Jericho. . . . What do you think Jesus would
> have made the Samaritan do if he had come upon the scene while the
> robbers were still at their fell work?[4]

Ramsey's voluminous writings on two areas of ethics, war and medicine,
remain highly influential to this day. He emphasizes throughout his work
on statecraft the unity of justice and charity (neighbor love), and he sought
to explicate how this works out, particularly in the ways that public servants

---

[4]Paul Ramsey, *The Just War: Force and Political Responsibility* (1968; repr., Lanham, MD: Rowman
and Littlefield, 1983), 142-43.

respond to criminals, terrorists, nuclear deterrence and the arms race, and great power conflict.

The story of the good Samaritan is a window into a number of Christian doctrinal themes, and we will look at a number of them that provide the foundations for a Christian approach to statecraft, including the difference between the individual and those responsible for serving and protecting the group, political order, justice, neighbor love, sphere sovereignty, vocation (calling), and stewardship. One implication of the good Samaritan parable is that death itself is not the worst thing. "It is destined for people to die once, and after this comes judgment" (Heb 9:27). Augustine rightly pointed out that we will all die sooner or later. He argued, and Ramsey is picking up this theme, that there are times when it is appropriate for us, especially if we can protect the weak or serve in the public trust, to put ourselves in harm's way. Reinhold Niebuhr, writing with World War II in mind, put it this way: "There are historic situations in which refusal to defend the inheritance of a civilization, however imperfect, against tyranny and aggression may result in consequences even worse than war."[5] Later in this chapter I will look at a few of the key thinkers in Christian history and how they distilled principles for decision making about the use of force.

There are three levels of analysis for thinking how society functions, and in particular the role individuals and governments play in issues of peace and security. The first level is the individual level, meaning my responsibilities at the most local level: my responsibility as a husband, as a father, as a neighbor, in my workplace, and in my local community. The second level of analysis is at the societal level, that of domestic politics and social life. This is where organizations, businesses, political parties, social movements, faith-based organizations and churches, and the organs of government operate. These collective organizations are run by people and work on behalf of people. They are responsible to promote interests of those they represent and to promote the common good. The third level of analysis is the international level, where most war takes place. This is the level primarily inhabited by the governments of countries, but it is also the realm of some international

---

[5]Reinhold Niebuhr, "The Christian Faith and the World Crisis," *Christianity and Crisis*, February 6, 1941, 4.

organizations and multinational corporations. There is no overarching government at this level, so it is incumbent on governments to defend their citizens from adversaries, from terrorists to ideological competitors. Again, the heads of those governments, agencies, corporations, and other entities are all people.

This way of seeing the world is important when one understands that an individual may have responsibilities across the levels of analysis. Here is a case in point. A friend of mine is a Navy admiral. When he is home on shore leave, much of his life is as a private citizen. His local responsibilities to his wife, children, the PTA, his local congregation, the Rotary club of which he is a member, his aging parents, and the like all take precedence. Some recognize these basic relationships as having a covenantal character, particularly as a member of a family, a local church, and as a citizen; thus the term "private" citizen is a bit of a misnomer. For my friend, these relationships, expressed as fatherhood, husband-hood, and so on, are one element of his *calling* in this life. But he has not stopped being a Navy admiral. If called to occupational service, as he was during ongoing Middle East conflicts, he goes to sea and he becomes an agent acting on behalf of the United States government and its allies at the third level of analysis. This is also his vocation, his God-ordained calling. He may be called on to make decisions that are literally life or death to defend his sailors, to protect those in foreign lands at risk of genocide, or to punish criminals, pirates, and terrorists. He does so under the legitimate authority entrusted to him by the president of the United States, the Congress, and US law. Moreover, his professional vocation is motivated by love, not hate: the desire to defend the lives, livelihoods, and way of life of his family, community, and country.

The admiral gives us a picture of how "turn the other cheek" is actually supposed to work. When he is home and his lawnmower strays over the neighbor's sprinklers, the admiral must take responsibility for that, even if it results in a tongue lashing. This is when turning the other cheek is an act of the fruit of the Spirit. Moreover, he is called to be patient and humble, often turning the other cheek as a husband ("love your wives, just as Christ also loved the church" [Eph 5:25]) and as a father ("do not provoke your children" [Eph 6:4]). Most importantly, if attacked for his faith, he must turn the other cheek. The greatest witness is to never deny Christ when we are mocked or attacked for the faith. That is when one must turn the other cheek even to the point of death.

Understanding the doctrine of calling (vocation), that God gives everyone skills and talents to be used for the common good, and recognizing that we live simultaneously in various roles with various responsibilities at the three levels of analysis can help us to best understand that God calls and empowers some individuals to employ force to protect, prevent, and punish.

Christians have doctrines that illuminate both the responsibility and restraint that need to be practiced in civic life. Catholics have a doctrine known as subsidiarity, the general principle that problems should be handled at the lowest level of analysis whenever possible. So the first institution to handle a problem should be a family, but when the family cannot deal with it, it goes to the neighborhood (including the local church and extended family), then local government, and perhaps if the problem is big enough, to state or federal authorities. Catholics and Protestants agree that God has created various institutions (i.e., family, church, government) and that he has given humanity the creativity to create additional institutions (e.g., business, education). In most cases, the immediate institutions—the family—can nurse an ill child, but local charity may need to support the family during a prolonged sickness. Government might have to be involved if this is not a localized illness but it is rather a spreading epidemic. Of course, when it comes to organized crime or foreign aggressors, it is those higher levels that are responsible to defend the citizenry.

Protestants, particularly in Reformed circles, emphasize a slightly different approach to the levels of analysis called sphere sovereignty. Like subsidiarity, sphere sovereignty begins with the idea that God is a God of order and he has instituted various arrangements of authority for our lives. The Bible does not give us a single model of civic government, and thus it is human creativity that has come up with different arrangements, such as constitutional monarchy and democracy, for organizing society. A basic political order, as I have written elsewhere, provides at least three features: basic law and order provided by law enforcement and government institutions (traditional security), governance (domestic politics and the provision of basic services), and international security (secure from immediate external threats). The principle of political order and good governance is entirely congruent with righteous leadership whether in Israel's oligarchic period (books of Joshua and Judges), monarchy, or the teaching of Romans 13 in the New Testament.

Sphere sovereignty recognizes government as one among many institutions in society (the second level of analysis—collective social life), including the family and the church. According to Dutch theologian, pastor, and later prime minister of the Netherlands Abraham Kuyper (1837–1920), we should think of society as full of different sectors ("spheres"): business, academia, church and religious organizations, education, the family, government, and so on. Each of these sectors has its own rationale and rules and should be largely independent within its own sphere of influence. All of these spheres are subservient to God. God intends for the skills and talents of humanity to interact for the common good, so Kuyper portrays society like a huge clock mechanism, with all of the interlocking gears having important independent functions but, at the same time, being interdependent and interlocking for the good of society.

Sphere sovereignty suggests that there are those whose role it is to protect domestic society, such as the military and law enforcement, so that all the gears of society can function properly. When we think back to Ramsey's expanded notion of the good Samaritan parable, we can see many of these principles at work. The application, when it comes to statecraft, is this: How do we pursue order, justice, and peace in a fallen world? Christian thinkers provide us with principles of statecraft that do just that.

CHRISTIAN STATECRAFT: KEY THINKERS AND THE JUST WAR FRAMEWORK

Christians have been writing about issues of war, peace, and security for two millennia. These approaches can take a number of names, the most common being "Augustinian," "just war," or Niebuhrian "Christian realism." Despite minor differences, all are forms of "Christian realism" that oppose fantastical, idealistic approaches to the tough dilemmas of politics and society (another chapter in this book looks at the uniquely Niebuhrian form of Christian realism). The approach of this chapter is to focus on the stream of classical just war thinking that goes back to the first centuries of

Christianity and is rooted in natural law as well as biblical texts. Before taking a look at a Christian critique of irresponsible pacifism and vengeful holy war, the following are three of the key historical thinkers who are widely recognized, across denominational lines, as seminal Christian exponents of just war statecraft.

Augustine. At the end of the fourth century AD, Augustine (354–430) pondered the conditions for the just employment of force in political life.[6] Augustine's formulation of the just use of force relies heavily on the notion of *caritas*, or charity: "Love your neighbor as yourself." In domestic society as well as international life, how does one go about loving one's neighbor? Augustine argues that within society, adherence to the rule of law, including punishment of lawbreakers, was a way of loving one's neighbors. When one loves one's neighbors, one refrains from harming them and supports the authorities in their efforts to provide security to the citizenry. Moreover, Augustine notes, neighbor love means protecting one's neighbors when they are attacked, even if one must apply force to protect them. Augustine uses Romans 13:1-5 to argue that sovereign authorities have a responsibility to order and to justice, including the use of the sword:

> Every person is to be subject to the governing authorities. For there is no authority except from God, and those which exist are established by God. Therefore whoever resists authority has opposed the ordinance of God; and they who have opposed will receive condemnation upon themselves. For rulers are not a cause of fear for good behavior, but for evil. Do you want to have no fear of authority? Do what is good and you will have praise from the same; for it is a servant of God to you for good. But if you do what is evil, be afraid; for it does not bear the sword for nothing; for it is a servant of God, an avenger who brings wrath on the one who practices evil. Therefore it is necessary to be in subjection, not only because of wrath, but also for the sake of conscience.

Augustine suggests that this is also true with regard to foreign threats: loving our neighbor can mean self-defense of the polity. Likewise, loving our foreign neighbors may mean using force to punish evildoers or right a wrong. Aquinas summarizes this thought of Augustine's in his *Summa*:

---

[6]Some material in this section is adapted from Eric Patterson, "Just War Theory and Terrorism," *Providence*, November 30, 2016, https://providencemag.com/2016/11/just-war-theory-terrorism/.

"True religion looks upon as peaceful those wars that are waged not for motives of aggrandizement, or cruelty, but with the object of securing peace, of punishing evil-doers, and of uplifting the good."[7] Oliver O'Donovan comments that Augustine's typology suggests "defensive, reparative, and punitive objectives" of the decision to go to war.[8]

In addition to neighbor love, Augustine's writings suggest a second reason for *jus ad bellum*: order. Augustine consistently privileges political order over disorder. The Augustinian conception of the universe is one in which God is the ultimate creator, judge, arbiter, and end. Although God allows sin and imperfection in this world, he nonetheless sustains the universe with a divine order. This order is mirrored in society by the political order with its laws and hierarchy. Augustine argues that although the city of man is a poor reflection of the city of God, nonetheless it is the political principle of temporal order that most approximates the eternal order.[9] During his lifetime Augustine witnessed the alternative: the breakdown of the Pax Romana, the looting of Rome, and ultimately the sacking of his home in North Africa in the final days of his life. Augustine's fear of political disorder was thus more than a distaste for regime change; it was dread of losing civic order with all of its attendant moral duties and opportunities.

Today, many Christians want to focus on the importance of loving one's neighbor but neglect Augustine's presupposition that political order is the foundation for society.[10] Augustine's argument is that the government has a responsibility to both domestic and international security—a responsibility that people serving in public office are duty bound to administer.

Thomas Aquinas. Aquinas (1225–1274) was the great scholastic expositor of Augustine. He argued that a war is just when it meets three

---

[7]This quotation from Augustine is referred to in Aquinas's statement following objection 4 in Saint Thomas Aquinas, *Summa Theologica: Complete English Edition in Five Volumes*, trans. Fathers of the English Dominican Province (New York: Christian Classics, 1981), II-II, q. 40, art. 1.

[8]Oliver O'Donovan, *The Just War Revisited* (Cambridge: Cambridge University Press, 1993), 53.

[9]Roger Epp, "The Augustinian Moment in International Politics," *International Politics Research Papers*, no. 10 (Aberystwyth, UK: Department of International Politics, University College of Wales, 1991).

[10]This debate—how to employ the law of love in a violent world—turned many Christian pacifists such as Reinhold Niebuhr away from pacifism and toward "Christian realism" in the 1930s and 1940s. The Christian realist argument reflects Augustinians' call for this-worldly policies to thwart evil, even if such policies dirty the hands of those engaged in fighting for justice and order. See Eric Patterson, ed., *The Christian Realists* (Lanham, MD: University Press of America, 2003), esp. chap. 1.

requirements: sovereign authority, just cause, and right intent. It is note-worthy that Aquinas began not with just cause or right intent, but with sovereign authority:

> In order for a war to be just, three things are necessary. First, the authority of the sovereign by whose command the war is to be waged. For it is not the business of a private individual to declare war. . . . And as the care of the common weal is committed to those who are in authority, it is their business to watch over the common weal of the city, kingdom or province subject to them. And just as it is lawful for them to have recourse to the sword in de-fending that common weal against internal disturbances, when they punish evil-doers . . . so too, it is their business to have recourse to the sword of war in defending the common weal against external enemies.[11]

In short, Aquinas saw most violence as criminal and lawless. The funda-mental purpose of the state was to provide a counterpoise to lawlessness. Ergo, the legitimate use of force should only be in the hands of the rightful authorities in order to promote security.

Aquinas also argued that states should be concerned with just cause. He writes, "Secondly, a just cause is required, namely that those who are at-tacked, should be attacked because they deserve it on account of some fault." He quotes Augustine: "Wherefore Augustine says: 'A just war is wont to be described as one that avenges wrongs, when a nation or state has to be punished, for refusing to make amends for the wrongs inflicted by its sub-jects, or to restore what it has seized unjustly.'"[12] Aquinas's conception of just cause is richer than the contemporary debate on self-defense because it includes punishing wrongdoing and restitution of some sort to victims. Indeed, it seems that Aquinas's just cause would support the use of force to curb aggressive non-state actors, protect individual human life via humani-tarian intervention, and punish rogue regimes that disrupt the international status quo.

Third, Aquinas said that the just resort to force requires just intent. Scholars and churchmen alike have long pointed out the dilemmas of ascertaining right intent. For the average soldier, the medievals solved this

---

[11]Aquinas, *Summa Theologica* II-II, q. 40, art. 1.
[12]This continues Augustine's quotation from above in Aquinas, *Summa Theologica* II-II, q. 40, art. 1.

problem by providing absolution to their troops before battle and sometimes providing it again after the battle for the survivors. This did not completely solve the problem of rage and bloodlust on the battlefield but sought a spiritual solution to a very human dynamic.

However, this says little about the sovereign's motivation. Contemporary politics makes the situation even more complex because most state decisions are not made by a sovereign individual such as a king or empress. Western governments are pluralistic, representing multiple voices and acting based on a complicated set of interests and ideals. However, Aquinas's focus on right intent does not necessarily call for agonizing over one's ethical motivations. He writes, "Thirdly, it is necessary that the belligerents should have a rightful intention, so that they intend the advancement of good, or the avoidance of evil." In other words, Aquinas's idea of right intent is that states should seek to advance the security of their people and avoid wars based only on greed or vengeance. Aquinas again cites Augustine: "Hence Augustine says: 'The passion for inflicting harm, the cruel thirst for vengeance, an unpacific and relentless spirit, the fever of revolt, the lust of power, and such like things, all these are rightly condemned in war.'"[13] Aquinas would likely agree that in contemporary international politics, the right intent of states is to seek their own security and then promote human life and flourishing around the world.

Vitoria. In the sixteenth century a Catholic friar and professor at the University of Salamanca, Francesco de Vitoria (1483–1546), responded to European defense against the Turks as well as Spain's activities in the New World using an expanded just war criterion based on Augustine and Aquinas. Vitoria, citing Augustine and Aquinas, argues that wars can be just if fought by legitimate authorities with right intent on behalf of a just cause. However, Vitoria asserts numerous limits on the prosecution of war, even on behalf of faith. For instance, Vitoria argues that it is wrong to kill noncombatants such as women, children, "harmless agricultural folk," "clerics and members of religious orders," and even enemy prisoners who are no longer a threat. Vitoria writes, "The reason for this restriction is clear: for these persons are innocent, neither is it needful to the attainment of victory that they should

---

[13]Aquinas, *Summa Theologica* II-II, q. 40, art. 1.

be slain. It would be heretical to say that it is licit to kill them. . . . Accordingly, the innocent may not be slain by (primary) intent, when it is possible to distinguish them from the guilty."[14] Vitoria's use of just war theory gives us guidelines that today we call proportionality and distinction (discrimination, noncombatant immunity).

Much more could be said about the ways Christians have continued to flesh out just war statecraft and thus created a foundation for what we today call the law of armed conflict and international humanitarian law. This is a seminal achievement that is rooted in Christian just war thinking. In recent decades Christians have continued to write in the tradition of Augustine and just war statecraft: Reinhold Niebuhr and his contemporaries called America to arms against the evil of the Nazis; Paul Ramsey explicated the ethics of nuclear deterrence; Jean Bethke Elshtain defined "equal regard" as the duty to protect the victims of genocide; Elshtain, George Weigel, and James Turner Johnson explained the twin evils of Saddam Hussein butchering his own people and neighbors *and* those who would deny the United Nations and governments for righting Hussein's wrongs; J. Daryl Charles and Timothy Demy demonstrated the nuances in various Christian denominational positions on just war thinking and addressed considerations of calling and vocation; Joseph Capizzi has written a masterful book on political order in Christian history; I have championed a robust *jus post bellum*; Marc LiVecche has extended Christian thinking to moral injury and the practical implications for sending and receiving soldiers; and the list goes on.

The shared set of principles that all of these thinkers generally agree on is made up of three elements: the morality of going to war (*jus ad bellum*), the morality of how war is fought (*jus in bello*), and the morality of war's ending (*jus post bellum*).

---

[14]Quoted in Richard Shelly Hartigan, "Francesco de Vitoria and Civilian Immunity," *Political Theory* 1, no. 1 (1973): 83. This discussion can be found in Vitoria's work *De Indis et de Iure Belli Reflectiones*, ed. Ernest Nys, trans. J. P. Bate (New York: Oceana/Wildy and Sons, 1964), §449, https://archive .org/details/franciscidevicto0000vito/page/n5/mode/2up.

JUS AD BELLUM

- **Legitimate authority:** Supreme political authorities are morally responsible for the security of their constituents and therefore are obligated to make decisions about war and peace.

- **Just cause:** Self-defense of citizens' lives, livelihoods, and way of life are typically *just causes*; more generally speaking, the cause is likely *just* if it rights a past wrong, punishes wrongdoers, or prevents further wrong.[a]

- **Right intent:** Political motivations are subject to ethical scrutiny; violence intended for the purpose of order, justice, and ultimate conciliation is just, whereas violence for the sake of hatred, revenge, and destruction is not just.

- **Likelihood of success:** Political leaders should consider whether their action will make a difference in real-world outcomes. This principle is subject to context and judgment, because it may be appropriate to act despite a low likelihood of success (e.g., against local genocide). Conversely, it may be inappropriate to act due to low efficacy despite the compelling nature of the case.

- **Proportionality of ends:** Does the preferred outcome justify, in terms of the cost in lives and material resources, this course of action?

- **Last resort:** Have traditional diplomatic and other efforts been reasonably employed in order to avoid outright bloodshed?

JUS IN BELLO

- **Proportionality:** Are the battlefield tools and tactics employed proportionate to battlefield objectives?

- **Discrimination:** Has care been taken to reasonably protect the lives and property of legitimate noncombatants?

JUS POST BELLUM[b]

- **Order:** Beginning with existential security, a sovereign government extends its roots through the maturation of government capacity in the military (traditional security), governance (domestic politics), and international security dimensions.

- **Justice:** Getting one's just deserts, including consideration of individual punishment for those who violated the law of armed conflict and restitution policies for victims when appropriate.

- **Conciliation:** Coming to terms with the past so that parties can imagine and move forward toward a shared future.

[a]This formulation derives directly from Augustine, as recorded in Thomas Aquinas, *Summa Theologica*, trans. Fathers of the English Dominican Province (New York: Christian Classics, 1981), II-II, q. 40, art. 1.

[b]These criteria are not enshrined in historic just war thinking but are distilled from various sources elaborated on by Patterson initially in 2004. See also Eric Patterson, *Ethics Beyond War's End* (Washington, DC: Georgetown University Press, 2012); and Patterson, *Ending Wars Well: Order, Justice, and Conciliation in Post-Conflict* (New Haven, CT: Yale University Press, 2012).

Figure 1. Just war criteria

Christians are rightly concerned about peace. Societal peace is a secure, rightly ordered community, at peace within itself and with its neighbors. Aquinas, following the Roman statesman Cicero, rightly said that the purpose of a just war is peace. Thus, Christians should be concerned with a prudential approach to the ethics of war's end (*jus post bellum*): postconflict settlements should exhibit restraint in their terms while pursuing justice (restitution, punishment), in contrast to a so-called victor's peace based on vengeance and destruction. A Christian approach to war's end is moral in seeking punishment and restoration as well as focusing on a shared, secure future rather than on revenge for historic or imagined grievances. Figure 2 demonstrates a model for how a sturdy framework of political order can lay the groundwork for efforts at justice and, ultimately, conciliation.[15]

Figure 2.

More specifically, *jus post bellum* requires moral accountability for past actions, including the decisions by leaders (*jus ad bellum*) that led to war in the first place. There should be accountability for those in power who are responsible for the advent of conflict; in fact, at times our military response is an act of justice. A Catholic successor to Vitoria, Francisco Suárez (1548–1617), wrote, "The only reason for it [war] was that an act of punitive justice was indispensable to mankind."[16] Generally, the breakdown of international peace is a complex set of circumstances, but in many cases war is directly attributable to the aggressive policies of a specific regime

---

[15]I developed this model in *Ending Wars Well: Order, Justice, and Conciliation in Post-Conflict* (New Haven, CT: Yale University Press, 2012).
[16]Quoted in O'Donovan, *The Just War Revisited*, 18.

or cabal within the regime, such as Hitler's Nazis or radical Hutus in Rwanda (1994). Leaders are responsible for peace and security; when they abrogate that obligation, it may be appropriate to hold them accountable in postconflict settlements.[17]

The same is true for *jus in bello* violations. Soldiers and their leaders on both sides are responsible for their conduct during the fighting. A richer notion of just peace is one in which steps are taken to hold those who willfully broke the laws of war in combat accountable for their misdeeds.

A related moral principle of *jus post bellum* is restitution. Of course, the destructive nature of war means that a complete return to the prewar status quo is impossible, and may not be desirable in cases of secession or civil war. Citizens, both in and out of uniform, have died. Vast sums have been expended. Natural resources and regions of land have been used up or destroyed. *Jus post bellum* takes the cost of war, particularly the cost in lives and material, into account and argues that when possible, aggressors should provide restitution to the victims. This principle applies both to inter- and intrastate conflict: at war's end aggressors should remunerate, when appropriate and possible, the wronged.

An additional moral concern that *jus post bellum* addresses is that of punishment. Punishment is punitive action against a wrongdoer. It may mean loss of rank or position, fines, imprisonment, exile, or death. Thus, punishment is the consequence of responsibility and an important feature of postconflict justice. Punishment is moral in that it moves beyond an abstract conception of accountability by employing sanctions against those responsible for initiating violence or transgressing the war convention and violating international law. As I will argue later in this chapter, punishment is a lost strand of just war theory.

Finally, a Christian approach to postconflict looks toward conciliation, defined as coming to terms with the past, so that we can see our former adversaries as partners in a shared peace. This is not easy. The principles of order and justice provide a foundation for political conciliation among nations that were formerly in conflict. Such conciliation is the ultimate step

---

[17]Material in this and the following three paragraphs is adapted from Eric Patterson, *Just War Thinking: Morality and Pragmatism in the Struggle Against Contemporary Threats* (Lanham, MD: Lexington Books, 2007), 83-84.

toward building a durable framework for domestic and international peace. One can see the role of Christians seeking justice and conciliation at the end of various conflicts. The fact that apartheid-era South Africa did not fall apart into civil war and later developed its Truth and Reconciliation Commission is largely due to the role that Christian teaching, expounded and modeled by people like Archbishop Desmond Tutu, played in laying out an alternative to mass violence. Abraham Lincoln routinely cited biblical texts about restoration and reconciliation ("bind up the nation's wounds") as his philosophy for how the Civil War should end. He was directly opposed by the Radical Republicans, his own party, who hungered for vengeance. President Woodrow Wilson, the son of a minister and for many years a practicing Presbyterian, developed his famous Fourteen Points as a vision for a postwar European, and global, order rooted in the golden rule.

MISTAKEN ALTERNATIVES TO JUST STATECRAFT: PACIFISM AND HOLY WAR

As noted above, the vast majority of Christians across denominations and down through history have been part of traditions that have affirmed just statecraft. Martin Luther and John Calvin specifically mention their intellectual antecedents, routinely citing Augustine in particular. Nevertheless, there are variants distinct from mainstream, biblical thinking on issues of war, peace, and security that should be briefly addressed: pacifism and holy war. When one carefully considers the doctrines outlined above, notably how neighbor love is to be enacted by responsible citizens and leaders in a fallen world, neither pacifism nor holy war offers a compelling alternative to loving, prudential, restrained action.

Pacifism. J. Daryl Charles (1950–) convincingly documents that Christian history provides no evidence that the early church took a unified pacifist position, although many second- and third-century Christians were apparently pacifists.[18] John the Baptist, Jesus, Peter, and Paul all engaged directly

---

[18]Charles reports on the historical context and position of early church fathers such as Tertullian (who thought that political and military service were forms of pagan sacrifice) and Origen—both of whom admit that Christians were serving in the Roman military. J. Daryl Charles, "Presumption Against War or Presumption Against Injustice? The Just War Tradition Reconsidered," *Journal of Church and State* 48, no. 3 (fall 2005): 335-69. Charles points out that even the Quaker pacifist Roland Bainton suggests that the occupation of soldiering was likely not completely off-limits to

with tax collectors, soldiers, and Roman public officials. Lewis captures the biblical ethic in his critique of pacifism. He interprets "turn the other cheek" as allowing for force in situations in which certain factors demand it, saying of this view:

> It harmonises better with St. John Baptist's words to the soldier and with the fact that one of the few persons whom our Lord praised without reservation was a Roman centurion. It also allows me to suppose that the New Testament is consistent with itself. St. Paul approves of the magistrate's use of the sword (Romans 13:4) and so does St. Peter (1 Peter 2:14).[19]

Notably, New Testament leaders, including Christ, never commanded soldiers or the other public servants to quit their work. John the Baptist instructed soldiers to avoid abusing their power. Jesus said that a Roman centurion had the greatest faith in Israel. Peter's first Gentile convert was a Roman centurion and his family, a man who was already a devout seeker of God.

Nevertheless, it is true that there were compelling motives for many Christians to be skeptical of serving the political authority of the day, which was sinful Rome.[20] Christians, like Jews, opposed the idolatry and emperor cult of Rome and were persecuted by taxation and later imprisonment, crucifixion, and martyrdom in the arena. A good illustration of what the church was teaching can be seen in Acts 15, the teaching that the Council of Jerusalem gave to newly converted Gentiles. Did Gentile followers of the Way have to undergo circumcision and live by the ceremonial obligations of the Jewish law? No, but they were enjoined to avoid meat offered to idols and abstain from sexual immorality. Why these two? Sexual morality is the fundamental basis for the purity of the family and thus a building block for God's design for society. Moreover, in the Roman and Near Eastern world, sexual promiscuity was not only rampant but also encouraged. For instance, some temples had cultic prostitutes, both male and female, and many

---

early Christians. See Bainton, *Christian Attitudes Toward War and Peace* (New York: Abingdon, 1960), 66, 81.

[19]Lewis, "Why I Am Not a Pacifist," 87.

[20]Frederick H. Russell discusses how the limited teaching of Christ on violence ultimately resulted in early church leaders, such as Origen and later Ambrose and Augustine, having to define a Christian position on military service, allegiance to the state, and war in general. See Russell, *The Just War in the Middle Ages* (Cambridge: Cambridge University Press, 1975), chap. 2.

politico-religious ceremonies disintegrated into debauchery and sexual immorality. Likewise, food offered to idols is suggestive of the many ways that
pagan religious practices were a part of the Greco-Roman world, including
the sacrifice of animals that later ended up in butcher's stalls, and thus
Christians were trying to avoid practicing or reinforcing idol worship.

Moreover, if one served in the Roman army, there were severe restric-
tions on marriage: Caesar Augustus had made it virtually illegal to marry
if one served in the legions (one could not legally marry until one had
served a decade or more).[21] This encouraged prostitution just outside the
camp gates as well as rape of the defeated as a common practice of warfare.
In the best cases, legionaries took common-law wives outside of legal norms.
In short, there were real consequences to public service in the Roman world,
but many people came to faith while serving in government administration
or in the military. Thus the church was not entirely pacifistic but tried
to find the best ways to counter *the idolatrous claims of the state on
the individual.*[22]

Over time a secondary pacifism did develop, as Christian scholars such
as Augustine and Aquinas differentiated between the citizen's duty to the
state, including military service, and the pacific duties of church leaders.[23]
In other words, those living the spiritual vocation (pastors, monks, priests)
were not to fight, but that did not mean that government was to leave them
unprotected, nor did it mean that their parishioners should not protect and
defend. Augustine famously made this point in a letter to a Roman military
officer named Boniface in AD 418. Augustine exhorted Boniface to fulfill
his calling and fight against temporal enemies who seek to destroy the peace,
while distinguishing it from the clergy's vocation of spiritual warfare.[24]

---

[21] Adrian Goldsworthy, *Pax Romana: War, Peace, and Conquest in the Roman World* (New Haven, CT: Yale University Press, 2016), 191.

[22] For a look at historical and contemporary Christian pacifism from its most famous contemporary defender, see John Howard Yoder, *The Original Revolution: Essays on Christian Pacifism*, Christian Peace Shelf Series (Scottdale, PA: Herald Press, 2003). A history of the application of pacifism in American politics is Theron F. Schlabach and Richard T Hughes, eds., *Proclaim Peace: Christian Pacifism from Unexpected Quarters* (Urbana: University of Illinois Press, 1997).

[23] For a brief introduction to this entire controversy, see James Turner Johnson, "Just War, as It Was and Is," *First Things*, January 2005, 19.

[24] Augustine of Hippo, *Letter* 189 (*NPNF*[1] 1:552-54), Christian Classics Ethereal Library, www.ccel .org/ccel/schaff/npnf101.vii.1.CLXXXIX.html?highlight=augustine,letter,boniface,war#fna_vii .1.CLXXXIX-p3.2.

For Augustine, the law of love includes punishment (consequences for immoral behavior) and justice (restoration of what was taken, righting past wrongs).

Fast-forward to the Reformation. Many of the concerns that the early church had about idolatrous Rome echo in the critiques Martin Luther, John Calvin, and others directed at the Roman Catholic Church. One splinter group from the Reformation is Anabaptism (not to be confused with today's Baptists), and this line of thinking is the foundation for Christian pacifism in the modern era.[25] The foundational statement of the Anabaptist movement is the Schleitheim Confession of 1527, which makes three key points that are a response to Old Testament forms of legal authority ("magistracy") and the teaching of Romans 13 that "the ruler wields the sword for your good":

1. The "use of the sword" (force) is "ordained by God" but "outside the perfection of Christ." Thus it is appropriate for "worldly magistrates" to "punish," "put to death the wicked," and "guard and protect the good." Within the church, however, the strongest use of force is "the ban" (excommunication).

2. Just as "Christ was meek and lowly," it is not appropriate for Christians to "employ the sword against the wicked for the defense and protection of the good." Christians should not take any job that would cause them to employ force (law enforcement, military) nor should they take an office (judge, certain political jobs) that would cause them to make judgments between unbelievers.

3. Christians should pray for those in worldly authority because those individuals do the important work of limiting evil in a fallen world. But Christians should not participate.[26]

---

[25]There is a second strain of pacifism, "nonviolent action," that has roots outside of Christianity in the social movement started by Gandhi. There is no historical evidence of carefully planned Christian nonviolent resistance strategies such as those led by Gandhi and Martin Luther King Jr.'s "nonviolent *direct* action" (the latter's term). King brought Christian theological elements of witness, neighbor love, and especially consideration of one's own motivations to classic civil-disobedience techniques.

[26]The classic statement of the Anabaptist tradition can be found at the website Anabaptists, www.anabaptists.org/history/the-schleitheim-confession.html. It is noteworthy that classical Baptists have not accepted this Anabaptist position. In fact, in 1524 the five Baptist churches of London

So, the authentically Protestant pacifist position since the Reformation is one associated with classic Anabaptists. It comes to a very different definition of Christian citizenship in this world from Augustine, Calvin, Luther, John Wesley, Roger Williams, and others. Classic Anabaptist pacifism says that the Christian should pray for those who restrain evil but not participate in public service because it will dirty one's hands and nullify the witness of the believer. Anabaptists do not believe that in the New Testament era God called some Christians to serve in public life. They do not believe that Christians have a responsibility to protect their fellow citizens except via prayer, witness, and humanitarian service.

More can be said in a later chapter about variants of pacifism that rely on personal feelings, a preference to not get involved in the mess of political life, merely sentimental solidarity with the vulnerable without a sense of responsibility to protect, and the like. But, at the end of the day, the Anabaptist model has not been embraced by the majority of Christians over the past two millennia because it denies doctrines of activated neighbor love via vocations of public service and stewardship. Indeed, when we think about Christian heroes such as William Wilberforce, who led the fight against the slave trade in the British Parliament; Abraham Kuyper, who defended a Christian model for politics as prime minister in the Netherlands; or Christians motivated to abolish slavery, stop genocide, and shutter concentration camps, we can conclude that just statecraft was not just for Moses, Hezekiah, and Nehemiah, but it is an honorable and necessary calling today. As

---

publicly dismissed the Anabaptist position. Here is an excerpt from the Schleitheim Confession:

VI. We are agreed as follows concerning the sword: The sword is ordained of God outside the perfection of Christ. . . . In the perfection of Christ, however, only the ban is used for a warning and for the excommunication of the one who has sinned, without putting the flesh to death—simply the warning and the command to sin no more. . . .

It will be asked concerning the sword, Shall one be a magistrate if one should be chosen as such? The answer is as follows: They wished to make Christ king, but He fled and did not view it as the arrangement of His Father. Thus shall we do as He did, and follow Him, and so shall we not walk in darkness. . . .

Finally it will be observed that it is not appropriate for a Christian to serve as a magistrate because of these points: The government magistracy is according to the flesh, but the Christian's is according to the Spirit; their houses and dwelling remain in this world, but the Christian's are in heaven; their citizenship is in this world, but the Christian's citizenship is in heaven; the weapons of their conflict and war are carnal and against the flesh only, but the Christian's weapons are spiritual, against the fortification of the devil.

Dietrich Bonhoeffer (1906–1945), who was martyred by the Nazis for his involvement in a plot to stop Hitler, concluded, "If we want to be Christians, we must have some share in Christ's large-heartedness by acting with responsibility and in freedom when the hour of danger comes. . . . Mere waiting and looking on is not Christian behavior."[27]

Holy war. Sometimes just war thinking is mistaken for holy war (jihad, crusade) or militarism. The holy warrior believes that violence can be employed in defense of or to further eternal values. In practice, holy wars are often reactions to threats that seem to undermine the basic ideals and existence of one's civilization. Thus the medieval Crusades (1095–1291) were largely a geopolitical response to the previous three centuries of Muslim warfare, beginning with the push of Islamic armies out of the Arabian Peninsula in AD 632 and advancing, within just a century, across the Levant to Persia in the East and, westerly, across North Africa and Spain, only to be blunted by Charles Martel at Tours (France) in 732. For the next three centuries, Muslim armies hammered at the doors of Christian polities, most notably attack after attack on the Eastern Roman Empire (Byzantium). The First Crusade, launched in 1095, was in response to a direct appeal from the Byzantine leadership, from their capital in Constantinople (today's Istanbul), for aid against this scourge. Thus, despite Hollywood depictions or the denunciations of al-Qaeda that the West is full of modern crusaders, we should recognize the geopolitics of many so-called holy wars in the past.

But what inspires the *individual* holy warrior? Of course, as skeptics like to note, it is entirely possible that material gain might stimulate participation, as it did for many during the creation of Spain's empire in the New World or for many ISIS (Islamic State) fighters. Nevertheless, many holy warriors are motivated by other concerns. For one, holy warriors are provoked to action by righteous indignation. Their most personal convictions have not only been questioned but also affronted and defiled. The holy warrior feels compelled to action in defense of those ideals held most dear— faith in God and the religious community. The holy warrior may also seek an eternal reward. This does not necessarily indicate a "death wish," but rather that the individual is convinced that her actions are in pursuit of

---

[27]Dietrich Bonhoeffer, *Life Together*, trans. John W. Doberstein (San Francisco: Harper & Row, 1954), 64.

transcendent ends and that such behavior will please the deity she worships. Of course, some holy warriors seek glory in both the here and hereafter in the tradition of early martyrs of their faith.

More could be said about holy warriors, but the basic principle is that holy war can be based on zealous love for one's faith and that this justifies employing violence. What is most disconcerting about holy war is that if the *end* is absolute—the defense of God's name—then it is difficult to provide any ethical rationale for limiting the *means* employed. Holy warriors are not content with a "settlement" because they are attempting to inaugurate God's kingdom on earth. Hence the "excesses" of holy war: the extermination of entire cities during the rapid expansion of early Islam, the Inquisition and wars of the Counter-Reformation, the quasi-religious philosophy of the kamikaze, and the fatwas of Osama bin Laden resulting in al-Qaeda's attacks on civilian populations. For the holy warrior, the end justifies any means.

In practice, holy wars are usually a downward cycle of violence among ethno-religious groups. In a terrible spiral of destruction, holy wars usually involve religious people giving justifications for widespread violence directed at all the members of a targeted community (including women and children, the vanguard of the next generation of the other). Nonmilitary "soft" targets are often attacked, and when this includes houses of worship, a new, diabolical dimension to the conflict is introduced because adherents feel that the sacred has been defiled. Sadly, most wars that follow this path dehumanize the enemy and justify mass bloodshed as a glorious obligation to prove oneself by defending the faith.

We saw elements of this in the Yugoslav Wars of the 1990s. What began as the disintegration of the multiethnic federated country of Yugoslavia turned into a nightmare of atrocities. Religious leaders became involved by giving nationalistic sermons, justifying the arming of citizens, and appearing at militaristic rallies. Photos of those rallies show the "three-fingered salute," associated in Orthodox Christianity with the Trinity, held aloft by crowds chanting for the destruction of their Muslim neighbors. Over time, houses of worship were deliberately demolished and the violence descended into scenes reminiscent of the Holocaust, where one side tried to exterminate the other based on the other's ethno-religious identity. That is so-called holy war in the modern era. It is an abomination, whether practiced by the Serbs or by the Islamic State.

But what does Christianity have to say about what appears to be holy war commanded by God in the Old Testament book of Joshua? Christians have long distinguished between God's commands in the taking of the Promised Land and later biblical and New Testament history. When it comes to the Old Testament case, we have significant teaching that Catholics, Orthodox, and Protestants have agreed on by the likes of Augustine, Calvin, Luther, and others. This teaching sees the period recorded in the books of Joshua and Judges thus: an omnipotent and loving God commanded all peoples to honor him, and in case after case humanity refused to do so. God, in his sovereignty, commanded that justice be rendered on various Canaanite peoples for their idolatry and immorality and divinely appointed the Israelites to employ that justice. It was a holy war in the sense that it was directly and divinely commanded by God although it was bound to a specific time and place. It is noteworthy that it was limited: Israel was not to employ force outside of geographical borders, nor was Israel to use it as a means of global conversion by force (there was a robust vehicle for voluntary conversion in Hebraic law). Israel was not rendering a verdict: God had done so directly, and his commandment was that Israel conquer the land and mete out God's judgment in a way that also returned Israel to its homeland. Christians believe that an omnipotent, good God is just in making such determinations but that this is a unique case in history and does not go beyond.[28]

From David onward, and especially in the New Testament era (which continues to this day), God gave no such commands to his people. Consequently, most Christians look skeptically on the papal claims that drove the Crusades to liberate Palestine, although in the main these were largely defensive wars responding to Muslim aggression and thus justified.[29] If a

---

[28]For an examination of the Canaanite warfare in its ancient Near Eastern context with hyperbole, see Paul Copan, *Is God a Moral Monster?* (Grand Rapids, MI: Baker Books, 2011); Copan and Matthew Flannagan, *Did God Really Command Genocide?* (Grand Rapids, MI: Baker Books, 2014); and Copan, *Is God a Vindictive Bully? Reconciling Portrayals of God in the Old and New Testaments* (Grand Rapids, MI: Baker Academic, 2022).

[29]See Jonathan Riley-Smith, *What Were the Crusades?*, 4th ed. (San Francisco: Ignatius Press, 2009); Riley-Smith, *The Crusades, Christianity, and Islam* (New York: Columbia University Press, 2008); Thomas F. Madden, *The New Concise History of the Crusades* (Lanham, MD: Rowman and Littlefield, 2013).

religious figure operates outside of Scripture and God's explicit divine command to enjoin a war of conquest on behalf of religious ends, it simply does not comport with classical Christian views, whether condoned by a pope in the eleventh century or a Serbian priest in the twentieth century. It is noteworthy that such calls to holy war are rooted first in the individual's clerical authority and second in the claim that holy war will purify the warrior (through struggle and sacrifice) and purify the land (by cleansing it of unbelievers). Consequently, the Crusades, though primarily a protective measure, may have technically been a "holy war" (or, better, "religious war") because an ecclesiastical official justified them, but that by itself does not make them "holy," "righteous," or "just." Christians do not believe that God has commanded total war on religious grounds in the New Testament era. It is only through the atoning work of Christ that humanity can be purified, not through individual works.

CONCLUSION: CHRISTIANS IN ALL PHASES OF WAR

Jesus' "turn the other cheek" idiom is often used in a way that loses sight of how Christians are called, both as citizens and especially in their differing vocations, to serve across all aspects of war and turmoil. Lewis understood this and illustrated it in the gifts given to the Pevensie children, who became the kings and queens of Narnia. Peter, as high king, was given a sword and shield. Susan was given a bow and, importantly, a horn. When that horn sounded the alarm, help would come. Lucy was given a small dagger for personal defense and a vial of precious healing ointment. Readers will recall that one of the most poignant scenes in the Narnia adventures is when Lucy, acting as a sister (private citizen), wants to focus her attention on her wounded brother Edmund rather than on caring for the crowds of wounded around her:

> They found Edmund . . . covered in blood, his mouth was open, and his face a nasty green color. "Quick, Lucy," said Aslan. And then, almost for the first time, Lucy remembered the precious cordial. . . . Her hands trembled so much that she could hardly undo the stopper, but she managed it in the end and poured a few drops into her brother's mouth.
> "There are other people wounded," said Aslan, while she was still looking eagerly into Edmund's pale face and wondering if the cordial would have any result. "Yes, I know," said Lucy crossly. "Wait a minute."

"Daughter of Eve," said Aslan in a graver voice, "others also are on the point of death. Must more people die for Edmund?"[30]

The point is that Lucy, in her role as queen and with the gift of a healing potion in her hands, has a responsibility to serve and heal, just as Susan has a responsibility to sound the alarm and Peter has a responsibility to protect and defend.

So, too, there are roles for Christians across the spectrum of insecurity. US military doctrine speaks of multiple phases of war and, to summarize, these range from the prewar state (insecurity, perhaps humanitarian crisis, perhaps the rise of authoritarian leadership, political belligerence) to the acceleration toward, and envelopment in, hot war, to the late conflict (negotiations going on, planning for the postwar, gearing up for postwar recovery, considerations of the new political order and justice), to the postwar phase. The goal for the latter is not just unstable peace that existed before the war. The goal is a better state of peace.

There are Christians who are called to serve in every phase of conflict. We want and need Christian diplomats who are working to soften disagreements, forge compromises, and even issue stern warnings. In some cases, these are "track two" diplomats, the term given to private-sector leaders (e.g., religious leaders, business leaders) who serve as private intermediaries to governments or their counterparts in other countries.

In areas where there is a humanitarian crisis, there are almost always Christians working via relief organizations (e.g., World Vision, Samaritan's Purse, Operation Blessing): they are there before the UN and Western governments arrive, and the faith-based humanitarians will be there long after the UN departs. When the bullets start to fly, we need principled Christians to be involved in the halls of power making decisions, like Daniel and Joseph, and we need principled Christians operating in the military, adhering to the moral principles of just war thinking. At war's end, Christians will continue to serve on the ground to ameliorate suffering. We also need Christians to bring their wisdom to negotiating the new political order, establishing reasonable justice, and seeking long-term conciliation.

To this point little has been said about forgiveness. Forgiveness is not easy to achieve between millions of people (collectives) via their governments. I

---

[30]C. S. Lewis, *The Lion, the Witch and the Wardrobe* (New York: Collier, 1950), 176-77.

have discussed political forms of reconciliation in the section on *jus post bellum*. However, there are a number of areas where Christians can work for conciliation at the individual level. In the church, pastors and spiritual leaders must preach that even in times of war, there is no place in the Christian heart for hatred. We fight for our country, for what is right, for our allies, to preserve human life and property, and for the vindication of rights. We do not fight for revenge, nor out of lust, hatred, or greed.

It is not only the warriors who need this message: it is especially needed for spouses, children, and parents of those in harm's way, the fallen, and the wounded. I recall the vitriol in my own grandmother's voice when one of my neighbors purchased a Japanese car in 1985, forty years after the Japanese surrendered. She could not imagine anyone buying anything from the "Japs who attacked us" on December 7, 1941. Pastors have a responsibility for leading their congregations through reflection, healing, and forgiveness.

Other Christians will serve in ministries of healing and conciliation. Some of this is the healing of the body, through the medical arts and sciences, whether triaging patients on the margins of battlefields or managing longer-term care and recovery of veterans at home. Many wounds are hidden but just as lethal, and we need Christian counselors, psychiatrists, and psychologists to serve as agents of healing for trauma, PTSD, moral injury, and moral bruising.[31]

In sum, there is no opt-out option for the people who call themselves Christ followers. Christians are called to serve in the time and place where

---

[31]It is beyond the scope of this chapter to go into the nuances of these categories. The best primer from an explicitly Christian perspective is Marc LiVecche, *The Good Kill: Just War and Moral Injury* (Oxford: Oxford University Press, 2021). Post-traumatic stress disorder (PTSD), recognized by previous generations with terms such as "shell shock," refers to a "broadly defined mental health disorder" emerging from "exposure to . . . or witnessing, a particularly kind of traumatic event, typically life threatening and of such intensity that it results in stressors outside the range of human experience." Note that PTSD's stressors are from "outside the sufferer," unlike other mental health problems (e.g., those associated with chemical imbalance). In recent years a different diagnosis, "moral injury," has been used to describe the "lasting psychological . . . impact of perpetrating, failing to prevent, or bearing witness to acts that transgress deeply held moral beliefs and expectations." An example might result from a US Marine killing a child in combat, despite the fact that the thirteen-year-old Afghan male was shooting a rifle at the Marine under foggy conditions. Marc LiVecche differentiates moral *injury* from moral *bruising*, the latter a term for times when it is not forgiveness that is needed (no moral wrong was done, though a tragedy occurred) but rather vindication (yes, a tragedy occurred; here are the steps toward coming to terms with something that was entirely not your fault). See LiVecche's excellent discussion of these issues with definitions and citations (*The Good Kill*, 21-25).

God has put them and utilize the skills and talents he has given them. Thus, whether preparing the hearts of the local church to prayerfully respond to injustice and violence, caring for the destitute in a hospital in Africa, fighting on the frontlines to stop a genocide in the Middle East, negotiating a just peace treaty in Europe, protecting one's locale from criminals and terrorists, or serving the psychiatric needs of veterans on the home front, there are many, many roles that Christians are called on to play across the various phases of conflict. These important domains reflect virtuous callings, and we, as Christians, are motivated by love of God and love of neighbor to fulfill our vocations in them.

A Nonviolence Response

MYLES WERNTZ

In Eric Patterson's presentation of the just war tradition, we find a portrayal of the intersection of Christian thought and practice that poses a deep challenge for the modern world. The description of moral reasoning Patterson offers, that of "just statecraft," bears little resemblance to the worst kinds of militarisms. It is a serious description and warrants a serious response.

In the space that follows, I will limit myself to the heart of Patterson's argument: the nature of Christian vocation vis-à-vis violence, and its relationship to public life. There are a number of stereotypes concerning the depictions of nonviolence that Patterson makes here; I address these in my own essay, and refer the reader there. In this space, I want rather to investigate two aspects of Patterson's essay: (1) the relationship of Christians to their society and (2) the implications of this vision for Christian vocation in a violent world.

UNTANGLING THE STATE IN THE JUST WAR TRADITION

Characterizing the just war tradition as "just statecraft," Patterson rightly rejects the baleful "checklist" approach to the just war and offers this version of the just war as the one that most clearly approximates the theological tradition. But his reading of the just war tradition as statecraft is hard to reconcile with the vision of both Scripture and theological tradition: to say that statecraft is the most workable notion of just war is different from saying that it is the most cohesive to the tradition, for reasons I will state shortly.

I will begin with the biblical warrant for this position. It is indisputable that the Old Testament packages together expectations of religious and political governance into one body. But the New Testament—with the decline of Israel as a nation—presents difficulties to carrying this vision of statecraft forward. Patterson connects the testaments by way of Romans 13:3, but this conflates governance as a principle of human organization with the *sanctioning* of governance.[1] To say that Christians should pay taxes as a matter of prudence is one thing (Rom 13:3), both as what is good for one's neighbor and for the sake of Christian formation: God affirms orderly social relations. But it is another thing to say that God sacralizes the act of statecraft. To test Patterson's hypothesis of divine sanction for statecraft, let us ask the counterfactual: Can we envision Paul commending his congregations to *join* the Roman army, since statecraft is sanctioned by God, as an act transposable out of the Old Testament's theocratic vision? If—and only if—the answer is yes can Patterson's narrative be sustained. Surely it cannot be the case that Rome is the rightful inheritor of *Israel's* political vocation: what Israel at its best means by "order" and what Rome means are not the same. While the Romans may have been expeditious governors, they were not just, nor were they analogically continuing Israel's vocation, and no early Christian apologist would call for Christian participation in statecraft on this basis.

Within Patterson's reading of the Christian tradition, the same elision occurs between order as a principle and the sanction of government as a divine vocation. Contrary to Patterson's assertion, in Augustine and Aquinas, what we find is not a full-blown theory of governance or statecraft (Augustine held that Rome was frequently a demonic parody of the city of God!), but a concern for Christian virtue; when Augustine instructs those outside the Christian faith, such as his writings to Boniface and to Faustus, he is defending the integrity of the two testaments of Scripture and what kind of virtues are becoming of creatures of God, not writing a full-scale political treatise. Aquinas, likewise, writes on war not as a theory of statecraft but as one writing a diagnostic for priests, that they might ascertain what sin has been committed and what the remedy might be.[2]

---

[1] For a better reading on this dynamic, see Scot McKnight, *Reading Romans Backwards: A Gospel of Peace in the Midst of Empire* (Waco, TX: Baylor University Press, 2019), 49.

[2] See Jean Porter, *Justice as a Virtue: A Thomistic Perspective* (Grand Rapids, MI: Eerdmans, 2016), 6-17. Aquinas writes these questions as part of what would have been used as a manual for priests needing guidance for applying penance, not as theories of governance. Thus his concern here is not for statecraft but for the kinds of virtue the soul is inclined to.

These distinctions matter precisely because, while Augustine and Aquinas are committed to the good of the common society, there remained a distinction between secular virtue and Christian virtue that could not be effaced. Patterson's description, however, equivocates between the gifts of the Spirit to the Christian and the vocation to statecraft, finding "stewardship" in Scripture to be a principle that is univocally applicable across life, contrary to what we find in the Scriptures, and in Augustine and Aquinas.

The roots of the just war that we find in Augustine and that is further developed in Aquinas are not ordered, in other words, toward providing guidance for magistrates, but in negotiating the nature of Christian virtue. In emphasizing virtue in their writings on war (Augustine's rightly ordered love, and Aquinas's emphasis on justice), both were writing for Christian congregations and for penitents asking questions about the Christian life. Neither was writing treatises of statecraft, but offering instruction in virtue. With the post-Reformation figures of Vitoria and Suárez, and with the rise of the secular state, this initial mooring is left behind, and these questions became questions of statecraft, not of virtue.

It is important to name this genealogy, because without it we make the erroneous assumption that Scripture and the theological tradition are primarily ordered to the governance of state. If we assume a natural companionship between them (as Augustine did not), then we are left with the assumption that statecraft and governance are naturally what Christian discipleship entails. This, however, would have been a great surprise to Augustine, and to nearly all the Christians who preceded him.

CHRISTIAN VOCATION IN A VIOLENT WORLD

The scriptural justifications for public political participation are important to sort out, because this sorting allows us to see what is at stake in describing the just war as statecraft. Perhaps in a pluralist context, this is the best one can hope for—that the world becomes restrained and accordingly less bad—and thus what the just war tradition can offer is a theory of governance that attempts to restrain the worst violence of the world. But does it follow that just war is the only option for achieving the ends of just war: public order and public service?

Patterson begins his defense of his model of just war by emphasizing the relation between war and public service. It is at this juncture that the distance between the just war and pacifism grows far less, I believe. There are multiple interpretations of the just war that hew close to pacifism in this way, that both are concerned with the protection of the innocent and with the prevention of loss of life.[3] It bears noting that many of the features he ascribes to the just war are common properties of those who do not hold to the just war, such as the need to protect the innocent, the need for countries to relate to one another well, the need for public order, and the desire for just relations to obtain among neighbors.

At the risk of being controversial among pacifists, let me concede another similarity: the pacifist is likewise *not* bound to the proposition that force is, in and of itself, a negative thing: force simply means the ability to accomplish something. Even in the most well-trod pacifist text, the Schleitheim Confession of the Anabaptists,[4] which forbids Christians from taking up the sword, hardly resigns the Anabaptists simply to talking nice to people in order to accomplish what is good, but employs the ban, the removal of someone from the fellowship.[5] To not only ask my son to do what is good but also to punish him when he does not is to exercise force, but it does not follow that lethal force lies behind my appeal to my son.[6] As I have suggested elsewhere, just warriors are not the only ones capable of working

---

[3]For these, see in particular Tobias L. Winright, "Two Rival Versions of Just War Theory and the Presumption Against Harm in Policing," *The Annual of the Society of Christian Ethics* 18 (1998): 221-39; and Drew Christiansen et al., "Must Just Peace and Just War Be Mutually Exclusive?," *Horizons* 45, no. 1 (2018): 105-27.

[4]As I discuss in my own essay, Schleitheim is not the view of most contemporary Christian pacifists.

[5]Michael Sattler, "The Schleitheim Articles," in *The Radical Reformation*, ed. Michael G. Baylor, Cambridge Texts in the History of Political Thought (Cambridge: Cambridge University Press, 1991).

[6]Patterson's case is significantly overstated, then, when he writes that the rejection of *violence* by pacifists logically entails a rejection of *force*. By linking so tightly "force," "the exercise of violence," and "public responsibility," Patterson rhetorically rigs the game such that the reader is left with the impression that a pacifist might not discipline their children for fear of violating this core principle. A broad swath of on-the-ground nonviolent movements—from the American civil rights movement to the Polish revolution of 1983 to the farmworker protests of the 1960s to the Christian Peacemaker teams—attest that it is irresponsible to suggest that pacifists do not care for the innocent in situations of violence. See Myles Werntz and David Cramer, *A Field Guide to Christian Nonviolence: Key Thinkers, Activists, and Movements for the Gospel of Peace* (Grand Rapids, MI: Baker Academic, 2022) for details of this vast body of practitioners and thinkers.

within categories that seek not only to stop wars, minister in the midst of violence, or work for peace in the wake of violence.[7]

It is not the exercise of force that divides pacifists and just war proponents here—whether to persuade, coerce, or even to nonlethally restrain—but the imagination of who counts as "the neighbor," or as we have seen, linking together discipleship, Scripture, and statecraft. In linking the vocation to love one's neighbors to one's neighbors *bound together by the same state* (consistent with the post-Vitoria traditions of just war), Patterson alters the Christian vocabulary surrounding being a neighbor, offering service, or justice such that one's concerns for order, justice, and vocation begin with those who are nationally proximate to them.

The question before us at this point is not simply whether just war as statecraft is theologically consistent, or what the Christian should desire with respect to their response to violence: the pacifist agrees with the just warrior that war offers less than is desirable for God's vision of creation. The just warrior does not hold that what just war offers with respect to war is an ideal for what creation is or that war comports to the perfections of God. War, for the just warrior, exists as an accommodation to a world in sin, a restraining ethic before the eschaton.[8] The Christian hope is one in which the nations come streaming into Jerusalem and in which Christ is made all in all.

To declare that hope as that which occurs beyond the edge of history, however, is to underplay the suffering that Christians might expect as they live out this vision of reconciliation in the present. There is no promise, either by the just war or by pacifists, that a violent world can be undone by violence. And as such, we must all continue to pray for the kingdom to come, and to offer ourselves as peacemakers in ways consistent with the one of whom the apostle Paul wrote, "Very rarely will anyone die for a righteous person, though for a good person someone might possibly dare to die. But God demonstrates his own love for us in this: While we were still sinners, Christ died for us" (Rom 5:7-8 NIV).

---

[7]Myles Werntz, "Terrorism and the Peace of Christ: Seeking Pacifism's Future in Theory and Practice," *Philosophia Christi* 18 (2016): 109-17.

[8]I take this to be properly Patterson's view.

A Christian Realist Response

A. J. NOLTE

I must start my response to Eric Patterson's essay with a cheerful confession that will become evident when the reader looks through my own chapter: not only is Patterson one of the top just war scholars writing in the United States today, but he's also an esteemed expert on Reinhold Niebuhr, the leading twentieth-century exponent of what I have called "dirty-hands" Christian realism. When one adds to this the fact that the differences between a just war and a Niebuhrian perspective are quite nuanced, it's no little surprise that there is a great deal in his chapter with which I agree, and a good deal, though perhaps somewhat less, with which Niebuhr would have agreed. It is no accident that Patterson, in other venues, has argued that just war statecraft is essentially Christian realist, though not Niebuhrian. Thus, in this response, I will attempt to sketch out what I think is the most important difference between Augustinian just war theory and the dirty-hands perspective—a theological issue at the root of the lesser-evil versus lesser-good distinction that divides these two approaches—the strengths and weaknesses of each, and the benefits of a possible synthesis.

As I describe in my chapter, Niebuhr's chief quarrel with Augustine is that he views the latter's pessimism about human nature as "too consistent"—a critique he also extends to Luther and Calvin.[1] In other words, notwithstanding the assumption one might make given his dirty-hands view of warfare, Niebuhr is actually more of an optimist than Augustine regarding human nature. Augustine, of course, was responding to the Pelagian heresy,

---

[1] On this point, see Daniel Rice, *Reinhold Niebuhr and His Circle of Influence* (Cambridge: Cambridge University Press, 2012), 158-59.

which essentially argued that human beings can save themselves from sin entirely through their own merits. This doctrine is problematic on a number of levels, and when combined with his opposition to the ultra-rigorist Donatists, who believed Christians could, and should, live in a pure fashion untainted by the world, Augustine's skepticism about human nature makes sense in context. For Augustine, the effects of sin were all but total, depriving humans of their ability to achieve any kind of real or full justice on their own. As Augustine scholar Robert Dodaro makes clear, "In view of the pervasive nature of original sin from Augustine's perspective, Christ is able to establish a just society only because, as the God-man, he alone is able to heal human beings of the ignorance and weakness which prevent them both from understanding the obligations of justice and from fulfilling them."[2]

Niebuhr, by contrast, viewed sin not as inherited corruption (the Augustinian view) but rather as "an inevitable taint upon the spirituality of a finite creature, always enslaved to time and place, never completely enslaved and always under the illusion that the measure of his emancipation is greater than it really is."[3] Niebuhr also differs from Augustine in that he sees within humanity a "capacity for justice," though he acknowledges that this capacity is counterbalanced by an "inclination to injustice."[4] Niebuhr's most famous critique was of unbounded optimism, and in this capacity, he affirmed the pervasive effect of original sin:

> No matter how wide the perspectives which the human mind may reach, how broad the loyalties which the human imagination may conceive, how universal the community which human statecraft may organize, or how pure the aspirations of the saintliest idealists may be, there is no level of human moral or social achievement in which there is not some corruption of inordinate self-love.[5]

Nevertheless, he thought Augustine's stark pessimism, reflected in his theology of the two totally distinct cities, was "too consistent to give a true picture of either human nature or the human community, even before the

---

[2]Robert Dodaro, *Christ and the Just Society in the Thought of Augustine* (Cambridge: Cambridge University Press, 2004), 2.

[3]Reinhold Niebuhr, *Beyond Tragedy: Essays on the Christian Interpretation of History* (1937; repr., New York: Charles Scribner's Sons, 1965), 39-40.

[4]Reinhold Niebuhr, *The Children of Light and the Children of Darkness: A Vindication of Democracy and a Critique of Its Traditional Defense* (New York: Charles Scribner's Sons, 1944), xxi.

[5]Niebuhr, *Children of Light*, 16-17.

advent of free governments, and was certainly irrelevant to modern democratic governments."[6]

Perry Hamalis finds Eastern Orthodox thought on this point to be quite close to Niebuhr, emphasizing that Eastern Orthodox thinkers share the Niebuhrian Christian realist understanding of "an abiding hopefulness about humanity's potential for goodness and holiness through God's grace and the right use of human freedom."[7] To briefly summarize a complex theological difference, Eastern Orthodox theologians tend to emphasize sin's nature as a stain on the soul that impairs the image of God rather than as an inherited corruption. Their approach is also less juridical and categorical than that of Western theologians: the question is less whether humans are legally guilty of sin, and more what effect sin has on the soul, the world, and one's fellow image bearers.[8]

I would argue that it is precisely because of this differing conception of sin that Niebuhr and the Eastern Orthodox take a different approach to war than Augustine and just war theologians. Because of their more optimistic conception of humanity, Niebuhr and the Eastern Orthodox share a "categorical rejection of death's 'blessedness,' or 'acceptability.'"[9] Hamalis says, "For the Orthodox, death is the enemy: it is contrary to God's will and essentially tragic," citing Metropolitan John (Zizioulas) of Pergamon: "The [Orthodox] Christian view is that death is never good; it is always an 'outrage.'"[10] This has direct implications in terms of war: "Even if war is the best available option, it is always tragic, always destructive, always a cause for mourning and for repentance."[11]

Augustine's understanding is quite different: his pessimism about human nature leads him to a corresponding pessimism about the good human beings can achieve. In his words,

---

[6]Rice, *Reinhold Niebuhr*, 158-59.

[7]Perry T. Hamalis, "Just Peacemaking and Christian Realism: Possibilities for Moving Beyond the Impasse in Orthodox Christian War Ethics," in *Orthodox Christian Perspectives on War*, ed. Perry T. Hamalis and Valerie A. Karras (Notre Dame, IN: University of Notre Dame Press, 2017), 348.

[8]I am indebted to Father Job Serebrov, a graduate of Saint Vladimir's Seminary and now a priest in the Anglican Church of North America, for his helpful comments on this theological summary of Eastern Orthodox conceptions of sin.

[9]Hamalis, "Just Peacemaking," 350.

[10]Hamalis, "Just Peacemaking," 350.

[11]Hamalis, "Just Peacemaking," 350.

This earthly city, which shall not be everlasting (for it will no longer be a city when it has been committed to perpetual pains) has all its good in this world, and rejoices in it with such joy as such things can afford. . . . Though united by a common nature, [it] is for the most part divided against itself, and the strongest oppress the others, because all follow after their own interests and lusts, while what is longed for either suffices for none, or not for all, because it is not the true good. Each part of it that arms against another desires to be the world's master, whereas it is itself in bondage to vice. . . . Yet one cannot say that the things this earthly city desires are not good, since it itself is, of its kind, better than all other human things. For it desires earthly peace for the sake of enjoying earthly goods, and it makes war in order to attain this peace; since, if it has conquered, and there remains no one to resist it, it enjoys a peace which it had not while there were opposing parties to contest it for the enjoyment of those things which were too little to satisfy both.[12]

Thus Augustine's belief that higher goods are unattainable for humanity leads him to an acceptance that the best attainable is, itself, a lesser good. Just war theory follows naturally from this premise, for once it has been accepted that a kind of peace in which earthly goods may be pursued is the highest good attainable in the political sphere, it also follows that war designed to preserve this good is, itself, not evil. And, to be fair, Augustine imposes more constraint on just war than his pessimism might suggest. As Dodaro explains,

Christ's unique status as a fully just human being means that he cannot serve as an example of repentance and dependence upon divine grace, which, Augustine concludes, believers require in order to live justly. The city of God on pilgrimage through the earthly city therefore requires as its "heroes" saints such as King David and the apostles Peter and Paul, whose public acts of penance make them suitable models for members of the just commonwealth ruled by Christ.[13]

Thus the model for a statesman, magistrate, or Christian soldier is not Christ, who is himself without sin, but the example of those righteous men who have held this vocation in the past.

---

[12]Augustine, *City of God*, quoted in *The Political Writings of St. Augustine*, ed. Henry Paolucci (Washington, DC: Regnery, 1962), 13-14.
[13]Dodaro, *Christ and the Just Society*, 4.

One point is worth making regarding the nonjuridical conception of sin held by the Eastern Orthodox and, to some extent, shared by Niebuhr. Just war theory is at pains to make clear that soldiers are not "guilty" of the blood of those killed in just wars. Thus, by just war standards, the dirty-hands conception is inconsistent: if war is necessary to prevent a greater tragedy, then how can we hold those who serve in it legally responsible? This is actually a strength of just war theory in some ways, as I believe it raises the bar above which a cause must rise if it is to be seen as both just and necessary. That is, the determination that those who fight in just wars must not be deemed "guilty" of the blood of those killed in war makes it incumbent on practitioners of just war statecraft to keep their standards consistent, and consistently high. That being said, I'm not sure that a dirty-hands perspective necessitates the opposite conclusion: that those who fight in necessary wars are, in some sense, "guilty" of the blood spilled in these wars.

Both Niebuhr and the Eastern Orthodox engage ethical questions on a practical, pastoral level. In Hamalis's words, "Orthodox ethics tends to work more personally and contextually, from the ground up, than theoretically and abstractly, from the top down."[14] I wonder, then, if dirty hands might be seen less as a legal judgment of guilt than a pastoral judgment about the effects of sin: those who have taken the life of another image bearer, no matter how necessary the cause, incur a kind of spiritual damage as a result, which must, in some fashion, be repaired.

I will conclude by tipping my hand as to my own personal views. The differences and distinctions between these conceptions of sin have been debated by some of the greatest Christian theologians in history. That said, I think a certain amount of synthesis is possible and desirable. On one hand, I think just war statecraft is probably better equipped to wrestle with broad questions of when war is just and necessary, what conduct in war ought to look like, and what an acceptable resolution to such a war should be, than a dirty-hands perspective. Recognition that peace and order are necessary albeit lesser goods both accurately assesses the limits of politics and curbs any enthusiasm for an "ends justify the means" approach. Notwithstanding the claims of some opponents of just war statecraft, from both East and

---

[14]Hamalis "Just Peacemaking," 342.

West, I see much less tendency for just war statecraft to slide into holy war than a dirty-hands perspective.

On the other hand, the strength of the dirty-hands approach is more pastoral and spiritual. With its insistence on the dignity and sanctity of every human life, this perspective reminds us not only of the moral seriousness of killing in war—just war statecraft has not forgotten this—but also of the spiritual cost of killing in war. Have we, as Western evangelical Christians, sufficiently grappled with the fact that there are those in our churches who, however necessary the cause, have been required to kill their fellow image bearers? Have we done what is necessary to help our brothers and sisters process this morally serious act? Leaving aside any question of moral guilt, have we recognized that this act has a spiritual cost that is itself an effect of the fall, into which the healing love of Christ must be brought? I believe the perspectives of Niebuhr and the Eastern Orthodox place these questions front and center perhaps more directly than an Augustinian just war perspective would do. Notwithstanding the theological differences that undergird these two traditions, then, I think there are symmetries between them that can enrich a robust Christian understanding of war.

A Church Historical Response

MEIC PEARSE

Eric Patterson begins his piece with an exposition of C. S. Lewis, with whom I, like so many of us, find it hard to disagree about anything. Nevertheless, I do disagree with Lewis—*not* in his acceptance that war may be unavoidable, nor in his discussions of the considerations that may cause us to fight, but in his sometimes mean-spirited depiction of pacifists.[1] As Stanley Hauerwas (himself a pacifist) says, "He made little effort to understand the most defensible forms of Christian pacifism," which are "not . . . because we believe that nonviolence is a strategy to rid the world of war, but because nonviolence is constitutive of what it means to be a disciple to Jesus."[2]

Similarly, I do not agree with Patterson's dismissal of Anabaptism as "an anomaly" (it is not hard to demonstrate the continuity of its ethos with that of the pre-Constantinian church), nor that a mere majority makes for a very compelling argument about anything—or we might all have to give up being Christians entirely.

And here we come to the crucial point that brings Lewis and the dismissal of Anabaptism together: in determining a *Christian* position, practical outcomes for society—the Kantian consideration of how it would be if everyone were to do something—is as far beside the point as is an

---

[1]"I am indebted to [this] society for my birth and my upbringing, for the education which has allowed me to be a Pacifist, and the tolerant laws which allow me to remain one." C. S. Lewis, "Why I Am Not a Pacifist," in *The Weight of Glory*, ed. Walter Hooper (London: MacMillan, 1949), 81. Even pacifists, one might reply, have to be born and brought up *somewhere*!

[2]Stanley Hauerwas, "Could C.S. Lewis Have Imagined a World Without War?," ABC Religion and Ethics, July 18, 2011, www.abc.net.au/religion/could-cs-lewis-have-imagined-a-world-without-war/10101312.

assessment of majorities. The nub of the question—and goodness knows, that is difficult enough—is, What would Jesus have *his followers* to do?

Politics may have its place, but it is something we do on our own time, like carpentry or teaching. It is compatible with being a Christian but subject to all the constraints of discipleship, and not to be confused with the faith itself. For Christianity is no more a program for running the body politic than it is a blueprint for building a wooden sailing ship or for a particular form of pedagogy.

This becomes particularly eye-catching in Patterson's description of one of the virtues ascribed to Reepicheep: "rightful patriotism." This expression alone is subject to a dozen possible definitions. Should Jesus have endorsed the Zealot party in Palestine? And if not, why not? And if the answer is, "Because the Romans were lawfully constituted authority," then the American rebels of the 1770s should presumably have just knuckled under. After all, they had far less to put up with than Palestinian Jews in the time of Jesus. And if we wish to argue *for* the rebels of the 1770s but *against* the Zealots of Jesus' day, we shall find soon enough that we have descended into the merest casuistry. And the reason for *that* is that just war arguments, both historically and in the present, always find in favor of the causes their protagonists were inclined to favor anyway, and against those about which they do not care.

My own point is not for or against any of these political positions, whether past or present, or even for or against Reepicheep's "rightful patriotism." (As it happens, I'm for it—though I would contend for my own preferred definitions of both the adjective and the noun.) My point is that none of these positions are, or can be, *Christian*. To talk that way is to make a category error. Sure, Reepicheep is an exemplar of civic virtue. But an exemplar of Christian discipleship? Not on the evidence of *The Voyage of the Dawn Treader*.

One of the most telling points in Patterson's essay is his quotation of Paul Ramsey: "What do you think Jesus would have made the Samaritan do if he had come upon the scene while the robbers were still at their fell work?" (p. 17).

Well, quite! I have no good answer to that one. And neither, I suspect, do pacifists. But perhaps that is just the point: Jesus does not propel us into imagining ourselves using force. That much we do all too easily for ourselves, almost every day. Jesus was surrounded by all manner of men who imagined little else. The specifically *following Jesus* aspect of following Jesus is to bind up the broken, to show mercy. And so the tale of the good Samaritan propels us into imagining that instead. The pacifist might add that exactly this delimitation of Jesus' parable is an implicit prohibition against the use of force, even to defend the good. I, as has been made clear elsewhere in this book, would not go so far: Jesus merely assumes we have our own ideas about force, but he does not sanction any of them—still less sanctify them—because that is not what his kingdom is about.

Patterson is right, as all would agree, in citing Augustine as one of the fountainheads of thinking about just war within the Christian tradition. He says, "Augustine argues that within society, adherence to the rule of law, including punishment of lawbreakers, was a way of loving one's neighbors" (p. 22). But Augustine's definition of "loving our neighbors" is a little too lax for me—and, I suspect, for most of us. He argues that punishing heretics and schismatics is a way of loving them also! (Indeed, everyone's favorite quotation from the great man—"Love, and do as you like"—is, *in context*, part of a sermon advocating persecution of schismatics!)[3] "Hate" has lately been redefined by the "woke" as daring to disagree with them. Similarly, if "love" is to be understood this counterintuitively, we may be headed for some very peculiar understandings indeed.

This brings us to the historical difficulty of so much connected with Patterson's argument—and all such arguments—for just war. He says, "The Bible does not give us a single model of civic government" (p. 20), which he intends on purely expository grounds, whereas I would contend that even to ask such a question of the text is to make a category error. Then he adds, "and thus it is human creativity that has come up with different arrangements, such as constitutional monarchy and democracy, for organizing society" (p. 20).

Well, neither of those two examples is among the "models" to be found in the Bible. So, why these two examples here? Why no mention of feudalism and serfdom? Absolutist monarchy? Rule by oligarchs? The Roman Empire—complete with slavery and crucifixion? After all, these are what

---

[3]Augustine of Hippo, *Ten Homilies on the First Epistle of John* 7.8 (*NPNF*[1] 7.504).

was on offer for most of Christian history and—here is the crucial point—
formed the context in which just war arguments were framed. Any arguments
that assume only present Western arrangements are "just" and to be defended as such would be the merest post facto rationalization.

Constitutional monarchy and democracy are products of recent times.
The latter was anathema not just to Augustine but to all of the Protestant
Reformers. Constitutional monarchy—though not under that phrase—
might have been acceptable to Calvin, though he would not have had it
allow even for religious toleration let alone all the other freedoms we associate with that form of government today.

Nor will it do to say that they were people of their time. For so are we.
They took as axiomatic all manner of political mechanisms that we should
reject. And the crucial element that formed Christian just war thinking—
and formed the thinking of Augustine and Protestant Reformers alike—
was the assumption of a "Christian state," with a single, compulsory church
(hence Augustine's "love" rationale for persecuting dissenters), *to defend
which a rationale was needed for participating in warfare.* This is why
Patterson rightly reminds us, "At the end of the fourth century AD,
Augustine . . . pondered the conditions for the just employment of force in
political life" (p. 22). Such a pondering had become necessary by his time,
but not before. Perhaps it was this circumstance that led him to rely for his
framework, not so much on Christian precedents (for, in truth, there were
none), as on the pagan Roman orator Cicero, on whose writings Augustine
was considered something of an expert, and whose writings he quoted
widely (and also paraphrased) in his own works, especially *City of God*.[4]

The Christian just war approach, then, is inextricable from a whole set
of assumptions about what Christianity is, which would no longer be
accepted—indeed, would be vehemently rejected—by all modern Christians except die-hard theocrats. For Christendom (the "Christian state"
model) has disintegrated over the past three centuries, and nobody—not
even Catholics, most Orthodox, or those Protestants who are proud to claim
lineage from Luther and Calvin—wants it back. Just war thinking may have
its place as part of a secular rationale—which is how it began under the

---

[4]Peter Brown, *Augustine of Hippo: A Biography* (Berkeley: University of California Press, 1970), 299.

pagan orator Cicero. But to continue to urge it as something *Christian* is like clinging to the beams of a ship that has already sunk.

Patterson is quite right to bewail that many Christians today "neglect Augustine's presupposition that political order is the foundation for society" (p. 23). But this is not peculiar to Christians in the West; the assumption that political order will somehow take care of itself is a generalized disease from which, as so often, Christians have failed to immunize themselves. But the needful concern for social foundations is something universal, in the sense that the society that neglects it will disintegrate and fall to rivals—as ours is in the process of doing. But to concede these points, with which I feel sure Patterson would agree, does not make the specifying of legitimate violence a part of Christian theology, for all of us will cast about for specifications that favor our own society, and we are looking here for something that is specifically Christian.

Would Patterson's example of his friend who is an admiral have been as persuasive, even to himself, had the friend been in the Russian Navy? Or the Chinese? How about the Iranian? "He may be called on to make decisions that are literally life or death to defend his sailors, to protect those in foreign lands at risk of genocide, or to punish criminals, pirates, and terrorists. . . . His professional vocation is motivated by *love*, not hate: the desire to the lives, livelihoods, and way of life of his family, community, and country" (p. 19, emphasis added). We are back with his choice of democracy and constitutional monarchy as orders that need defending: modern, Western, his (and, of course, mine).

The reality is that this entire approach has its origins in secular thought forms (which is no argument against it all, of course—unless we wish to make it a part of *Christian* theology); that it became part of Christian thinking at the point where the original purpose of the faith was subverted by alliance with the (extremely ruthless) Roman Empire; that its criteria (see Patterson's figure 1) have been used as a legitimation by all sides in pretty much every conflict since; and that these criteria have been re-rationalized in the present as a defense of precisely *our* kinds of society, with which we feel comfortable. In view of all this, I would contend that we are a very long way from home.

None of this is to deny that Christians can ever fight, or play a part in public life—or, in particular, help in making peace (Patterson points out the contribution of Archbishop Desmond Tutu in post-apartheid South Africa). But it is to insist that the attempt to codify this is futile—partly because war is a radical evil that weaponizes all moral (or merely "moral") criteria in the various causes of the protagonists, and partly because fighting for some particular social order is not part of our calling. Jesus' kingdom is "not of this world," for we have here "no lasting city, but we seek the city that is to come" (Jn 18:36; Heb 13:14 ESV).

Just War Rejoinder

ERIC PATTERSON

First, allow me to thank each of the other contributors for their serious engagement with my chapter. Each made helpful, interesting points, and the sophisticated reader should be encouraged toward prayerful reflection on a complete reading of the book.

Second, I would like to conclude with three comments that are formed as a response to the responses of fellow contributors. They have to do with *vocation, love,* and an understanding of where we are at in *redemptive history.*

One of the reasons I disagree with pacifism is the way that it separates nearly all "holy" vocations from "unholy" public service. In this it makes the mistake that many adolescents make about Christians in the professions. It is typical for the evangelical youngster and, unfortunately, his parents to mistakenly think that "real" ministry is professional service as a pastor, worship leader, youth pastor, or missionary. Unfortunately, we have created a hierarchy of callings based on a sacred-secular distinction: church work is sacred; all else is substandard, second-class, and secular. The ramifications of this faulty theology are numerous, including the authoritarianism found in some evangelical pulpits (at this writing there are still ongoing ripple effects of Mark Driscoll and others' authoritarian tendencies), the guilt that some parishioners feel for not being in "full-time" ministry, and so on.

The Bible, and the Reformation's recovery of key doctrines such as the priesthood of all believers, denies these quasi-gnostic sacred-secular distinctions. God made the world and it was good. He made male and female and declared them "very good." Despite the fall, God's imprint is on humankind, including the skills, talents, and aptitudes God has given us.

Unfortunately, we too often make a terrible sacred-secular distinction in our work. We talk about "Christian lawyers" and "Christian politicians" as if there were a singular Christian law or politics. Would we say the same thing about plumbing or carpentry? Is there "Christian plumbing"? Of course, the answer is no. Plumbing should cohere to the basic principles of gravity as God ordained the universe. If one tries to violate the basic laws of gravity—which is the foundation for how pumps, flows, valves, and other plumbing apparatus operate—then you will find yourself in a big mess. *Good* plumbing follows the natural order that God created: it is not created through an atmosphere of Christian pop music playing while a toilet is replaced, nor is it sanctified by fish symbols on T-shirts and business cards. There are people who are Christians who pursue the vocation of plumbing. They should both excel at the craft of plumbing and behave with honesty and integrity in their dealings with customers and employees. The same holds true for a doctor who is a Christian (there is no such thing as distinctly Christian limb-setting or Christian amputation), the grocer who is a Christian (Christian arrangement of turnips?), the electrician who is a Christian, or the public servant who is a Christian. All licit occupations, which exclude, say, prostitution and drug dealing, are valid callings for the Christian.

This brings us back to the many vocations of public service: judges, police, firefighters, soldiers, elected officials, and those appointed to public service. There is simply no biblical doctrine that erases these professions as acts of worship to the Lord and as acts of loving service to one's fellow citizens. That was not the case in the Old Testament, which includes not just public service within the nation of Israel but also the service of Joseph, Daniel, and Nehemiah to foreign, pagan monarchs. Christians believe that God equips and empowers for service in this world. We compromise the value of professions, of God's calling, if we make negative sacred-secular distinctions that privilege "ministry" above "secular jobs." Pacifists often go a step further by denigrating those jobs that are implicated by the use of force in some fashion.

In my chapter on just war thinking, I recalled Paul Ramsey's famous query about the good Samaritan, which I will paraphrase thus: if the good Samaritan had arrived earlier, what should he have done? Turned the other cheek and allowed the robbers to beat him as well? Turned out his pockets?

Cravenly hidden himself? Called for help? One can think of many implications of the good Samaritan story when the reader pulls back for just a
moment and thinks about this as both a private event and a public one. In
addition to ministering to the fallen Jew, the good Samaritan, at the very
least, may have gone to give testimony to local law enforcement (themselves
likely faithful Jewish constables). He may have lobbied local officials to
invest more resources into rooting out brigands and increasing expenditure
on public safety. On the front end, he might have intervened had he been
at the right place at the right time. All of these possibilities suggest the
longer-term, wider application of neighbor love that is inclusive of both the
wounded individual and practical efforts to ensure such does not happen
again to one of my other neighbors.

This bridges the concept of vocation (calling) with the doctrine of love.
How does one do neighbor love in the world in which we live? One of the
other contributors reminds us that rightly ordered love is important for the
Christian. C. S. Lewis may help us here. In *The Four Loves*, Lewis discusses
expanding circles of love of neighbor. Lewis begins with one's own neighborhood: it is entirely right to feel comfortable in, to love, one's own backyard.
Lewis is speaking about both the intimacy of one's closest obligations (i.e.,
family) and the consolation that many people feel in their most familiar,
home setting. This is a localized love and has ramifications for the duties
that one rightly feels toward one's immediate neighbors. Expanding circles
of attachment, of love, is what we call patriotism: genuine love for one's
home and community. A humble form of this love should make us respect
the love others feel for their own communities: they likely feel the same way
about their own country. The proud Texan can love American history while
affirming that the French, Japanese, and Israeli feel the same way about their
own nations. All of this is appropriate as God has placed us in a specific
time and place.

Often the pacifist, or the otherworldly Christian, sees such patriotism as
taboo because they claim that it gives a moral carte blanche to partisan
projects and idolatrous nationalism. That need not be the case. Lewis responds to this by admonishing us that patriotism should express a set of
lessons: "The past is felt both to impose an obligation and to hold out an
assurance ... [from] our fathers." He calls it our "saga," which includes

veneration of the good while being clear-eyed about the bad. In the American case, that saga is all the good of the Founding era—the powerful ideas and institutions associated with the Declaration of Independence and Constitution—as well as the painful, persistent advance of fundamental rights and freedoms over the past two centuries. In other words, true love of neighbor—at the collective level—should force us to consider the sins of the past alongside the milestones, and it should exhort us toward greater neighbor love in our own day.

Lewis also reminds us of disordered love: collective love that is self-aggrandizing, that excludes some neighbors while elevating others. He cautions against "revolutionary idealism" masked as patriotism, which characterized the Nazis, Soviets, and others. The revolutionaries of his day, whether ideological or "racialist," idealized and idolized their own groups and their own interests. They were willing to wage "wars of annihilation" because they had a superiority complex that gave them a carte blanche justification to remake the world in ways that benefited themselves. This is the ultimate wrongly directed neighbor love in its most exclusive sense. Lewis would have recognized the same violent chauvinism in groups like ISIS, Boko Haram, and Burma's military junta today. The answer to such forms of chauvinistic collective love is not to abandon public life, but rather to counter such idolatries, from newsprint to education to the church to, in some cases, the actual battlefield. How else will a good Samaritan avert another Holocaust?

In conclusion, Protestants especially have emphasized that redemptive history looks like this:

Creation → Fall → Redemption → Restoration

This approach is expressed in the life of each individual believer, and it is the corporate experience of humanity, because the Bible is clear that a full restoration is coming when Jesus Christ is declared "Lord of all." A mystery of the New Testament is how best to understand the "now and not yet" aspect of Christ's kingdom. The kingdom has been proclaimed, but it is not fully consummated. This has implications for how one views the appropriate New Testament response—we "live" in that New Testament—to issues of neighbor love and the use of force. For instance, theological liberals tend to operate with a heavy emphasis on the righteousness or goodness of creation and focus attention not on individual human sinfulness but rather on the corruption of human institutions. Pessimists so emphasize the fall and original sin as to be fatalists: Why make any effort to better the world when all is doomed to destruction? A third category takes an idealistic approach to restoration, creating a false dichotomy between Christians and the rest of the world, as if full restoration had already happened. This idealism is the mistake made by utopian Christian pacifists. Some pacifists say that they realize the world is fallen but that Christians need to be witnesses to an ultimate understanding of peace. That is the type of idealistic Gandhian peace that counseled the Jews to all surrender to the Holocaust. It is hard to imagine any New Testament writer to have counseled such.

In contrast, the argument I am making—and that many in the Augustinian, just war statecraft, and broadest Christian realism tradition(s) assert—is this: evangelicals must have an adequate theology that is rooted in the entirety of redemptive history. We must recognize that we live in the time where Christ's kingdom is only partly revealed: we live as God's beautiful creation marred by sin, redeemed by Christ, and thus at work redeeming the world in which God has placed us. We will not bring about the final restoration, only God will. But we are called to live in continuity with the principles of both the Old and New Testaments, fulfilling the various callings that God has assigned to us, so that we can demonstrate fidelity to God and love of our neighbors in every walk of life. Christians will not do so by avoiding public life, by standing aside without responsible action to prevent wrong, right past wrongs, and punish wrongdoing. We are not called to avoid public service, as the Anabaptists suggest, nor to simply comment from the sidelines. We are called to active engagement to advance neighbor love through law, justice, and peace.

2

A NONVIOLENCE VIEW

A Nonviolence View
Christian Pacifism

MYLES WERNTZ

Christian pacifism turns on a relatively simple premise: that the killing of another human in the act of war is inconsistent with the gospel of Jesus Christ, and as such, Christians are called to abstain from war. But the logic of Christian nonviolence, distinguished from liberal optimism and from utopian dreaming, is rooted in the person of Jesus Christ as a revelation not only of the way of human union with God but of the very nature of God. In this chapter, we will go over not only what Christian pacifism is and is not but also some of the historical and scriptural roots for it, as well as how it responds to two particular issues of conflict: terrorism and surveillance.

DEFINING CHRISTIAN PACIFISM: WHAT IT IS NOT

To begin, we must establish a distinction between "pacifism" and the broader category of "nonviolence," in two ways. First, "pacifism" exists with reference specifically to issues of warfare; the broader category "nonviolence" names a broader posture toward the use of violence in which relations toward nonhuman life, the character of our social relationships outside war, and even our manner of argumentation become objects of consideration.[1] The verbiage of nonviolence is far more expansive, with pacifism a specification of these larger concerns.

---

[1] There are important debates, for example, about the ways in which the commitments of Christian pacifism extend to issues of policing and of human relationships to animals, but these are beyond the scope of this essay. For introductions to these particular topics, see Gerald Schlabach, *Just Policing, Not War: An Alternative Response to World Violence* (Collegeville, MN: Michael Glazier, 2007); Charles C. Camosy, *For the Love of Animals: Christian Ethics, Consistent Action* (Cincinnati, OH: Franciscan Media, 2013); and Andy Alexis-Baker and Tripp York, eds., *A Faith Embracing All Creatures: Addressing Commonly Asked Questions About Christian Care for Animals* (Eugene, OR: Wipf & Stock, 2012).

Because Christian pacifism is a political specification of nonviolence (popularly understood), Christian pacifism is sometimes understood as simply "whatever violence is, Christian pacifism is the opposite." This is unhelpful, for two reasons. First, trying to oppose violence supposes both that we can have an exhaustive description of violence and that we can then avoid being involved with those activities. Such an approach is doomed to failure, not only because of the intertwined nature of human life, in which I will unwittingly contribute to the bodily harm of those whom I do not know, but also because harm to human life proliferates in ways beyond the physical. Second, equating pacifism with nonviolence might lead one to assume that pacifism is simply a withdrawal from public life, if one understands nonviolence as a withdrawal from all forms of violence. In some discussions by just war proponents, "violence" names the illegitimate violation of human bodily integrity, whereas justified punishment—the killing of aggressors in war, for example—does not count as violence, having been authorized and legitimated by right authorities for a justified cause. Thus, by renaming pacifism as nonviolence, pacifism then is positioned as not engaging issues of public life *at all*. As I will show shortly, this is not a proper description of Christian pacifism.

Christian pacifism, as both a positive ethic and one that engages public life, surely involves a rejection of one form of committing harm to humans (war) and a disengagement from one form of public life (war), but many of the misunderstandings of Christian pacifism come from its being seen as nothing other than a negative position. But before we can establish the contours of what Christian pacifism *is*, let us clear away some popular misunderstandings.

1. Christian pacifism is not rooted in optimism about conflict in the world. Christian pacifism is not fundamentally a matter of optimism, either with its prospects of resolving all conflicts or about the human condition as such. While there are certainly secular analogs which propose that through reasoned dialogue and democratic processes, pacifism can both resolve conflict and prevent conflict, Christian pacifism does not rest its case on such successes. This is not to say that these empirical studies are without merit! Over the last forty years, a variety of methodological tools and ethnographic studies have begun to demonstrate the role nonviolence plays in conflict resolution, both with respect to international conflicts and internal civil wars.[2]

By contrast, *most* forms of Christian nonviolence freely assume that, because of sin, we will always hear of wars and rumors of wars.[3] Likewise, to be a Christian pacifist—one who thinks that killing in war is inconsistent with the Christian life—is not to think optimistically about the success of nonviolence in resolving conflicts, but to place the teachings of Christ at the center of one's approach to conflict in the world. To think that engaging in war resolves conflict is to take a foreshortened approach to conflict; war certainly accelerates the end of this particular conflict but in doing so frequently creates the conditions and fractures that will lead to and justify the next conflict.[4]

If the Christian pacifist is to be accused properly of anything on this point, it is hope, for key to the theological structure of pacifism is eschatology. The Christian pacifist trusts that the same God who teaches disciples to turn the other cheek and who leads the church to seek the peace of the city as the Spirit is the same God who overcomes the evil of the world with the words of his mouth. As Stanley Hauerwas frames it, "The eschatological convictions that shape Christian nonviolence assume this is God's world," that moral actions of the Christian are always undertaken within a description of war as a corruption of God's world, not its cure.[5] It is hope in the Christ who calls disciples to a particular way of living in the world that drives forward the Christian pacifist, not optimism that nonviolence will end all conflicts. An eschatology which emphasizes that the

---

[2]The foundations of more recent work can be found in Gene Sharp's trilogy, *The Politics of Nonviolent Action* (Boston: Porter Sargent, 1973). More recent and influential figures such as Sharon Erickson Nepstad and Erica Chenoweth have expanded on Sharp's methodology. See Erica Chenoweth and Maria J. Stephan, *Why Civil Resistance Works: The Strategic Logic of Nonviolent Conflict* (New York: Columbia University Press, 2012); Sharon Erickson Nepstad, *Nonviolent Struggle: Theories, Strategies, and Dynamics* (Oxford: Oxford University Press, 2015); *Nonviolent Revolutions: Civil Resistance in the Late 20th Century* (Oxford: Oxford University Press, 2011).

[3]I say "most" here, for reasons I will delineate in a moment. Christian nonviolence has taken many forms and is thus not susceptible to a singular knock-down argument against it.

[4]One of the recent developments within just war thought is that of the *post bellum*, what happens after conflict. This is, I take it, a laudable development. For an analysis of how conflict frequently creates the context of the next conflict, see Gideon Rose, *How Wars End: Why We Always Fight the Last Battle* (New York: Simon and Schuster, 2010).

[5]Stanley Hauerwas, *War and the American Difference: Theological Reflections on Violence and National Identity* (Grand Rapids, MI: Baker Academic, 2011), 39.

one who is the judge of history has come into history already to call forth a people who bear witness to the reality of creation is not encompassed by a pacifist witness, but neither can it neglect it, for this is one of the enduring features of the New Testament's description of the church. Such an eschatology, however, does not rest on the absence of violence but rather—as is amply displayed in the New Testament—the suffering witness of the church in the midst of a creation eagerly awaiting the fullness of its redemption.

2. Christian pacifism is not one singular position or approach. The most common example that comes to mind when people think "Christian pacifism" is that of the Mennonites, or perhaps the Amish (a distant cousin of the Mennonites).[6] But Christian nonviolence, as I will detail later in this chapter, is not a recent invention from the sixteenth century, nor is it simply a position enacted by one minor branch of Christians prevalent in the American Midwest. Over the last nineteen hundred years, Christian nonviolence has shown itself to not be one thing. The early disavowals of Christian participation in the military by numerous church fathers are not the same as that of Martin Luther King Jr., nor are they the same as that of the Ghanaian Mercy Oduyoye or of the American Episcopalian William Stringfellow or of the sixteenth-century German Anabaptists. Christian pacifism is a pluralized and global Christian tradition that has sought to work out what it means to be a disciple of Jesus Christ in the midst of a violent world while simultaneously not killing one's enemies.[7]

There are various conversations that occur among advocates of Christian nonviolence, such as whether destruction of property is consistent with nonviolence, or whether pacifism entails separating entirely from war or possibly admits ministering within it as a chaplain or a medic. This is one of the gifts and liabilities of Christian nonviolence: it does not have one singular center of gravity, nor are its proponents unified on all of the

---

[6]For an introduction to this family of the Christian church, see C. Arnold Snyder, *Following in the Footsteps of Christ: The Anabaptist Tradition* (Maryknoll, NY: Orbis, 2004).

[7]My forthcoming book with David C. Cramer, *A Field Guide to Christian Nonviolence* (Grand Rapids, MI: Baker Academic, 2022), will discuss the different streams of Christian nonviolence. For the basic typology, see David Cramer, "A Field Guide to Christian Nonviolence," *Sojourners*, January 2016, https://sojo.net/magazine/january-2016/field-guide-christian-nonviolence.

particulars. There is, broadly, a family resemblance among the different groups that emphasizes a divergence between killing in war and the Christian life, though the theological reasons for doing so vary widely.

Noting the variety here is significant, not only because it defuses the common objection of Christian pacifism as sectarian (a criticism associated with one subgroup among Christian pacifists), but because it emphasizes the transnational and transcultural nature of Christian pacifism. Whereas modern Christian just war thinkers tend to come from a distinct Euro-American lineage, drawing on specific Catholic and Reformed roots, Christian pacifism's lineage is broadly ecumenical and global, with major thinkers emerging from all eras, and from nearly every Christian tradition, from the early Pentecostals to the Quakers to Catholics to Baptists.[8] If Christians take seriously the notion of catholicity—that the Spirit of Christ operates in the breadth of the church toward the end of unity—then the presence of such a diverse theological body coming to the same conclusion is not to be overlooked.

In the same way that Christian pacifism is not the provenance of one tactic, likewise it is not necessarily linked to one set of liberal optimist pre-sumptions: Vatican II includes it as a viable option for Christians to take, a position recently reaffirmed by Pope Francis, though fellow pacifists such as Methodists Ellen Ott Marshall and Stanley Hauerwas would take issue with some of the theology that undergirds this affirmation. This theological plu-rality creates some of the tensions present within Christian pacifism: what one thinks about the state of humans in sin will affect what peace is hoped for, as does whether one comes from the magisterial tradition of Protestants or the Anabaptist traditions, with their disagreement over the theological status of the state, to name two examples. While grouped together under the basic affirmation of the incompatibility of the Christian identity with taking human life, there is a bevy of theological divergences that renders some va-rieties subject to some criticisms, but no variety subject to all criticisms.

---

[8] Jay Beaman, *Pentecostal Pacifism: The Origin, Development, and Rejection of Pacific Belief Among the Pentecostals* (Eugene, OR: Wipf & Stock, 2009); Meredith Baldwin Weddle, *Walking in the Way of Peace: Quaker Pacifism in the Seventeenth Century* (Oxford: Oxford University Press, 2001); Anne Klejment and Nancy L. Roberts, eds., *American Catholic Pacifism* (Westport, CT: Praeger, 2009); Paul Dekar, *For the Healing of the Nations: Baptist Peacemakers* (Macon, GA: Mercer University Press, 1993).

3. Christian pacifism is not the same as "quietism" or "withdrawal from society." In the same way that the Christian committed to pacifism is not an optimist, Christian pacifism is not defined by some imagined separation from the world, as if by removing ourselves into a commune we could keep ourselves unstained by the violence of the world. If we take sin to be an enduring feature of creation, it is folly to assume that any approach toward violence leaves the Christian immune morally from its effects. Claims by other approaches to war will accuse Christian pacifism of keeping its hands clean while others do the work, but this both underestimates the depth of violence in creation and overestimates the concern Christian pacifism has for its own moral purity with respect to war.

To name going to war as intrinsic to being involved in society lays one's cards fairly clearly with respect to what one thinks "being involved in society" includes—namely, being willing to participate in lethal action in defense of justice. This is, quite simply, conflating a variety of issues—just valuation of the world, faithful participation in God's world, the moral status of violence, and the theological status of created life after the incarnation of the Son, to name just a few! If being willing to support violence in the defense of justice constitutes "being involved in society," then one's definition of society is interwoven with violence as a necessary feature (a questionable premise), or the essential character of public institutions is seen to be violence, necessary if only to keep even worse societal ills at bay.

Scripturally, violence is simply one of the most notable features of sin in the world; beginning with Genesis 3, violence becomes inextricably linked to the advance of human life in the world, both within the line of Abraham and outside of it. Adopting a Christian understanding of sin entails, among other things, assuming that there is no corner of creation—either church or world—that does not suffer some of the effects named by violence.[9] Even the early Anabaptists, one of the most well-known groups to propound the

---

[9]As contemporary philosopher Slavoj Žižek observes, our experience of subjective violence is possible because we exist within a field of violence which he names as objective violence, in *Violence* (New York: Picador, 2008), 11-14. Without accepting the metaphysics of Žižek's claim—that the fundamental law of existence is one of conflict—Žižek is correct that in a world afflicted by sin, there is no "withdrawing" into a pure space freed from violence. It is for this reason, among others, that penitence is a necessary component of all Christian social ethics: there is no one righteous, not even one.

refusal to take up the sword, did not propose that their separation from the world somehow made them immune from sin and interpersonal offenses; the Schleitheim Confession, in which this separation between church and world appears, proposes rejecting the sword not out of a desire for moral purity but out of seeking unity with Christ.[10]

To be a pacifist, as I will describe shortly, does not entail abandoning society, for violence is not something any creature in a world under the fall can escape. Rather, Christian pacifism means inhabiting this world suffering from violence in a way that does not promise to avoid all suffering, but to engage the world's suffering in a way that mirrors Christ. This is a difficult word: that discipleship (and in this case, a faithful account of Christian pacifism) is bound up with suffering. For the work of the Spirit is not, contrary to much modern pneumatology, about avoidance of death, but of being the presence of Christ to a creation that will eventually suffer death.[11] Likewise, Christian pacifism does not propose that, even if withdrawal from "the world" were a possibility, it would somehow avoid entanglement with violence.

WHERE DID CHRISTIAN PACIFISM COME FROM?

Before we embark on describing what Christian pacifism *is*, a brief historiography is in order. The arguments surrounding the prevalence of Christian participation in war in the earliest centuries are complex, but rely on three general themes: (1) how widely these opinions were held, (2) whether these were absolute prohibitions or pastoral counsel, and (3) the degree to which popular practice followed these writings.[12] It is my evaluation, given the geographical ubiquity of these arguments—with prohibitions issued from

---

[10]Michael Sattler, "The Schleitheim Confession," in *The Radical Reformation*, ed. Michael G. Baylor, Cambridge Texts in the History of Political Thought (Cambridge: Cambridge University Press, 1991), 173.

[11]Ephraim Radner, *A Profound Ignorance: Modern Pneumatology and its Anti-modern Redemption* (Waco, TX: Baylor University Press, 2019).

[12]John F. Shean, *Soldiering for God: Christianity and the Roman Army* (Leiden: Brill, 2010), 105–77, makes the sociological argument that the opinions of elite Christian leaders on this point ruptured Christian congregations and did not speak for the laity. See also John Helgeland, Robert J. Daly, and J. Patout Burns, *Christians and the Military: The Early Experience* (Philadelphia: Fortress, 1985), 1, who argue for ambiguous thinking among early Christians. More recently, George Kalantzis, *Caesar and the Lamb: Early Christian Attitudes on War and Military Service* (Eugene, OR: Cascade, 2012) has challenged the ambiguity of this evidence.

throughout the ancient Christian world—that the normativity of the prohibition of violence was most likely the pastoral norm prior to the fourth century AD.[13]

Because of the way in which involvement in the military also involved obeisance to the imperial cult, the reasons for opposing involvement in war by Christians take multiple forms. Some documents, such as the Didache (ca. 80–120), a catechetical document, reiterate the teachings of Jesus from Matthew 5:41-48, instructing Christians to not strike back when struck.[14] This straightforward appeal to the words of Jesus is echoed by Justin Martyr (ca. 100–165) in his *First Apology*, where he notes that Christians have "turned from the way of violence and tyranny," and in his *Dialogues with Trypho*, in which he notes that "we who were full of war and the slaughter of one another . . . have in every part of the world converted our weapons of war into implements of peace."[15]

Other writers moved beyond a straightforward moral prohibition rooted in the instruction of Jesus to more sacramentally oriented objections. Throughout his *Apology*, Tertullian (ca. 160–ca. 220) makes the case that the Roman religion is bound up with Roman wars, that their victory in war was caught up with their devotion to the gods. As he puts it,

> There can be no compatibility between the divine and human sacrament, the standard of Christ and the standard of the devil. . . . Moses, to be sure, carried a rod; Aaron wore a military belt, and John (the Baptist) is girt with leather. . . . But how will a Christian go to war? Indeed how will he serve even in peacetime without a sword which the Lord has taken away? . . . The Lord, by taking away Peter's sword, disarmed every soldier thereafter. We are not allowed to wear any uniform that symbolizes a sinful act.[16]

To be sure, there were Christians in the military during this early period. But significantly, while there are accounts of Christians in military service

---

[13]Kalantzis, *Caesar and the Lamb*, 42-46.

[14]Michael Holmes, ed., *The Apostolic Fathers: Greek Texts and English Translations* (Grand Rapids, MI: Baker Academic, 2004), 246-70.

[15]Kalantzis, *Caesar and the Lamb*, 82-85. See also the material from Athenagoras, *Plea on Behalf of the Christians* 35 (Kalantzis, *Caesar and the Lamb*, 90-91), which follows this line of argument. Cyprian of Carthage, *To Donatus* 11, also notes the divergent forms of virtue present in Christians and soldiers of Rome (Kalantzis, *Caesar and the Lamb*, 151).

[16]Tertullian, *On Idolatry* 19.1-3, in Kalantzis, *Caesar and the Lamb*, 119-20.

during this period, there is no extant writing advocating that Christians should volunteer themselves for the military, or should view Christian service to the world in this way. By contrast, conversion to the faith often involved martyrdom or decommissioning prior to the fourth century.

Many historiographies of Christian pacifism will point to the late fourth century as a tide change with respect to the question of war, a question that will not concern us here.[17] Clerics, beginning with the canons issued from church councils by the late fifth century, were forbidden to engage in bloodshed of any kind, such that the face of missions that was carried forth by the mo-nastics was consistent with the stance of the earliest Christians.[18] The canons, forbidding bloodshed by monastics, developed alongside penitential codes that were administered throughout the fifth and sixth centuries. In these peni-tential codes, penance was required for killing in war, as bloodshed constituted a defilement of the soul, which had to be atoned for. In canons ranging geo-graphically across the Roman world, Christian soldiers were prohibited from rejoining worship until penance had been done.[19] For despite the emergence of a nascent just war tradition, participation in war by Christians was not seen as a universal good, insofar as this form of order making involved killing.

This emphasis is carried forth most notably in the Reformation era by the Anabaptists, as seen in the Schleitheim Confession, drafted by German and Swiss Anabaptists in 1527. In these articles, we find that "Christ himself forbids the violence of the sword and says 'Worldly princes rule, but not you.'"[20] It is important to note, however, that the duality described here is not in any way new, but a return to an older vision of the Christian and war that had, through the Middle Ages, been restricted to clergy.

Christian pacifism in the twentieth century has diverged now into nu-merous streams. Some varieties have focused on tactical and practical

---

[17]One objection to the bevy of pre-fourth-century resources is that these are judgments rendered by non-ecclesiastical voices, as opposed to church canons. This is dismissed, however, as these writings are reaffirmed by the canons of councils, and by seeing these lay writers as *reflecting* eccle-siastical opinion. To assume that these are rogue writers offering judgments over against ecclesi-astical opinion is a distinctly Protestant read of the situation, particularly considering the lengths to which these writers go to stay within the developing theological mains of Christian reflection at most other points.

[18]John T. McNeill, "Asceticism Versus Militarism in the Middle Ages," *Church History* 5 (1936): 3-28.

[19]For a full list of these penitential practices, see John T. McNeill and Helena M. Garner, eds., *Medieval Handbooks of Penance* (New York: Columbia University Press, 1938).

[20]Sattler, "The Schleitheim Articles," 177.

political approaches, such as the Just Peacemaking approach of Glen Stassen. Some varieties have focused on the training and moral formation of Christians, such as Stanley Hauerwas, Ellen Ott Marshall, and Howard Thurman. Among Christian pacifists there are various disagreements about the role of the state, about the nature of force, and practical questions of suffering. But what binds these diverse approaches together—and has bound the diversity together across history—is a common commitment that war is incompatible both with the good of God's creation and the good of the Christian, and is to be forsaken in favor of other means of peacemaking.

DEFINING CHRISTIAN PACIFISM: WHAT IT IS

To return to the distinction between pacifism and nonviolence, the term *nonviolence* is defined linguistically as whatever violence is not. There is far more to nonviolence than this, but the impression is that if one refuses to engage in violence, then one is withdrawing from the world. This is where "pacifism" as a positive concept entails not only refraining from killing in war but also working for peace by other means. As will be detailed more shortly, pacifism has developed far beyond the simple refusal to kill to a more complex version of peacemaking, which emphasizes mediation in conflict and addressing social causes that lead to conflicts. So, as a globally encompassing, transhistorical tradition of moral inquiry, what is Christian pacifism? I'd like to lay out four points that, I suggest, constitute a full-orbed vision of the position, points that describe what I take to be true not only to the tradition of reflection but also to the diverse practitioners who have contributed to Christian pacifism.

   1. The taking of life in war is incompatible with the Christian life. On its face, Christian pacifism seems to be positioning itself in a place of moral superiority: that those who do not kill in war are morally superior to those who do. Scripturally, this is a fallacy: the Pharisees are criticized on this very point, of attaining a level of righteousness that they use to position themselves above others. On the contrary, this first point is simply stating, as with many other things within the Scriptures, that there are certain actions that do not cohere to the person and work of Jesus. Killing in war is one of those actions. The most immediate objections to this scripturally come from the Old Testament, in which there is not just openness to war but on occasion the declaration of war by God on nations, and the command for the people of God to go to war. It is at this point that the question of a scriptural account of pacifism has to travel through some uncomfortable and thorny territory, for the Old Testament has a far different description of peacemaking than the example enacted and proclaimed by Jesus of Nazareth.

Without denying the validity of the Old Testament accounts surrounding *haram* (Heb., "place under the ban," "utterly destroy," or "remove from use"), I want to offer these two reasons for staying with the New Testament primarily in exploring our topic. First, when the earliest Christian exegetes read these texts, they approached them in multiple ways, but never, prior to the fourth century, in sermons or church councils or treatises or private letters, as examples or inspiration for Christian practice.[21] Origen, the most influential biblical interpreter of the first two hundred years of the church, in his sermons on the book of Joshua, treated them allegorically.[22] For Origen, these passages were placed by God within the Scriptures to provide spiritual instruction about how Christians are to approach the use of violence within the world. Others, such as Cyprian of Carthage, used military metaphors approvingly, but as an analogy to praise the martyrs of the church.[23] But in any event, the Old Testament descriptions were not seen (in the first three centuries at least) as normative for Christian practice, not only because of an emerging distinction between Christians and Judaism, but also because—if Jesus is God in the flesh—then what may have been proper for one era and permitted by God had been abrogated by Christ's own teachings. We are not permitted, as it were, to go behind God's economy as displayed in the Scriptures, and to seek precedents where precedent is no longer permitted.

This approach of the early church in reasoning this way is typological: there is a consistency of God's revelation of Scripture such that there is not a break in God's activity between testaments but rather an expansiveness to it. We find this way of reading was pervasive in the early church, as it helped Christians to be able to profit from practices of the Old Testament without repeating them, by seeing in the Old Testament its spiritual import for the

---

[21]The history of Christian pacifism will be addressed shortly.

[22]Origen, *Homilies on Joshua*, trans. Barbara J. Bruce, ed. Cynthia White, Fathers of the Church (Washington DC: Catholic University of America Press, 2002), 94.

[23]Kalantzis, *Caesar and the Lamb*, 148-54.

world after the incarnation.[24] As such, the Old Testament is not set aside so much as it is read according to the work of Christ. As André Trocmé argues, Jesus—in becoming the *goel* (Heb., "the mediator") of the people—redeems the people of God through a nonviolent approach of laying down his life for the people both of his own day and those to come. As such, the ways of God's mediation for the people in Christ set the stage for what it means for Christians to engage violence as well.[25]

As William Cavanaugh argues, in the Old Testament the only validity for taking life is at the explicit command of God, particularly in light of the prohibition against murder. Cavanaugh then proposes that if the people of God may only kill at the command of God, and if we as Christians believe that Jesus is the fullness of the Godhead, there seems to be only one option: we cannot follow God without also being bound by the ways in which the law (as in the Sermon on the Mount in Matthew) is expanded. Christians cannot, in other words, maintain peace in a way that would violate the explicit utterances of God incarnate, Jesus Christ.[26]

One objection here is the distinction between murder and killing: The former is prohibited by the Old Testament as an unjust action by a private individual, and the latter is apparently left permissible in service to justice by the proper authorities. This argument of Cavanaugh also helps to orient us as we approach the New Testament as well. Cavanaugh's insistence that disciples do what they see Jesus doing guides our reading of these passages; disciples are to follow the example of their Lord, leaving God to be God. Disciples are to follow what they see their Lord doing, not—in the case of one reading of Romans 13—to act presumptuously on behalf of Christ in ways that supersede what Christ has taught. The argument is made sometimes that Jesus never asked the Roman centurion of great faith (Mt 8:5-13) to cease being a centurion. But this commendation of the centurion as one of great faith over against the Pharisees is worlds apart from saying that we can imagine Jesus or Paul asking Christians to sign up to be a Roman centurion as a way of being a disciple.

---

[24]For an introduction to this way of scriptural interpretation, see John J. O'Keefe and R. R. Reno, *Sanctified Vision: An Introduction to Early Christian Interpretation of the Bible* (Baltimore: Johns Hopkins University Press, 2005).

[25]André Trocmé, *Jesus and the Nonviolent Revolution* (1962; repr., Walden, NY: Plough, 2003), 145.

[26]William Cavanaugh, "Killing in the Name of God," *New Blackfriars* 85 (2004): 510-26.

2. The refusal to take life in war does not mean abandoning the good of the world. This stereotype of Christian pacifists runs deep, stemming from the connection of Christian pacifism with only its most well-known variety: the sixteenth-century Anabaptists. In the Schleitheim Confession of the sixteenth century, one of the hallmark confessions of the German Anabaptists, there are a number of interlocking commitments by which Christians make themselves known as part of the "perfection of Christ," including a refusal to take up the sword. Their commitment to pacifism was, as I have argued, intrinsic to the Christian life, in that to be a Christian is to imitate Christ. Their baptism inducted them into a new way of life described by Jesus and affirmed by the apostolic witness. But even among the Anabaptists, there was disagreement as to what it meant to hold to Jesus' teaching on the sword. Balthasar Hubmaier, one of the best-known Anabaptist theologians from this period, makes a powerful case that "sword" and "lethality" are different, and that preservation of order does not entail the taking of life.[27] As such, he encouraged Anabaptists to be involved in civic affairs and tending to the public good.

From other corners, the stereotype of pacifists likewise does not hold up. Dietrich Bonhoeffer, the Lutheran martyr and theologian who never renounced his writings in *Discipleship*, in which he took a hard line on whether Christians could commit violence against others, also took up posts within Nazi Germany to defeat the Nazi bureaucracy from within. When one turns to pacifists such as Mercy Agamba Oduyoye, we find that the way to actualize the peace of Christ is by taking the disciplines of the church into public venues of peacemaking around gender and violence.[28]

If anything, peacemaking as displayed throughout the New Testament is a materialist venture, a calling of God interlaced with suffering, patience, prayers for one's enemies, trust in the deliverance of God, and seeking the peace of the city. The New Testament does not treat war as a special species of conflict, for two reasons. First, contrary to the distinctions placed between the public and private uses of violence, as articulated by Martin Luther and others, the New Testament does not pose two levels of actions when

---

[27]Balthasar Hubmaier, "On the Sword," in Baylor, *The Radical Reformation*, 181-210.
[28]See my article, "Broadening the Ecclesiocentric Claim: Possible Futures for Christian Nonviolence," *Journal of the Society of Christian Ethics* 39, no. 2 (2019): 303-18.

describing the use of violence. Rather, when describing the differing forms of violence, Jesus links them together along a continuum as members of the same genus.[29]

In recent years, a great deal of literature has emerged showing the ways in which—in a variety of contexts, including conflict mediation, revolution, and civil wars—nonviolence has an empirical track record of resolving conflicts. Since the 1970s, volumes of work have shown through historical examples and disciplined deployment that the use of nonviolence tactically and strategically works to resolve conflict without the use of wide-scale military action (Mt 5:21-26). As an empirical strategy, nonviolence has been shown to "work," as the late Glen Stassen put it.[30] This being said, Christian pacifism's validity does not rest on its workability so much as its fidelity to Scripture and to theological wisdom.

Finally, on this point, pacifism does not necessarily commit one to forsaking the use of force, even if it does commit one to not killing your enemies: the beating of a sword into a plowshare is not the same as killing one's enemy. The destruction of nuclear facilities, the use of targeted embargoes, and even the use of nonlethal policing are debated among pacifists—not as a matter of seeing how far one can go without breaking the letter of the command, but out of an understanding that the things which facilitate destruction in the world are part of what is confronted by the kingdom of God entering into the world. For Christ's coming into the world is not only a revelation of who God is and how God is; Christ's coming is also a judgment on death itself and all that would facilitate the destruction of God's creation. If pacifism is a moral action that seeks to imitate Christ, then it follows that limited destruction of those facilities, weapons, and structures that create war are not prima facie out of hand.

---

[29]Mt 5:21-22 in this case does not divide the public act of murder from the private act of hate. The response here is that killing for an authorized purpose is a public act in a way that the killing by an unauthorized agent (murder) is not. What this fails to see is that the horizon of authority, under which the discussion of Mt 5:21-22 occurs, is one that encompasses church (Mt 5:23-24), courts (Mt 5:25-26), and private actions (Mt 5:21-22). Jesus is uninterested in restricting his instruction to one of these venues over against another. The difficulty with divorcing war from private violence is, among other reasons, that it moves war beyond morality entirely; either war is coextensive with ordinary moral experience or it is not, and to render war a different species of violence is to place war under a different criteria of moral action than the encompassing one presented by Jesus.

[30]Glen Stassen, "The Unity, Realism, and Obligatoriness of Just Peacemaking Theory," *Journal of the Society of Christian Ethics* 23 (2003): 171-94.

3. Pacifism is not solely fulfilling a command but also entering into a life of discipleship and virtue. Far from being simply slavish adherence to a singular verse in Matthew, Christian pacifism is, as I observed with the Schleitheim Confession, about entering into a way of discipleship, a way of discipleship in which one joins by the Spirit of God into a life of virtue and holiness. Again, this is not some kind of holiness that is worked out in seclusion from creation, but a holiness that one becomes by virtue of participating in the work of God in creation. This theme, written on by Dorothy Day, Stanley Hauerwas, Bernard Haring, Ellen Ott Marshall, and others, emphasizes not only that those who refuse violence in the world know what it is to be the children of God but also that in doing so, they bear witness to others what God is like.

In Christian reflection, the virtues consist of not only those that are acquired—things like courage and wisdom—but those that are given only by God—things like faith, hope, and love. But the thing about the virtues is that even the best of human virtues—courage, for example—is not negated by God's work in the Spirit, but made what it was meant to be. Consider this example from Thomas Aquinas, one of the most pivotal figures in Christian history and a proponent of the just war perspective. In Aquinas's work, we find that the courage of the soldier remains second to the perfected courage of the martyr, the one who is conformed to Christ in bodily practice, virtue, and confession.[31]

One can certainly refuse to go to war for any number of reasons. Perhaps a person lacks courage, or perhaps one thinks the war to be unjust, or because one's commitment to one's family and life ranks higher than one's love of country. But the refusal to kill for the pacifist is different from these cases because in refusing to kill, one is not stepping away from one thing into a place of safety, but taking on a different yoke of discipleship that will lead to places one does not wish to go. As I indicated in the first point, to refuse to kill one's enemy is not to say that we cease to have enemies, but to say that there are some things worse than dying—namely, refusing the call of Christ.

Pacifism, as the public expansion of the scriptural vision of peacemaking, does not answer all of the questions posed by the world when it comes to

---

[31]Thomas Aquinas, *Summa Theologica*, II-II, q. 124.

violence. Several decades ago, famous American just war thinker Paul Ramsey asked the question of whether a pacifist could even enter into a conversation around war, if they operate from the presumption that war is out of bounds.[32] Ramsey's question assumes, however, that one needs to be open to lethal force in order to make arguments about what constitutes justice, peace, equity, or the human good.[33]

In sum, Christian pacifism is not simply about following a command but about entering into a call of discipleship that joins Christ by the Spirit in a world of violence. It is not about avoiding the violence of the world, but entering into it as Christ's witness to the inbreaking kingdom of God. It is not about denying the revelation of Scripture, but reading it the way that Scripture reads itself: as culminating and being fulfilled in Jesus, the Son who died and was resurrected in our place, the Jesus who—in the words of Paul—put to an end the hostility between humanity and God and among humanity, and invites his body to inhabit the world in this form.

4. Christian pacifism refuses an ultimate divide between the private and public. One of the disagreements that emerges as Christians debate war and peace is the relationship between private convictions and public actions. The divide between public and private authority is a long-standing tenet of both magisterial Protestant and Catholic just war accounts. In particular, what holds for private morality is not the same as what is warranted in public engagements, and what a private citizen can do is different from what a public authority can command. As indicated earlier, Christian pacifists reject this divide between public and private morality. This is not to say that the Christian pacifist expects states to be pacifist, but rather that the obligations of Christian ethics are not mitigated according to one's public station or profession. To be sure, what it means to be a faithful Christian is differentiated according to one's marital status or age, but what it does not mean is that one's public station creates a new metric for discipleship.

As a pastoral question, this logic is disastrous for those who are Christians in the military. The division between public and private morality

---

[32]Paul Ramsey, *The Just War: Force and Political Responsibility* (Lanham, MD: Rowman and Little-field, 2002), 259-80.

[33]In my article, "Terrorism and the Peace of Christ: Seeking Pacifism's Future in Theory and Practice," *Philosophia Christi* 18 (August 2016): 109-18, I follow the trifold schematic of just war thought to show that, contra Ramsey, the concerns of the just warrior are shared concerns of pacifists.

encumbers them with two divergent forms of morality: what is done in war and what is done in the normal course of civilian life. In circumscribing war as a self-authorizing field, Christian military personnel can never integrate their moral life, for their moral life in combat remains subject to a law that is totally different from their domestic one. Allowing justified killing in combat under the authority of a commanding government, but disallowing analogous actions in private life means that the soldier can never fully come home.[34]

As just war thinker Joseph Capizzi affirms, a Christian vision of war and peace must be rooted in the ongoing moral life of a people, and not divorced from it.[35] While he and I will disagree about what that vision of war and peace entails, this fundamental insight—which pushes back against war as a discrete moral realm of action, and against war as an amoral form of statecraft—is correct. The alternative to war as bearing out a fundamentally different measure of moral existence bifurcates the moral world into a place where Christ is not truly the measure of all in all but rather the governor of merely our intentions or of some form of existence beyond history.

CHRISTIAN PACIFISM AND MODERN CONFLICT

With both an accurate portrayal of Christian pacifism in hand, along with a brief account of its development, let us now turn to two practical questions of conflict: terrorism and enhanced surveillance. That a cohesive account of Christianity and war must answer these questions stems from the prior assumption that the truly faithful Christian must be willing to engage evil with lethal force. As I have indicated already, for Christian pacifism, this is a flawed assumption that then makes us ask the wrong kinds of questions such as, How can a Christian engage terrorists and still be peaceful? Just war and realism have their versions of this, broadly assuming either that a private morality and a political vision have little overlap, or, if they do, that

---

[34]Pertinent here is the literature on moral injury, which describes the phenomenon of the divided moral life within soldiers. See in particular Robert Emmet Meagher and Douglas A. Pryer, eds., *War and Moral Injury: A Reader* (Eugene, OR: Wipf & Stock, 2018); Rita Nakashima Brock and Gabriella Lettini, *Soul Repair: Recovering from Moral Injury after War* (Boston: Beacon, 2013); and Jonathan Shay, *Achilles in Vietnam: Combat Trauma and the Undoing of Character* (New York: Simon and Schuster, 1995).

[35]Joseph E. Capizzi, *Politics, Justice, and War: Christian Governance and the Ethics of Warfare* (Oxford: Oxford University Press, 2015), 26-43.

a vision of Christian peace as articulated here is largely mitigated by the presence of sin in the world. However, sin, as a reality within creation, is never described by the New Testament as that which mitigates the Christian moral vision. Rather, Christian moral vision is called into conflict with sin, but *not on the terms established by sin.* To engage sin under sin's terms is to cede the high ground to creation's corruption rather than to engage the world as the world in which Christ has already won the victory over death. As such, the Christian approach to issues of conflict is, in some ways, hamstrung from the beginning by being constitutionally unable to avail itself of any and all possible tactics and modality in conflict.[36]

Christian pacifism and terrorism. Terrorism offers a new species of conflict for consideration, in that terrorism definitionally falls outside the typical framework of state-on-state warfare.[37] Conducted by non-state actors with the intention of inflicting fear into a particular subgroup of a population, terrorism has historically been more closely associated with piracy than standing armies.[38] Terrorism emerges in many documented cases out of an exhausted political process that mutates the political process into violence. In discussions of terrorism it is easy for this basic point to be obscured.

For the Christian pacifist, the turn to violence to counter terrorist violence is unsatisfactory, for the reasons outlined above. Defenses of war and the illegitimacy of terrorism frequently rest in no small part on this distinction: that a state is justified in its use of violence in defense of its subjects, while a subgroup of a people cannot justly conduct this kind of violence for political ends.[39] It is worth observing that the justification of state authority here is, in one way, special pleading: before *any* nation is a nation, it is a

---

[36]This is not to say that the Christian pacifist cannot think carefully about issues of conflict; all the more reason to think well about these things!

[37]For a fuller treatment of this question, in relation to the categories of just war thought, see my "Terrorism and the Peace of Christ," 109-18.

[38]For the official definition of terrorism, see U.S. Code, title 22, sec. 2656f(d), and U.S. Code, title 18, sec. 2331 (1). On the ongoing status of terrorism with respect to legitimacy and violence, see Christopher D. Mercado, "Redefining Legitimate Authority: Just War in the Era of Terrorism," *Journal of the Indiana Academy of the Social Sciences* 14, no. 1 (2010): 117-25.

[39]Others such as Michael Walzer, *Just and Unjust Wars: A Moral Argument with Historical Illustrations* (New York: Basic Books, 1992), 197-206, have defined the difference as one of order versus chaos, of aiming at policies versus persons, and of playing by established norms versus violation of norms in conflict. While these descriptions are correct, I take them to be post hoc objections stemming from a more fundamental objection of the authority of the state to go to war.

subgroup engaging in tactical conflict against a superior force. To distinguish in this way is to characterize the behavior of the people of Israel in Joshua as terrorism, as established by modern definitions. I have already indicated the ways in which Christian pacifism broadly treats the question of violence in Scripture, but to construct a pacifist response by simply dismissing terrorism as a kind of political violence analogous to state military action will not suffice. For terrorism presents a real and pervasive form of violence that a Christian pacifist must not only account for but also offer a response to.

To begin, let us put the uncomfortable truth on the table: no account of Christianity and war can offer a full solution to the suffering of the innocent. When we remove the stereotyped objection to Christian pacifism, that it ignores the suffering of the innocent in favor of its own piety, and consider that no account of Christian participation in war can avoid death, then the question becomes: What account of war is able to approach not only friends, but also enemies, as those for whom Christ has died? As Augustine counseled his congregation,

> If you are able, and are not bad yourself, then pray for the evil person to become good. Why do you treat those who are bad violently? You reply, "Because they are bad." As soon as you treat them violently, you add yourself to them. Let me give you some advice. There's some evil person you despise? Well, don't let there be two. You criticize him, and then join him? You swell the ranks you're condemning. Are you trying to overcome evil with evil? To overcome hatred with hatred? Then there will be two lots of hatred, and both will need to be overcome. Can't you hear the advice your Lord gave through the apostle Paul, *Do not be overcome by evil, but overcome evil with good?*[40]

In other words, opposition to violence cannot be done in a manner that perpetuates the conditions and attitudes that created terrorism as a possibility to begin with. The aim here is not only rectitude and justice but also the restoration of peace. And so, if what pacifists propose with respect to conflict is peace without the use of lethal ends, then a variety of options open up. Let me briefly highlight two.

---

[40]Augustine, Sermon 302, "On the Feast of St. Laurence," in *Augustine: Political Writings,* ed. E. M. Atkins and R. J. Dodaro (Cambridge: Cambridge University Press, 2001), 113.

1. The rule of law. In recent years, pacifists have been fond of extending the term *violence* to cover political process as well as political acts of physical violence, viewing politics as war by other means, such that international law merely relocates conflict rather than ending it. The Just Peacemaking movement provides one counterexample of the ways in which positive law—the statutes laid down by a legislature, court, or other human institution—might be an aid to the reduction of war without directly being incompatible with the christologically grounded mandate to turn the other cheek. Glen Stassen argues that, if we read the teachings of Jesus not as perfectionist ideals but as realistic initiatives by which we might participate in the grace of Christ, the call to nonviolence for Christians is not at odds with positive law. In fact, as he argues in *Just Peacemaking*, affirmations of national security, ad hoc treaties and negotiations, and bilateral disarmaments are in fact precursors and extensions of the Christian call to nonviolence.[41]

For a pacifist to embrace the role of civil law is not to baptize the law, but to call civil law to account, reigning in procedural justice by the love of Christ, judging positive law by a natural law rooted in the incarnation. Terrorism, in certain cases, is a (disordered) response to an unjust law, resulting from a grievance that resorts to political violence to achieve political ends. In this case, the pacifist encourages the development of brokered settlements, democratic process, and the amendment of law. Not all grievances are justified grievances, but to the extent that terrorism is a political act against the backdrop of a political breakdown, emphasizing the rule of law—binding on all parties and to which all parties must be accountable—is one tool among others. As Tertullian suggested in the third century, Christians should prize both public order and the rejection of war for the same reason: the order that Christ gives to creation.[42] Pacifists should hear Tertullian clearly here: that fidelity to Christ's removal of Peter's sword goes hand in hand with a commitment to civic and moral order, as both are fulfilled in Christ's restoring work of creation.

---

[41]On this, see Glen Stassen's own *Just Peacemaking: A New Paradigm for Peace* (Cleveland: Pilgrim, 2008), as well Stassen, ed., *Just Peacemaking: Ten Practices for Abolishing War* (Cleveland: Pilgrim, 1998).

[42]See Tertullian, *On Idolatry* 18.

2. Presence in suffering. As I claimed above, it is folly to assume that any Christian approach to war and peace promises to end suffering, as suffering is a feature of a world under sin; there is no way around this. Accordingly, particularly in times and spaces of terror, pacifists need to ask in what ways they can respond to the question of human suffering in the midst of conflict. As the New Testament amply lays out, the Christian is called to be present in the midst of suffering, and to suffer for the name of Christ. With respect to war and terrorism, it follows then that the Christian should be willing to take on that suffering rather than let it fall on others.

But presence to suffering is not strictly to be conceived of in terms of presence to the innocent suffering—that is, those who have been targeted by terrorism. Rather, presence to suffering, from a Christian perspective, must include presence to the enemy as well. This is enshrined within just war thinking in terms of treatment of the captured enemy, but, following Oliver O'Donovan, Christians—when they encounter an enemy—are bound to treat them as not-enemy. Commenting on Thomas Aquinas's permission to kill an assailant, O'Donovan writes,

> On any interpretation, Thomas permits acts that may foreseeably kill the assailant—on the presumption that we have a greater responsibility to save our own life than our assailant. This presumption is dubious. True, our own lives are the more familiar responsibility, since we dutifully eat and drink and take precautions against illness every day, while saving another's life is a rare occurrence. Yet when another's life does fall into our hands to risk or to preserve, our primary business is with it, not with ourselves, *even if that life happens to belong to our enemies.*[43]

On the one hand, the pacifist can find common cause with themes present in the recent Responsibility to Protect movement, which contends that governments have a responsibility to alleviate the unjust suffering of another country's people.[44] If pacifists allow for my first proposal—that political order retains theological legitimacy *in principle* (not withstanding corrupt instantiations of order)—then pacifism can follow the lead of the

---

[43]Oliver O'Donovan, *The Ways of Judgment: The Bampton Lectures, 2003* (Grand Rapids, MI: Eerdmans, 2005), 210 (emphasis added).

[44]For an introduction, see Alex J. Bellamy, *The Responsibility to Protect: A Defense* (Oxford: Oxford University Press, 2015).

Responsibility to Protect movement, and work to alleviate the suffering of innocents in a proactive fashion, though not in the fashion envisioned by the movement itself. For the Christian concern for suffering extends beyond the innocent and must account for and minister to the aggressor as well.

This second theme of presence to suffering dovetails with the first for the Christian pacifist in this way: addressing the roots of conflict rather than waiting until conflict erupts to adjudicate the matter. For terrorism and war do not spontaneously emerge as forms of mass psychosis or madness but as the final result of long-standing interpersonal and political conflicts. The two approaches named here, then, help perform the ongoing work of mediation and conflict that both address conflict before it happens and helps to secure a lasting relation between combatants after the conflict.

Christian pacifism and surveillance. If Christian pacifism, as I have suggested, is not simply about a refusal to kill but an active making of peace before, during, and after conflict, then this brings into view questions of surveillance. If the primary purpose of a Christian ethic were to defend the nation-state, then surveillance would mean paying attention to those who would seek to do our nation harm, and to do so in a way deemed necessary by the nation. Christian pacifists, as committed as they are to the common good, do not hold to this presupposition, even if care, concern, and love for one's neighbor are premium values. For, as indicated by O'Donovan above, the scope of Christian concern includes the good of one's enemies and their lives.

If Christian pacifists—or any Christian—can speak intelligibly of surveillance or intelligence-gathering techniques, they must first be converted, as it were, and not described as prima facie justifiable techniques. As I have argued, our account of what we do in conflict must itself be brought under a Christian framework, beginning with how and why we pay attention to others. In an era when privacy is persistently under threat both by prying tech companies and from increasingly invasive nation-states, we must be clear that attention—and indeed, increased attention in the name of safety— is not to be dismissed out of hand. But what *kind* of attention we pay matters a great deal.

Simone Weil, in her essay on prayer, describes the act not as first conversation with God so much as it is learning to pay attention to God, to tarry with God; accordingly, to pay attention as a Christian is first an act of love toward that which is not ourselves.[45] Framing attention as a form of love shifts the conversation about how to treat both active and potential enemies into a different space. The difference here, for the Christian pacifist, is that any "paying attention" that happens occurs from within the gaze of the Christian who knows that love is the form of their attention. We pay attention to others—enemy and friend—because God has attended to us as friends while we were still the enemies of God (Rom 5:8). It is only in love, then, that we are able to pay attention in a way that does not allow prudence to become pragmatism. To be cognizant that there is a threat and to act accordingly is a mark of prudence, but to pay attention with the intention of turning the enemy into a friend is the mark of prudence infused by love.

Paying attention to others—now understood not as "others" but as our distant neighbors—for the sake of defending our proximate neighbors undermines any ability to deprive a distant neighbor of the dignity due our proximate ones. To put this in a concrete form, the dignity and love with which we pay attention to enemies is that which is due to friends. Jeff McMahan, in an important essay on this question, has contended that the act of attacking or of ill intent creates a moral asymmetry: that what is owed to the unjust combatants is not what is owed to the just.[46] For McMahan, even participation without knowing objectively that one's cause is unjust does not mitigate the objective disparity between sides of a conflict; this moral asymmetry then warrants the use of interrogative techniques, for example, on an enemy that one would never use on a citizen. But the scandal the Christian pacifist position presents here is not that there is an obliteration of nationality or citizenship, but that one may not treat the enemy as anything other than not-an-enemy because of God's actions toward us in Christ: the only attention that is due to anything mirrors the attention given us by God in Christ.

The logic of the "ticking time bomb" to justify so-called enhanced interrogation techniques have been shown, since their inception after the 2001

---

[45]See Simone Weil, "Attention and Will," in *Gravity and Grace* (New York: Routledge Classics, 1999), 116-22.

[46]Jeff McMahan, *Killing in War* (Oxford: Clarendon, 2009), 38-103. McMahan is assuming, as with terrorism or any war of aggression, that the cause does not justify the ends or means of war.

attacks on the World Trade Center in New York, to have yielded little to no valuable information.[47] Even if international conventions had not already roundly rejected torture as out of bounds, and even if there were credible information that was obtained through these techniques, the corrupted form of attention present in torture is impermissible for the Christian. For beyond the damage that is done to the enemy, damage likewise is done to the one who performs the techniques. For two centuries, as attested to by the canons of church councils, summaries of apostolic teachings, and dominical sayings, the act of violence committed in war was counted incompatible with one's baptism.[48] This was not solely because of the bloodshed committed, but because of the damage to the soul done in the act of harming another human. As the Canons of Hippolytus (third century) read, "A Christian must not become a solider, unless he is compelled by a chief bearing the sword. He is not to burden himself with the sin of blood. But if he has shed blood, he is not to partake of the mysteries, unless he is purified by a punishment, tears, and wailing."[49] That the canons ask for purification from violence before partaking of Christ's body is not to say that the one who commits violence to another person cannot be of the church, but rather that what has happened *to the one who commits violence* has done real damage to the soul and must be atoned for. As mentioned briefly earlier, to treat violence against others in the service of protecting others as a self-justifying venture, we condemn the ones who commit torture or who go to war to never being able to be reconciled. When harm done to an enemy is viewed in this way—as doing damage to one's soul—the logic of Christian pacifism becomes most clear: what is at stake in how we engage with the very real violence in the world has grave ramifications, most eminently for what it means that we are to be the image of Christ in a world broken by the violence of sin.

To respect a person's nature as a divinely made creature of God is also to facilitate their growth in the grace of God, which does not preclude

---

[47] For a summary of the practical and theological failures of the arguments of the "ticking time bomb" argument—that the compressed time before the attack warrants enhanced interrogation— see George Hunsinger, "Torture *Is* the Ticking Time-Bomb: Why the Necessity Defense Fails," *Dialog: A Journal of Theology* 47, no. 3 (2008): 228-39.

[48] For the documents themselves, see Kalantzis, *Caesar and the Lamb*, 188-95.

[49] Kalantzis, *Caesar and the Lamb*, 192-93.

increased attention to some rather than others. In this way, Christian non-violence commends a measure of surveillance in keeping with appropriate levels of attention; the argument can be made that surveillance is inherently a form of violence, but surveillance can be done in service of maintaining control over sub-state actors, or in the interest of prudential attention to groups known to be involved in conflict. For nonviolence, if the end of conflict is peace, then nonviolence could commend surveillance toward that end in ways that invite further inclusion within society rather than using surveillance to isolate and alienate certain members of society.

CONCLUSION

This description of Christian pacifism does not provide a panacea against the violence of the world, nor does it propose to offer a theory by which war may be ended. Neither Christian pacifism nor any other theory of Christian participation in war can credibly offer that. But what Christian pacifism does provide is an approach to the Christian's involvement in war that is biblically grounded, theologically rooted in the breadth of the Christian tradition, and practically attuned to the suffering of creation.

In attending to Christian pacifism as an opportunity to engage with the human suffering of conflict in different ways, a fulsome Christian witness has emerged over the last forty years, involving peacemaking teams, attention to the causes of conflict, building up nonviolent movements globally, and fostering the common life of churches as the firstfruits of the kingdom of God. As conflicts—both internationally and domestically—continue to multiply, it is time to take up the challenge of pacifism, which is part of the freeing yoke of Christ. Let us not fear conflict, but step into it as bearers of Christ's peace, seeing the enemy as also those for whom Christ has died.

A Just War Response

ERIC PATTERSON

Myles Werntz's chapter on pacifism and nonviolence is thoughtful and well-researched. Although I strongly disagree with many of his presuppositions and his conclusions, primarily on theological grounds and due to certain weaknesses in Hauerwasian theology, nevertheless the chapter has been carefully prepared. These remarks will start by elaborating Werntz's basic framework (what Christian pacifism is and is not), consider problems in his explication of early Christian positions, and then look at problems that arise from neglecting Christian doctrines of vocation, stewardship, and justice.

First, Werntz helpfully summarizes his position in seven points:

- The taking of life in war is incompatible with the Christian life.
- The refusal to take life in war does not mean abandoning the good of the world.
- Pacifism is not solely fulfilling a command but is also about entering into a life of discipleship and virtue.
- Christian pacifism refuses an ultimate divide between the private and public.
- Christian pacifism is not rooted in optimism about conflict in the world.
- Christian pacifism is not one singular position or approach.
- Christian pacifism is not the same as "quietism" or "withdrawal from society."

There are many areas of agreement possible here, the most important being that robust Christian pacifism need not be utopian, need not involve societal withdrawal, need not create false divisions between public and private, and is not a single position or approach. That being said, there are problems with the Christian pacifist position as elaborated here.

Werntz provides lengthy documentation of some of the earliest Christian voices on issues of soldiering and killing. Before I get into some of these historical issues, there are a number of areas where poor distinctions put this chapter on a weak footing. As I have written elsewhere in this book, it is important to distinguish *force* from *violence*. Force can be loving in intention and provide order and justice, whether punishment by a parent, protection by law enforcement, or the actions of military personnel. Violence is unrestrained, unlawful, typically beyond just authority, and usually motivated by lust, greed, or hatred. Just as we can distinguish between firm family discipline as opposed to child-beating, so too we can tell the difference between appropriate deterrence and punishment versus police brutality and distinguish between limited, lawful military force as opposed to total war and torture.

It is noteworthy that the author carefully says "killing in war" throughout the chapter, providing a footnote suggesting that there is some difference between the military profession and two other professions: domestic law enforcement and care for animals. I do not understand the role of the latter in this context, but it is a faulty distinction to wall off domestic law-enforcement activities from the duties of the armed forces. There are two reasons for this. First, these are professions of life and death, particularly when it comes to the gray areas of cross-border criminal networks; the intersection of local, federal, and international authorities; and the global nature of even localized wrongdoing.

Second, creating these false distinctions also shows theological disregard for the notion of callings or vocation. No one is entirely a private citizen, nor is one's occupation a private matter: we all serve, as God has placed us, in this time and this place with the talents, aptitudes, and opportunities that God has given us. What this means is that it is impossible to wall off our nine-to-five vocation from the other roles we have. I have a day job and for nearly a quarter century have served in the National Guard on weekends and summers. I am also called to serve in my local church, as a husband, as a father, and in various community roles. I am to be a peacemaker with others, as much as possible, in all these roles. The military parent is to love his wife, not exasperate his children, and turn the other cheek to his neighbor as much as possible. But that does not mean that he should cease from intervening if he sees a man beating a woman on a street corner. It also does not mean that he should not pursue his calling of protecting and defending the basic political order that makes human flourishing possible. Soldiers, police, magistrates, and public servants all have a role to play in promoting order and justice, and that entails the inevitable threat and use of force to, as Augustine wrote, punish wrongdoers, right past wrongs, and prevent future wrongs.

It is also important to challenge some of the elements of the historical argument made in this chapter. Let me sketch out briefly what appears to be the most logical evolution of early Christian thinking on the use of force, emphasize the problems mentioned in Acts 15 (e.g., food offered to idols and sexual immorality), and apply these to Christian thinking on peace and security prior to AD 500.

But first, we simply cannot disregard the Bible itself. None of the apostles suggested that the Old Testament should be put away. Hence, it is noteworthy that, in clear opposition to New Testament and early church thinking, many contemporary pacifists create two false distinctions. The first is that Old Testament models do not apply to the New Testament era. That is simply wrong. Moses, David, Nehemiah, Joseph, and others continue to be models of moral leadership. The Wisdom literature, which has much to say about just governance and stewardship, is not abandoned in the New Testament era. It is true that the early church did not expect the structures of their day to last because they thought that Christ's return was imminent. They were not all that interested in the social and political order in the first century following the resurrection because they anticipated the eschaton. That does not mean they threw out the teachings and models of the Old Testament.

The second false distinction is that the church was pacifistic until the reign of Constantine, and then it suddenly became intertwined with politics and statecraft. The unspoken implication here is that the church somehow sold out its spiritual purity when it was recognized by Constantine. But, again, this does not accord with the facts. We know that the New Testament features several public servants, none of whom is chastened for such work: the centurion and his servant in the Gospels, the convert Cornelius in Acts, a city treasurer named Erastus greeted by Paul in Romans, and others. What happened is that as the church grew, people from every walk of life accepted Christ. This included magistrates and military personnel.

One of the things that is most confusing in the record is the contradictory writings of the early church father Tertullian, cited extensively in Werntz's chapter. Tertullian's *On Idolatry* and parts of his *Apology* make it seem impossible for the soldier to be a Christian. The reason for that did not have so much to do with killing as it had to do with idolatry and immorality. Recall that when the Jerusalem Council, in Acts 15, met to decide on the inclusion of Gentiles in the church, new Christians were expected to abide by the basic moral law of the Old Testament (e.g., the Ten Commandments as summarized by love of God and love of neighbor), but they did not have to abide by the Jewish ceremonial laws, such as circumcision and the kosher diet. Due to the culture, the Jerusalem Council did emphasize two things: avoid sexual immorality and food offered to idols, associated with the widespread pagan practices that permeated much of Greco-Roman life. These were the same prohibitions that newly converted Roman soldiers would have been taught, and it would have been difficult for them. There were many holidays, festivals, and oath-taking ceremonies that idolized the emperor and the Roman pantheon. Moreover, because Roman soldiers were forbidden to marry, a wide variety of illicit sexual practices, from prostitution to illegal families, was routine.

Tertullian, however, also commended Christians in the military. His *Apology* recounts a famous episode, noted by others including Marcus Aurelius and Eusebius, when Christian legionaries in the Twelfth Legion knelt and prayed for rain. Lightning from heaven scared off the enemy troops, and rain provided desperately needed water for what became known as the "Thundering Legion." Tertullian wrote a later work called *On the Military Crown* (*De Corona*), which discusses the work, and challenges of idolatry, faced by Christian magistrates and soldiers. Origen (185–254), the other major voice cited by Werntz and others, pointed to the service of Christians in the military as a sign that Christians did not want the downfall of government. Origen says that there may be righteous causes and that it is just to defend one's country, though he is skeptical that Christians can keep themselves free from the idolatry of the Roman apparatus.[1]

As we leave this section of contested early church history, it is important to note something else about Werntz's chapter. When one looks carefully at the chronology of the chapter, one finds massive jumps in time. Page 75 is a case in point. The chronology jumps five centuries and then leaps another millennium, all in the space of about two paragraphs. This cherry-picking of history is, unfortunately, common for those making the pacifist argument. That is because it is easier to focus on the tiny minority of pacifists, whether in religious orders or among the fringe of Anabaptism, than it is to look at the much wider trends that are mainstream to Catholicism, Lutheranism, Presbyterianism, Anglicanism, Wesleyanism, and their descendants through the twentieth century. None of these major traditions, which make up all but a tiny minority of the West's Christians, has pacifistic theologies. Much more is said about why they do not in my chapter on just war in this book.

It is important that we circle back to the issue of what is meant by *nonviolence*. What has happened over the past several decades is a conflation of "pacifism" with "nonviolence" or what Martin Luther King Jr. called "nonviolent direct action." It is important to assess what is meant by "nonviolence," including its roots and the unfortunate confusion that some make between civil disobedience and illegitimate forms of rebellious violence, such as terrorism.

The vast majority of Christian pacifism has involved some form of opting out of participation in the use of force, such as entirely avoiding government service, whether due to one's clerical status (priest, monk) or to theological position such as the Anabaptist's Schleitheim Confession of 1527, which holds that government is important for restraining evil and promoting good, but that Christians cannot be implicated in violence by public service. The reason that nearly all Protestants reject this view is not to degrade the real tension of appropriately being in God's world and yet not fully of it but rather because such forms of dualism are actually gnostic in character.

---

[1] The best resource for pastors and scholars on these issues is Tim Demy and J. Daryl Charles, *War, Peace, and Christianity: Questions and Answers from a Christian Perspective* (Wheaton, IL: Crossway, 2010). See esp. pp. 113-20 for more material on Origen, Tertullian, and other church fathers.

Protestants, especially evangelicals, believe in the full arc of redemptive history, from creation through fall and redemption to restoration in the next life but also in this life. Evangelicals do not take the position that Luther castigated as "contempt of the world." God made the world, and despite the fall, there is much good in this world. We are called to be stewards and citizens in this world at the time and place where God has placed us. Theological dualisms like Gnosticism are typically heretical.

In the twentieth century, most efforts at nonviolent action have been inspired by Gandhi's form of mass people-power action. King testified to the importance of Gandhi's model for the civil rights movement's civil disobedience. But some distinctions are in order. First, Reinhold Niebuhr rightly pointed out that Gandhi's so-called nonviolence was, to use Niebuhr's terminology, "violent." Niebuhr explained that mass strikes that closed factories, resulting in loss of wages, loss of jobs, and families going hungry, are a form of violence by other means. They harm families and children. Another bizarre example is Glen Stassen's so-called Just Peacemaking. During the 1999 Kosovo campaign, in which the West intervened to stop ethnic cleansing in the Balkans that was being launched by the same diabolical Serbian regime that had murdered millions of Muslims just five years earlier, Stassen advocated sending human shields to stop the war. What many forget is that Stassen wanted Westerners to go to Serbia to stand as human shields so that NATO would be unable to attack the Serbian military. These forms of nonviolence have a great deal of moral cloudiness.

Now, when it comes to the US civil rights movement, there is much to be admired. It is important to note that what King and his associates were doing was rooted in Christian theology: they were breaking unjust laws in order to uphold higher laws of human dignity. They were willing to suffer, per Werntz, to do so. All that King really wanted was for Black Americans to have the same laws applied to them as were applied to White Americans: the same opportunity to travel, use public services, be safe in all parts of town, enjoy the fruits of their labor, and participate fully as citizens. Hence, when his organization applied for a parade permit or the opportunity for a public event, and it was denied unfairly, his organization broke the law and held the march anyway. King said that the first steps of such nonviolent direct action were to assess the situation and purify one's heart before taking public action, so that one is sure to be acting out of love and not hate.

King made a poignant observation about the difference between Gandhi and Bonhoeffer. Gandhi had the benefit of facing a democratic government, even if it was a constitutional monarchy. The British response was limited within the boundaries of law and culture. In contrast, Bonhoeffer faced an entirely different foe in demonic Nazism. A different approach was called for to fight the Nazis. King concluded that his approach to nonviolent action was best suited for changing the internal dynamics of the United States. He resolutely opposed those, like Malcolm X, who called for violent overthrow of the system. There is a difference between civil disobedience in a quasi-democratic society (breaking unjust laws to demonstrate how they are unjust and call for reform) and rebellion, revolution, or terrorism.

This is also important because there is some fashionable talk that "one's man's terrorist is another man's freedom fighter." This is simply not the case. It is another example of not making right distinctions. Bonhoeffer was no terrorist: he sought the good of Germany and the world and felt compelled to participate in a scheme that would bring force against the murderous Nazis. George Washington refused to stoop to terrorism, and he executed those under his command who used the war as an opportunity for rape, brutality, or theft. King, Bonhoeffer, Washington, and others understand that God's moral order, in this world, includes law and political institutions. These are not to be left entirely in the hands of those who would misuse them. We know this because in both the Old and New Testaments God has called and equipped individuals to serve in every licit walk of life, including in government, law enforcement, and the armed forces.

A Christian Realist Response

A. J. NOLTE

Myles Werntz's account of Christian nonviolence makes perhaps the best case for this position one can make. I have some quibbles with the account of church history he presents—most of which I address elsewhere in this volume—but on the whole, this chapter represents an excellent and theologically well-grounded treatment of the subject. Werntz's account of nonviolence has two other notable strengths: he is not utopian in his claims regarding what Christian nonviolence can achieve, and he proposes a number of approaches to preventing war and making peace that are in and of themselves worthy projects in which the church is, and rightly ought to be, substantively engaged.

Before outlining the core difference between nonviolence and what I have called a "dirty hands" Christian realist position, let me elaborate on some points of agreement. The two positions would agree that no Christian position on war can ever provide a perfect solution. They would agree that, in some sense, there are grounds for optimism about humanity rooted in the reality of Christ's incarnation and looking toward eschatological hope. I believe they would share a certain skepticism about the self-justifying tendency of states and nations where war is concerned, rooted in a recognition that "there is no political community that is entirely free of idolatry."[1] Finally, they would share the understanding that our ethical view of war should, in some sense, mirror the conduct of Christ.

---

[1]Perry T. Hamalis, "Just Peacemaking and Christian Realism: Possibilities for Moving Beyond the Impasse in Orthodox Christian War Ethics," in *Orthodox Christian Perspectives on War*, ed. Perry T. Hamalis and Valerie A. Karras (Notre Dame, IN: University of Notre Dame Press, 2017), 349.

The main disagreement between Werntz's position and the dirty-hands Christian realist tradition, typified by diverse thinkers from the Cappadocians to Reinhold Niebuhr, lies in the question of how Christ ought to be emulated. Werntz clearly aligns Christian nonviolence with what might be fairly described as an "already" approach to modeling Christ: "To engage sin under sin's terms," he argues, "is to cede the high ground to creation's corruption rather than to engage the world as the world in which Christ has already won the victory over death" (p. 84). While a dirty-hands Christian realist would certainly agree that Christ has won the victory over death, such thinkers have, I argue, emphasized the need to live in a fallen world where that victory remains far from complete. We might call this a "not yet" perspective.

Werntz is quite right to point out that modern Christian nonviolence must accept that no human being, apart from Christ himself, can have hands that are truly clean from sin. (I would suggest that much of the early Christian opposition to participation in war he cites is, in fact, motivated precisely by a sacramental emphasis on clean hands at the altar, and this is certainly the reason for the prohibitions on use of force by clergy that still persist today.) Yet I think Niebuhr envisions a somewhat different emulation of Christ—a more sacrificial one. Just as Christ takes onto himself the burden of our sin, so must Christian soldiers and statesmen, out of what Niebuhr calls the "law of love," use force to defend their neighbor from cases of grievous evil. For the Orthodox fathers, such as Basil of Caesarea, the approach is quite similar: war is necessary for the defense of one's neighbor against violent and dangerous men; penance is required for those who have killed in war; but the traditional penance for willful murder, which is a thirty-year prohibition from Communion, is reduced to three years.[2] Thus the dirty-hands Christian realist squares the circle between the necessity and, as Werntz points out, inevitability of war, and the recognition that killing in war remains a destruction of a human being made in God's image. Yet killing in war, for the dirty-hands perspective, is also necessary. Against

---

[2] For a fuller treatment of this topic, see Valerie A. Karras, "Their Hands Are Not Clean: Origen and the Cappadocians on War and Military Service," in Hamalis and Karras, *Orthodox Christian Perspectives on War*, 125-58. For the point on the differing lengths of penance imposed for murder and killing in war, see p. 148.

this argument, Werntz points out social-scientific evidence that nonviolent approaches can prevent or de-escalate conflict in many instances. Where this is possible, I believe both just war advocates and dirty-hands Christian realists would agree that such methods are preferable to war. Yet what of those situations where use of force alone can deter or prevent injustice? Such examples shaped Niebuhr's thought. In the face of the twin totalitarianisms of Nazism and communism, Niebuhr understood that only force could prevent tyranny.

I suspect a Christian nonviolence proponent might respond to the circumstances Niebuhr faced in one of three ways. The first is the approach of thinkers like Tertullian and Origen, who prayed for the victory of Roman arms, but argued that Christians themselves should not participate in war. However, the societies who stood against Nazi Germany and Soviet Russia were themselves majority Christian, meaning that a general Christian abstention from military service would have made any forceful defense impossible. Second, the Christian nonviolence proponent might engage in passive resistance, civil disobedience, or other disruptive acts designed to impede tyrannical power. Such an approach was characteristic of the Polish Solidarity movement in the 1980s. Solidarity's success, however, did not come in a vacuum, but in the context of an aggressive and, at the time, highly controversial American campaign of forceful deterrence directed at the Soviet Union. Likewise, the heroic Danish resistance and other civil-disobedience-oriented movements protesting the Nazis did some harm to the German war effort and some good to some civilians but, on their own, proved entirely insufficient to defeat the totalitarian scourge. Third, the Christian pacifist might look to eschatological hope: even the tyranny of this world will, in the fullness of time, be overcome by Christ, and as Christians, our responsibility is to live into that heavenly reality. This is not quite the withdrawal from the world of which Werntz wishes to absolve nonviolence, and there is undoubtedly some truth to it. But, to use Niebuhr's term, it seems to fall short of the burdens the law of love imposes on us where our neighbor is concerned. To pray for our neighbor's soul in the face of violence is, for Niebuhr, necessary but not sufficient; where the capacity to act in defense of one's neighbor is present, failure to do so represents an abdication of our responsibility.

This responsibility to act is at the heart of the difference between a modern nonviolence perspective and a modern Niebuhrian one, and may also mark a shift of emphasis between the effective nonviolence of Origen and the nuanced view of the Cappadocians, which I take to be basically congruent with Niebuhr. As Valerie Karras argues in her analysis of Origen and the Cappadocians, this shift is perhaps due more to a change in circumstances than a shift in the underlying theology. At the time of the Cappadocians, she explains, "the luxury of a pure pacifism is no longer practicable in a world where Christians dominate. Nevertheless, even within the limits of defensive action, the common thread of a moral abhorrence of war so forcefully argued by Origen and other pre-Constantinian Christian writers continues to underlie the more nuanced and pragmatic approach of the Cappadocians."[3]

The seamless way in which Origen's priestly conception of the church as a whole was adapted to the clergy in the East—and, to a large extent, in the West as well—indicates to me a continuity of intent, combined with an understanding of the pragmatic necessities imposed on a Christian-majority society. Patristic nonviolence is, in this reading, somewhat positional, and the reason this positionality is not made clearer is that it was impossible for Origen to imagine a world in which Rome would become Christian and Christ would not immediately return. In short, for Origen, there was no necessary bias toward action on the issue of Christians in war, because the church was a decided minority (less than 10 percent of the empire's population by many estimates, which is a smaller proportion of the population than was enslaved at Rome's height). By contrast, in the much different circumstances faced by the Cappadocians, universal nonviolence was, indeed, a luxury.

Reinhold Niebuhr's bias toward action is perhaps made most plain in his disagreement with his brother Richard over a military response to Japan's invasion of China, as chronicled in the pages of the *Christian Century* in the 1930s. The title of Niebuhr's essay, "Must We Do Nothing?" also neatly encapsulates the general thrust of his thought. In responding to the eschatologically pacifist approach of his brother, Reinhold argued that "it would

---

[3]Karras, "Their Hands Are Not Clean," 149.

be better to come to ethical terms with the forces of nature in history, and try to use ethically directed coercion in order that violence may be avoided."[4] He finds such eschatological hope historically implausible: "The hope that a kingdom of pure love will emerge out of the catastrophes of history is even less plausible than the Communist faith that an equalitarian society will eventually emerge from them."[5] Niebuhr acknowledges that his brother's pacifist stance "both in its ethical perfectionism and in its apocalyptic note is closer to the gospel than mine."[6] Yet Niebuhr found himself faced with an unresolvable paradox in the attempt to construct an ethic out of the pure love of the gospel: "I cannot abandon the pure love ideal because anything which falls short of it is less than the ideal. But I cannot use it fully if I want to assume a responsible attitude towards the problems of society."[7]

Here we return to Niebuhr's rejection of either a too consistent optimism or a too consistent pessimism. For Niebuhr, nonviolence might lead to either extreme but was incapable of constructing a Christian ethic in which responsible action could be taken to achieve real progress. In his words, "as long as the world of man remains a place where nature and God, the real and the ideal, meet, human progress will depend on the judicious use of the forces of nature in the service of the ideal."[8]

Werntz would doubtless argue against Niebuhr's categorical assertion that pacifism cannot constructively operate in the space between the real and the ideal. I suspect Niebuhr would doubtless agree that the active and positive contributions Werntz highlights are the kinds of things that enable some kind of genuine progress. Yet Niebuhr's persistently tragic view of history led him to a recognition that, in the end, force must inevitably be deployed at least to constrain tyrannical violence, thereby making space in which progress can be made. But the nonviolence proponent might argue that human progress is, after all, not really the point or the purpose of the church, or at least, is a point it may achieve only by the salutary example it

---

4Reinhold Niebuhr, "Must We Do Nothing?," *Christian Century*, March 30, 1932, republished at United Church of Christ, www.ucc.org/who-we-are/about/general-synod/general-synod-resolutions-regarding-environmental-justice/beliefs/beliefs_theology/beliefs_theology_must-we-do-nothing/.
5Niebuhr, "Must We Do Nothing?"
6Niebuhr, "Must We Do Nothing?"
7Niebuhr, "Must We Do Nothing?"
8Niebuhr, "Must We Do Nothing?"

can set by serving as a model and guide for ethical human behavior. Niebuhr would, in theory, agree. Yet he might question a model of Christlike behavior that leaves the primary cost of violence to be borne by our neighbors and not ourselves. Is it truly a Christlike witness, he might ask, for Christians to pass on to our non-Christian neighbor the spiritual cost of taking human life in defense of others? The nonviolence proponent must respond either with the argument that such defense is not truly necessary (utopian optimism) or that, for example, the difference between earthly freedom and earthly tyranny is of insufficient import to make defense of the former and prevention of the latter a goal Christians should pursue (excessive pessimism). For his part, Niebuhr firmly rejected any kind of false moral equivalence between attacker and defender, tyranny and freedom. Earthly peace and freedom might be relative and imperfect, but for Niebuhr, they are worth defending nonetheless, even if that defense requires the tragic but necessary ultimate sacrifice: killing those made in the image of God.

A Church Historical Response

MEIC PEARSE

As Myles Werntz states from the outset, Christian pacifism starts from the simple premise that killing a human being is inconsistent with the gospel. It is that central difficulty with which all nonpacifists need to wrestle—with the danger that their arguments may become finally incredible, even to themselves. As I indicate in my own essay, I can certainly point to a counterconsideration so weighty as to outbalance even this simple precept of pacifism; it is when I attempt to detail circumstances and protocols around uses of force "consistent with the gospel" that my "personal incredulity gag reflexes" kick in, and I wander away, muttering something about casuistry. His point that "Christian pacifism is not fundamentally a matter of optimism" (p. 68) is an extremely important one. Christian pacifism has—or should have—nothing in common with secular-liberal convictions about human goodness, and the idea that all actual conflicts are mere misunderstandings that would somehow come right if we just talked and listened long enough. (Such persons usually chatter about "negotiations"—forgetting that, implicit in the very idea of "negotiation" is, on both sides, an "or else" that generally refers to the use of some kind of force.) Failing this, secular-liberal-type pacifists tend to insist that all conflicts are rooted in social grievances—grievances that might be ameliorated if the goodies were just spread around more evenly.

The genuinely Christian pacifist shares none of these delusions, knowing instead that human beings are incorrigibly sinful, and that almost every conflict will stem from a mixture of causes, some of which should inspire sympathy in others, and some of which will be the merest patina of verbiage over darker motives. For the Christian, the pacifist imperative stems not from optimism, whether about "the arc of history" or about human beings. Indeed, it is not predicated on calculation of outcomes at all. The command not to kill comes in spite of the possible (or even likely) outcomes of such moral restraint. And that, of course, is the point at which many of us, including the present writer, are sadly unable to stay the course.

Despite Werntz's sound, good sense in distancing Christian pacifism from facile optimism, he seems to backtrack a few pages later, when he suggests that the "definition of society" as "interwoven with violence as a necessary feature" and with violence as "the essential character of public institutions" is "a questionable premise" (p. 72). Far from all this being questionable, I should wish to insist on just such a thing. Werntz could be challenged to show us long-term (or at least medium-term) viable examples in which the implicit threat of violence played no role. And if, by way of answer, he were to point to Amish communities or anything similar, it would be easy to show that those depend, for their safety from enemies without, on the forces of the state where they live, which provides a protective shield of violence in which the Amish themselves play no part. We are back with the baby in the cradle, the helplessly ill person, and Liechtenstein.

Werntz's historical insight is undoubtedly sound, however, when he states that engaging in *this particular war* "frequently creates the conditions and fractures that will lead to and justify the next conflict" (p. 69). One need look no further than the two world wars—the first creating the seedbed for the second—to see his point, though many other examples could be proffered. The blood feud of the Middle Ages (or of Albania and Montenegro in more recent centuries) is an extreme example of this dynamic.

Even so, it remains far from clear to me that merely walking away from World War I in (say) 1915 would have led to a more peaceful world. Very many combatants fight merely because they have to—because failing to do so would lead either to the death of oneself and one's family, or because it would lead to conditions too intolerable to live with. As the old wisecrack goes, "A fight is the one thing that, if a man asks you for one, you simply have to oblige him."

Werntz is perfectly correct to point out that "modern Christian just war thinkers tend to come from a distinct Euro-American lineage, drawing on specific Catholic and Reformed roots" (p. 71), a lineage he contrasts with the diversity of Christian pacifist traditions—and in this he is seeking to wrest the claim to (small-c) catholicity from the protagonists of the just war tradition. But aside from debates around breadth and catholicity, I should like to emphasize that the "Euro-American lineage" and the "specific Catholic and Reformed roots" are the direct lineal descendants of a very particular need emanating from the late fourth and early fifth centuries: to square the teachings of Jesus with Christianity's new status as the rationale for governing society as a whole. And since such a thing is impossible, it was the teachings of Jesus that had to give. If Werntz is too kind to make this point bluntly against his opponents, I (saying it softly) am not.

Indeed, the evidence for that pre-Christendom tradition is seen within the very provisions for exceptions made by the Christendom model itself. As Werntz rightly points out, even within supposedly Christian, war-fighting states, "clerics, beginning with the canons issued forth from church councils by the late fifth century, were forbidden to engage in bloodshed of any kind" (p. 75). It was all part of a pattern whereby many of the expectations previously incumbent on all Christians now devolved solely on clergy and monastics.

This is why, historically, pacifists have more generally been met with among Anabaptists of many kinds, Quakers, some Baptists, early Pentecostals, the (Plymouth) Brethren—all groups that rejected the very idea of a *corpus Christianum*, or a Christian state. To be sure, there are and have been Christian pacifists in other traditions, such as Catholics and Anglicans—but, with the deepest possible respect, they have had to cast into oblivion the historic meaning of their churches in order to reach that position.

I would venture to quibble with Werntz over his interpretation of the Schleitheim Confession—by common consent, the most important of the early evangelical Anabaptist confessions of faith. In Werntz's reading, the author (Michael Sattler) rejected "the sword not out of a desire for moral purity but out of seeking unity with Christ" (p. 73). To the contrary, the entire document is concerned with separation—that is, with purity. And the refusal to take the sword is part and parcel of that: "The sword is an ordering of God outside the perfection of Christ."[1] That sounds like a concern for "moral purity."

Clearly, Werntz agrees with (or comes close to agreeing with) the view of the relationship between the Old and New Testaments that I outline in my own essay. He says, concerning Old Testament texts about the destruction of persons and places (*haram*), that "when the earliest Christian exegetes read these texts, they . . . never, prior to the fourth century," saw them "as examples or inspiration for Christian practice" (p. 77). Quite so. The Old Testament does indeed give the advocate of Christendom what she seeks: a model for running society along theocratic lines. But it does so only at a price. And part of that price is to disregard the ways in which the first three centuries of Christian exegetes actually did use those texts, and the ways in which they saw the relationship between the testaments.

The other part of the price is the need to gloss over the rather appalling way in which the state of ancient Israel—the presumed model for the Christian Roman Empire (or Elizabethan England, or the United States of America)—came together. For it did so in the way that all states come into existence: it expelled or exterminated the existing inhabitants and claimed the territory for itself. If the parallels with early America are painful to contemplate, it is only because the events are closer to us in time, and so better documented than many other instances. But a reading of Bede relates how the Angles and Saxons (that is, the English) came into possession of southern Britain. And the brutalities of the Romans in subjugating the various peoples who lived south and west of the Rhine-Danube are sufficiently recorded to give us a tolerable impression of the process. For this is

---

[1] The main body of the text is no place for a detailed history lesson. But the Schleitheim Confession consists of seven articles—and the fourth (i.e., the middle of seven) is about "the separation that shall take place from the evil and the wickedness which the devil has planted in the world, simply in this; that we have no fellowship with them, and do not run with them in the confusion of their abominations." All seven provisions (with the arguable exception of the fifth, "The shepherd in the church") are concerned with the *boundaries of the church and separation* from those outside. At a time when all of Western Europe was arguing about competing doctrines of Communion, Schleitheim was concerned with *who may take it*. Christians may not be magistrates because "the rule of the government is according to the flesh, that of the Christians according to the Spirit." The Confession's concern for "moral purity" could hardly be more clear.

what a state *means*. Only the degree and duration of violence required to bring it about will vary between cases.

As Werntz says, "Before *any* nation is a nation, it is a subgroup engaging in tactical conflict against a superior force" (pp. 84-85). Seen in this light—the correct light, I would contend—"the behavior of the people of Israel in Joshua" is exactly equivalent to what we might now denounce as "terrorism" (p. 85). In making the wincing comparison, Werntz intends, of course, to show the absurdity of using Old Testament models as a blueprint in Christian theology and ethics. Quite right.

However, precisely this argument highlights the unavoidable nature of a state's responsibilities. What happened to the Gauls when confronted by the Romans; the Britons when invaded by the English; the North American nations when confronted by European encroachments that ultimately swept them all away—was appalling. What was done to them was wicked. That they failed to survive is a tragedy. Yet precisely these terrible fates highlight the duty incumbent on all states to defend themselves and their peoples. One need hardly be a slavish adherent of Hobbes to insist that this is their first duty, in the sense that the state that fails to provide adequately for it will be swept away. And most such transitions are attended by far more bloodshed than simply a change of rulers.

It is this, final consideration, it seems to me, that makes the commitment to pacifism finally untenable. The world is thus. All states that now exist came about as a result of violence—either offered or actualized. They maintain their present existence the same way—the smaller states subsisting on the indulgence of the stronger whose interests, for the moment, they serve.[2]

And all of them will pass out of existence as and when they are unable to maintain themselves against future aggressors. If they are lucky, they might merely be absorbed, their populations humiliated for generations. If unlucky, their peoples may be entirely eradicated. And so, in the meantime, they defend themselves; they make alliances; and they prepare.

---

[2]The example of interwar Czechoslovakia is instructive. Pushed for by local nationalists, the country would not have come into existence but for the destruction of the Austro-Hungarian Empire in war, and then the determination of the victor powers in 1919 to create it. Successful and prosperous, it nevertheless was dismembered in 1938–1939, when an aggressor (Nazi Germany) proffered overwhelming violence, and its friends Britain and France saw their interests as better served by placating Hitler than coming to the rescue.

A Christian pacifism that forswears participation in "the world"—as the Schleitheim Confession proposed—is greatly to be respected and admired. Even so, its renunciations seem too drastic for most modern Christians, accustomed to toleration and thus to some participation in wider society, to embrace. And once that point is conceded, then the need to fend off localized Armageddon—the obliteration of the state and population in which we happen to live—seems only reasonable. But codifying what might or might not be allowable in the unspeakable evil that is *actual* war: that, I contend, will remain permanently beyond us.

Nonviolence Rejoinder

MYLES WERNTZ

The relationship of Christianity to war, as this book shows, consists of divergent claims, difficult conversations, and careful moral reasoning. Being a pacifist, as I am, is one way in which the Christian moral life unfolds, and one that I am bound to defend, for no other reason than I think it true. The form of the world's violence continues to change, and gratefully, Christian pacifism learns and changes with it, not bound to simply repeat the past but to change faithfully with the times.[1] I am grateful for the other writers of this volume for their time and attention to Christian pacifism, and offer this as a clarification of some of their misreadings, as well as a chance to make my final case.

THE VOCATION OF THE CHRISTIAN PACIFIST

Since Luther first argued that the Christian should offer himself as the hangman, arguments for the just war (such as Patterson's) consistently evoke the specter of vocation, that the Christian pacifist neglects or limits the Christian's role in the world. As my chapter indicates, nothing could be further from the truth: to describe a Christian commitment to the world does not entail abandoning the world, even if it swears off using violence against it. What I put forward— far from H. Richard Niebuhr's "The Grace of Doing Nothing"[2] or

---

[1]See here Mark Douglas, *Christian Pacifism for an Environmental Age* (Cambridge: Cambridge University Press, 2019) for an exemplary approach to retrieval and reappropriation as it occurs within Christian pacifism.

[2]H. Richard Niebuhr, "The Grace of Doing Nothing," in *War in the Twentieth Century*, ed. Richard B. Miller (Louisville, KY: Westminster John Knox, 1992), 6-12.

sixteenth-century Anabaptism—is much better understood as taking up the vocation of the peacemaker.

To be a Christian peacemaker is not to segregate oneself from the world (which even pacifists such as the Anabaptists and Quakers did not ultimately do!),[3] but to engage in issues of public life—and yes, public safety—in ways that seek to address violence *before* it erupts. The classic categories of the just war carefully detail the logic for whether a conflict is just, but say little about the need for there to be public ways of reconciliation that occur on an ongoing basis. Christian pacifism, by beginning from the presumption that violence is both unnatural to us as creatures of God and inconsistent with the person of Christ, asks the question, What kinds of peacemaking need to occur consistently, then? What practices are needed if violence is off the table?

Framed this way, being a Christian pacifist is not a matter of perfection, but a matter of penitent discipleship. It is not that a commitment to Christian pacifism as such makes one perfect, but that the way of discipleship involves commitment to Jesus, in the ways of Jesus. Being a Christian in the world is never a safe vocation, and means—and we must be frank about this—swearing off some options that remain in front of us, particularly when it comes to the exercise of violence.

THE CHRISTIAN PACIFIST, THE SCRIPTURES, AND CHURCH HISTORY

The intent of discipleship, then, is not simply to "purify one's motives," cleaning oneself of hatred and animus so that we can then take up the "dirty work" of violence with pure hearts. Christian pacifism is frequently (and in these responses) accused of a soft variety of Gnosticism, treating the world as unworthy of engagement. But to clean oneself of vices, only to take up again the practices that foster the vices, is the real gnostic break: that a pure heart and virtues cannot find purchase in a broken world. As I have

---

[3]To make the claim that Anabaptist nonviolence, in its practice, is all like Schleitheim is neither true to Anabaptism in the sixteenth century nor true of contemporary Anabaptists. See Michael G. Baylor, ed., *The Radical Reformation*, Cambridge Texts in the History of Political Thought (Cambridge: Cambridge University Press, 1991), and one contemporary restatement, A. James Reimer, *Toward an Anabaptist Political Theology: Law, Order, and Civil Society* (Eugene, OR: Cascade, 2014).

described them, Christian pacifists do not keep themselves from the world but remain present to it.

To argue this is not, as some of my interlocutors have stated, to be a selective reader of Scripture: it is to be a *canonical* reader of Scripture, one committed to the notion that Scripture has both a telos and a direction. To be a canonical reader is not to imagine that all parts of Scripture should be read as flat examples, as if the virtues of the patriarchs and of the kingdoms could be read without the Gospels as their completion. Scripture reads itself in this way, reading prophecy as completed in Christ, and the stories of the patriarchs not as commending their violence but their faith. As my chapter indicated, early Christians did not seek to make Christians into soldiers, but soldiers into Christians, an act that frequently involved their martyrdom.

That Christians did not uniformly heed the counsel of their bishops or of church councils should surprise no one who has ever been to church. Some pacifists have thus held to a "Constantinian fall" of the church, in which there was a pristine age of pacifism followed by a thundering retreat. My chapter does not hold to this, contrary to some of my interlocutors' assumption that it does, but acknowledges rather that the consistent witness to not taking up arms remained, albeit in an emaciated form, in the prohibition against clerics taking up arms. That Christian pacifism was not a prominent ethic for many centuries is no strike against it; the Reformers frequently pointed to ways in which the Scripture's practices had fallen into disrepair (though were not abandoned), and this is no different.

That Christian pacifism reemerges most vigorously among the early Anabaptists is well known. I find it telling, however, that none of my interlocutors engage my (correct) claim that Christian pacifism does not remain there, and takes up homes in many different ecclesial contexts. After the Reformation, we find it spreading into various traditions, taken up by early Pentecostals, by the first generations of the Restorationist movement, by Catholics and Presbyterians, Methodists, and Baptists—all of them finding resonance within their own theological traditions for the truthfulness of Christian pacifism's claims.[4] The charges of sectarianism and theological

---

[4]For details on how four very different theological traditions arrived at this conclusion during the Vietnam era, see my *Bodies of Peace: Nonviolence, Ecclesiology, Witness* (Minneapolis: Fortress, 2014).

obscurity, in other words, simply do not stick, for Christian pacifism is in truth an ecumenically engaged position.

THE FUTURE OF CHRISTIAN PACIFISM

Well-known proponents of Christian pacifism in the last century, such as Stanley Hauerwas, did so much to help recover this tradition for a broader audience, and we all owe them an incalculable debt. But, as I have indicated, the future of Christian pacifism is not one in which we will all look like Hauerwas, or like the early Anabaptists, or like the early Catholic Church. It will exhibit family resemblances to these forebears, but Christian pacifism does not live or die by their examples. The future of Christian pacifism is one that is willing—as I have indicated—to learn from the best of the past reflections on war, wherever they may be found, and to reappropriate them in our own evolving conflicts and entanglements with violence. There is no shortage of new challenges, as war continually moves from being interstate to intrastate, and as new questions of technology, terrorism, and intervention are broached.

But, as much as the future of Christian pacifism will be done by prolif-erated Christians in various contexts and various theological traditions, the future of Christian pacifism will inevitably mean returning again and again to the source: to the person and work of Christ, who creates a body in the world founded on the presumption that, while we were crucifying Christ, Christ died for us anyway (Rom 5:8). As Christians continue to shelter victims, to work for public forms of justice, and to seek the peace of the city, we must never forget that our sheltering, working, and seeking are condi-tioned by the example and person of the one who calls us. To sever our ethics from this source—in the name of historical distance, of expedience, or virtue—is to risk making our public Christian witness unintelligible at best and absent at worst.

3

A CHRISTIAN

REALIST VIEW

A Christian Realist View
Necessary War and "Dirty Hands"

A. J. NOLTE

To speak of "political realism" from a Christian perspective is, of necessity, to speak of Christian realism. Before delving into the question of what Christian realism is, something must be said of what it is not. First, Christian realism is quite distinct from the modern international-relations-theory paradigm known as neorealism. Neorealism's concord premise is that realist international-relations theory can be justified apart from a reliance on either human nature or history.[1] Kenneth Waltz, John Mearsheimer, and the other neorealists sought to build a theoretical model for state behavior with actual predictive power and scientific rigor. This was a far different project from that of even secular classical realists such as Hans Morgenthau, who saw international-relations theory almost as a branch of the philosophy of history.[2]

This leads to a distinct difference between classical realism and neorealism with respect to the necessity of morality and moral judgment. As will be discussed below, Morgenthau quite explicitly considered the attempt to apply a realist understanding to statecraft a moral project, and was in regular and close dialogue with Reinhold Niebuhr, the most prominent Christian realist of his time.[3] By contrast, neorealists see their conclusions about history less as an attempt to bring moral judgment to bear on tragic

---

[1] Kenneth Waltz, "The Anarchic Structure of World Politics," in *International Politics: Enduring Concepts And Contemporary Issues*, ed. Art Robert and Jervis Robert, 10th ed. (New York: Pearson, 2011), 37-59.

[2] Richard J. Hoskins, "Reinhold Niebuhr and International Society: The Concord of Christian Realism and the English School of International Relations Theory" (PhD diss., University of Chicago, 2016), ProQuest Dissertation Publishing (AAT 10052894), 13-14.

[3] Daniel F. Rice, *Reinhold Niebuhr and His Circle of Influence* (New York: Cambridge University Press, 2012), 170.

realities than a project of scientifically determining the proper course for a state to take in international relations.[4] Normative moral judgments, for the neorealist, do not enter into the calculus.

Second, Christian realism is not merely the justification of realpolitik for its own ends: power for the sake of power. To be sure, Christian realists place a heavy emphasis on the centrality of power dynamics in international relations. However, they are every bit as concerned with the moral use of power as the other Christian traditions, though they approach questions of morality through a distinctive lens.

Finally, Christian realism is, or at least can be, distinct from the just war tradition, but this distinction must be carefully drawn, and many historical and contemporary thinkers have a foot in both camps. It has been argued that the difference between just war and Christian realism is that the former sees war as a lesser good, while the latter sees it as a lesser evil. Much of the difference between the two traditions can be found in this general vicinity, but a careful reading of the Christian realists does not, I think, fully support the "lesser evil" understanding with respect to Christian realism.

WHAT IS CHRISTIAN REALISM?
A WORKING DEFINITION

The uniquely Christian realist view of war stems from a conflict of moral imperatives best described as tragedy or irony. On one hand, Christian realists tend to emphasize the sacred nature of human life made in the image of God. On the other, the effect of sin is to interject self-love into human action—a tendency only intensified by the state.

The ineradicable effect of sin, then, is to place power and domination at the heart of human relations, making war an inevitability. The defense of one's fellow image bearers requires the destruction of other image bearers, which is the irony and tragedy of war. Though most Christian realists shy away from the lesser-evil terminology embraced by classic realists such as Morgenthau, they emphasize the effect of war on individuals and societies: war changes the nature of individuals and the character of states in ways that have lasting and often negative effects even if the war is necessary.

---

[4]Henry R. Nau, *Perspective on International Relations*, 5th ed. (Los Angeles: Sage, 2017), 44, 76-77.

Inaction, however, poses yet greater moral costs, and so failure to act also has tragic and negative effects, which are usually borne by one's neighbor rather than oneself. Thus, while the just war tradition emphasizes the conditions under which war might be morally justified, Christian realism's emphasis is on the cost of war—a cost they often measure in terms of "dirty hands" and damage to society. Yet these tragedies are eclipsed by the greater tragedies they believe inaction would cause.

Christian realism, then, is less a fixed principle, such as pacifism, or a tradition of moral reasoning, such as the just war tradition, and more a disposition toward war, history, state power, and international relations. As Eric Patterson says in the introduction to an edited volume on the modern Christian realists, "The Christian realists were not a school in the sense of a defined ideology or statement of purpose; rather, Christian realism was a movement that viewed politics ethically and pragmatically."[5]

Christian realism takes as its starting point the paradoxical condition of humanity: at once made in the image of God yet also fully subject to the catastrophic realities of sin. Thus, as the modern Christian realist par excellence Reinhold Niebuhr explained, humanity is caught in the tension between his freedom as an image bearer and his finitude imposed by sin and death.[6] This tension drives the self-interested human conduct that makes war inevitable. Christian realism recognizes the tragedy of war, and Christian realists tend to shy away from an assertion that war is a lesser good. Yet at the same time, Christian realism also will not pretend that war is not necessary, and though it is to be avoided where possible, it must be prosecuted in those necessary circumstances.

In what follows, I will explore the distinctive contributions of a Christian realist disposition to our understanding of war and the use of force by examining ancient and modern expressions of Christian realism, and laying out how I believe Christian realists might respond to some contemporary challenges in ways distinct from the just war tradition.

---

[5] Eric Patterson, introduction to *The Christian Realists: Reassessing the Works of Niebuhr and His Contemporaries*, ed. Eric Patterson (Lanham, MD: University Press of America, 2003), 1.
[6] Robert Lovin, introduction to Reinhold Niebuhr, *The Nature and Destiny of Man: A Christian Interpretation* (Louisville, KY: Westminster John Knox, 1996), xiii.

THE CHRISTIAN REALIST DISPOSITION IN SCRIPTURE AND THE EARLY CHURCH

Old Testament precedents: clean hands and a priestly people. There is a striking essay in Reinhold Niebuhr's edited volume *Beyond Tragedy* titled "The Ark and the Temple," in which Niebuhr meditates on 1 Chronicles 28. It is here that David announces that the Lord has forbidden him to build the temple, for, as the Lord says to him, "You are a warrior and have shed blood" (1 Chron 28:3 NRSV). For Niebuhr, the significance of this Old Testament example is the transformation of the code of ethics by which God deals with his people: from the "tribal" and "warlike" ethics of the ark to the "peaceful" and "universal" ethics of the temple.[7]

For Christian realism more broadly, however, this passage is critical at a more basic level: it underlines the need for purity at the altar of the Lord. Of course, this theme is picked up widely in Leviticus and other Old Testament sources, but 1 Chronicles 28 is perhaps the clearest Old Testament example of a paradoxical reality: even righteous war on God's behalf has such a lasting impact on David's character that he is seen as the wrong person to build God's house. It is his son Solomon, whose name in Hebrew might be translated as "peaceful one," who is ordained by God to build the temple (1 Chron 28:5-10).

Strikingly, it is not because of David's sins—many of which are chronicled in detail in the Bible—that he is prevented from building the temple but as a result of his warfare, much of which was not only righteous but also specifically sanctioned by God. It is not to David's moral discredit that he fought for the Lord, and indeed, it is credited to him as righteousness before God that he desires to build a temple for the Lord. Rather, if this passage is taken at face value, David's inability to build the temple is a tragic necessity: he fulfilled his purpose as a warrior king, but the building of the temple required a different sort of king, consecrated to a different sort of purpose.

Clean hands and tragic necessity in Origen and Tertullian's conceptions of war. Christian realists might read the otherwise quite confusing teachings of early church thinkers such as Origen and Tertullian on warfare and Christian participation in the military in light of the biblical tradition of

---

[7]Reinhold Niebuhr, *Beyond Tragedy: Essays on the Christian Interpretation of History* (New York: Charles Scribner's Sons, 1965), 61.

ambivalence and contradiction toward war and violence exemplified in the story of King David and the temple, that extends through the Old to the New Testament and beyond.

On one hand, Tertullian and Origen believed that military service was inappropriate for Christians. As Tertullian asks rhetorically, "Shall a Christian be free to walk around in a sword, when the Lord has said that whoever takes the sword shall perish by the sword? Shall a son of peace, who would not even go to law, be embroiled in battle? Shall he administer chains and imprisonment and torture and punishment, though he will not even take vengeance for wrongs done himself?"[8] In some ways, Origen is even more radical than Tertullian, arguing that a Christianized state should properly be a state without war: "If as Celsus suggests, all the Romans were convinced and prayed, they would be superior to their enemies, or would not even fight wars at all, since they would be protected by divine power which is reported to have preserved five entire cities for the sake of fifty righteous men."[9]

However, closer inspection shows both men's views to be somewhat more complex. For example, the same Tertullian who argues against Christian military service asserts that believers "are ever making intercession for all the emperors ... [for] a secure rule, a safe home, brave armies, a faithful senate, an honest people, a quiet world and everything for which a man and a Caesar can pray."[10] Origen is even more emphatic in asserting the value of Christian prayer for the Roman state:

> While others fight, Christians also should be fighting as priests and worshippers of God, keeping their right hands pure and by their prayers to God striving for those who fight in a righteous cause and for the emperor who reigns righteously, in order that everything which is opposed and hostile to those who act righteously may be destroyed. ... And though we do not become fellow-soldiers with him, even if he presses for this, yet we are fighting for him and composing a special army of piety through our intercessions to God.[11]

---

[8]Tertullian, *The Military Chaplet*, in *From Irenaeus to Grotius: A Sourcebook in Christian Political Thought*, ed. Oliver O'Donovan and Joan Lockwood O'Donovan (Grand Rapids, MI: Eerdmans, 1999), 26.

[9]Origen, *Against Celsus*, in O'Donovan and O'Donovan, *From Irenaeus to Grotius*, 41.

[10]Tertullian, *Apology*, in O'Donovan and O'Donovan, *From Irenaeus to Grotius*, 25.

[11]Origen, *Against Celsus*, 43.

For Origen and Tertullian, prayer was an inherently political act of very real and material benefit to the empire. Prayer was the primary responsibility of Christians to the state, and could only be fulfilled if the Christians kept themselves pure of all defilement.

Origen and Tertullian's opposition to Christian military service, then, stems not from a categorical rejection of war, but from their concern that Christians maintain clean hands. As early Christian scholar Philip Wynn explains, "If blood embodied the potential pagan pollutant of Christian society, the hands were the avenue whereby the contaminant could be communicated across the boundary between Christianity and paganism . . . and thus had to be purified from the consequent contamination."[12] Thus the early Christians will actually be impaired in their task of prayer if they participate in war, and so, paradoxically, Origen implies that Christian military service would cause harm to the health of the Roman state.

In short, then, Origen and Tertullian seem to have recognized a clear distinction between Christian participation in war, and the underlying righteousness of the war itself. In this context, it is particularly striking that Origen, though vehemently opposed to Christian participation in war, also uses the term "righteousness" in conjunction with wars waged by the emperor.

I believe a Christian realist might find Origen's and Tertullian's understandings of warfare quite familiar. These early Christian thinkers would agree with Christian realists that war is a tragic necessity and has a negative effect both on states and individuals that engage in it. At the same time, war cannot be avoided until the fallen world is completely re-created in Christ. In short, significant elements of early Christianity share a Christian realist understanding that both recognizes war's necessity and, at times, righteousness, while retaining a real anxiety about dirty hands in relation to killing in war.

The Christian realist Cappadocians? The conversion of Constantine to Christianity posed new challenges, and created new opportunities, for a Christian theology of war. On one hand, Christianity's legalization put an end to the idolatry of the Roman state. On the other hand, as more and

---

[12]Phillip Wynn, "War and Military Service in Early Western Christian Thought, 200–850" (PhD diss., University of Notre Dame, 2011), ProQuest Dissertation Publishing (AAT 3492609), 77.

more of the empire converted, it became clear that Origen's eschatological hope would be disappointed, and so if the state was not to be destroyed, and righteous war was to be fought, Christians would have to do the fighting.

Even before Augustine in the West, three Greek theologians known as the Cappadocian fathers began to grapple with these new realities, coming to conclusions that, like the thought of Origen and Tertullian, resonate more with Christian realism than the other traditions.

The most significant statement from the Cappadocians on warfare comes from Basil of Caesarea, and is worth quoting in its entirety: "Our Fathers did not reckon killings in war as murders, but granted pardon, it seems to me, to those fighting in defense of virtue and piety. Perhaps, however, it is well to advise them that, since their hands are not clean, they should abstain from communion alone for a period of three years."[13]

There are a number of complexities to unpack here. First, it seems as though Basil considers killing, even killing in war, always to be murder.[14] This seems to me to be contrary to the just war theory, which would tend to make a legal and pastoral distinction between killing in war and murder, so long as the former occurs in a just war. At the same time, Basil argues that pardon should be given for it if it is done in defense of piety and virtue.[15] As evidence of this, the typical penance Basil assessed for a murder done out of rage or premeditation was thirty years, not the three years recommended here for killing in war.[16] In canon eight, Basil elucidates a hermeneutic of differentiated intent, with the implication being that killing in a war in defense of "piety and virtue" must be pastorally differentiated from murder committed because of rage or premeditation.[17] As with all penance, the purpose of that which Basil assesses is, at least in part, for the good of the soldier.[18] Critical to this distinction is an approach to sin, found in many

---

[13]Saint Basil, *Letters, Vol. II, (186–368)*, trans. Sister Agnes Clare Way, CDP, Fathers of the Church (Washington, DC: Catholic University of America Press, 1955), 23, quoted in Valerie A. Karras, "Their Hands Are Not Clean: Origen and the Cappadocians on War and Military Service," in *Orthodox Christian Perspectives on War*, ed. Perry T. Hamalis and Valerie A. Karras (Notre Dame, IN: University of Notre Dame Press, 2017), 145-46.

[14]Karras, "Their Hands Are Not Clean," 146.

[15]Karras, "Their Hands Are Not Clean," 146.

[16]Karras, "Their Hands Are Not Clean," 148.

[17]Karras, "Their Hands Are Not Clean," 148.

[18]Karras, "Their Hands Are Not Clean," 148.

Greek thinkers of the early church, which emphasizes a "stain on the soul" rather than moral guilt. Thus the purpose of penance is not to legally expiate sin in order to satisfy God's justice, but rather to restore one's soul to a level of purity commensurate with reception of the sacrament and transformation more and more into the image and likeness of God. This clarifies Basil's intent: killing in war will have a deleterious effect on the spiritual health of the soldier, and so, pastorally, this effect must be seriously and substantively addressed to heal the soldier's relationship with God, self, and church. Though it is outside the scope of this essay, Basil's approach seems, at a casual reading, to have some commonalities with modern psychological research on killing in war.

Basil's stance, like that of Origen, partakes in a certain moral ambiguity.[19] As Valerie Karras explains, "The Cappadocians certainly evince a pragmatic acceptance of the reality, and even the necessity, of Christian soldiers serving in a Christian army in defense of a Christian state. . . . Nevertheless, even within the limits of defensive action, the common thread of a moral abhorrence of war so forcefully argued by Origen and other pre-Constantinian Christian writers continues to underlie the more nuanced and pragmatic approach of the Cappadocians."[20]

Ambrose of Milan and the pre-Augustinian roots of just war in the West. Even as the Cappadocians articulated an understanding of warfare we might call Christian realist, the seeds of a more formal just war tradition were beginning to flower in the West. This process began not with Augustine, but rather with the man to whom he attributed much of his intellectual development as a Christian: Ambrose, bishop of Milan.

Fortunately, we have a quite remarkable account of Ambrose's thoughts on Christian conduct in war. During a military campaign, Ambrose's close friend the emperor Theodosius perpetrated a massacre against a rebel garrison at Thessalonica. On returning to Milan, the acting Western imperial capital and Ambrose's bishopric, Theodosius likely expected a warm reception from his close friend and ally the bishop. Instead, Ambrose excommunicated Theodosius and refused to greet him on his return to the city—which was itself a very serious political act in the Roman Empire.

---

[19]Karras, "Their Hands Are Not Clean," 148.
[20]Karras, "Their Hands Are Not Clean," 149.

Explaining his actions in a letter to the emperor, Ambrose says,

There was that done in the city of the Thessalonians of which no similar record exists, which I was not able to prevent happening; which, indeed, I had before said would be most atrocious when I so often petitioned against it, and that which you yourself show by revoking it too late you consider to be grave, this I could not extenuate when done.[21]

This letter is particularly striking because Ambrose was both a personal friend to Theodosius and had received Theodosius's support against a heretical bishop and his followers patronized by Theodosius's predecessor. Nevertheless, Ambrose remains firm; Theodosius cannot be given the sacrament, or even acknowledged by Ambrose, until he does penance for his sins, and public penance at that.[22] The precedent that even a Christian emperor is limited in what he can demand from the church was one for which Ambrose fought consistently. Yet here he extends that precedent further, claiming for the church the right to judge a Christian emperor for his conduct in war, and to establish clear moral guidelines within which rulers must act.

Ambrose, then, quite clearly falls into the just war camp: he believes righteous war can be conducted by Christian emperors, and he does not impose penance for participation in war, or even killing in war, on its face. Yet Ambrose articulates a category of "wrongful killing" that is so significant it merits not just penance, but public penance, from an emperor. It is unclear whether Ambrose intends to make a clear distinction from Basil of Caesarea, but it is clear that the consequences of his approach led to a distinct approach to warfare.

Augustine on war: at once Christian realist and just warrior. The final important figure we must discuss in the context of Christian realism in the early church is also a man who owes much of his intellectual development as a Christian to Ambrose: Augustine, bishop of Hippo. Unsurprisingly, given his intellectual debt to Ambrose, Augustine is rightfully seen as a formative figure in the Christian just war tradition. I would argue that the unique contribution of Augustine was to combine a Christian realist

---

[21]Ambrose of Milan, *Letter* 51.6 (*NPNF*[2] 10:451), Christian Classics Ethereal Library, www.ccel
.org/ccel/schaff/npnf210.v.xi.html.

[22]Ambrose, *Letter* 51.

disposition with moral reasoning that is firmly in the just war tradition. As discussed below, this Augustinian approach would be followed by many, but not all, modern Christian realists post-Niebuhr.

The key to both Augustine's "sober realism" with respect to the state and his assertion that war is a lesser good is his understanding of sin's pervasive effects on one hand, and divine providence on the other. With a conception of sin shaped by his opposition to the ultra-rigorist Donatists—who believed that lapsed Christians could no longer serve as ministers—and the Pelagians—who asserted a real absence of original sin and the unconstrained ability of human beings to live without its effects—Augustine developed very strong conceptions of both sin and grace.

It is to Augustine that we owe much of Western Christianity's emphasis on the total inability of human beings, in their natural state, to cooperate with God, or seek the good in any meaningful way. Augustine did not deny that goods existed among fallen human beings, but he views them entirely as an outworking of divine providence. In his words, "Not by constraint of human will, which ever remains subject to a hierarchy of normative laws, but by an artful granting or withholding of power to accomplish what has been willed, God's providential design is inexorably realized in human history."[23] The second interpretive key to Augustine's political thought, his much more famous doctrine of the two cities, can be understood in light of this difference. Augustine saw the city of God as the highest and most perfect good, while the city of man is in all ways inferior, but not actually evil. The best summary of Augustine's view of the city of man comes from Henry Paolucci:

> Worldly political regimes, St. Augustine holds emphatically, exist for the mutual restraint of the wicked. The peace they enforce is a genuine good—yet clearly a good of the sort that results when the violently insane are bound in straitjackets to prevent them from destroying one another. Such peace is to be accounted a true good even if those who bind are neither less demented nor less violent than those who are bound. It suffices only that they be more powerful.[24]

---

[23]Henry Paolucci, introduction to Augustine, *The Political Writings of St. Augustine*, ed. Henry Paolucci (Chicago: Regnery, 1962), x.
[24]Paolucci, introduction, xix.

This evocative image captures a tension running throughout Augustine's thought with respect to the state. On the one hand,

> This earthly city, which shall not be everlasting (for it will no longer be a city when it has been committed to perpetual pains) has all its good in this world, and rejoices in it with such joy as such things can afford . . . though united by a common nature, [it] is for the most part divided against itself, and the strongest oppress the others, because all follow after their own interests and lusts, while what is longed for either suffices for none, or not for all, because it is not the true good.[25]

On the other hand,

> One cannot say that the things this earthly city desires are not good, since it itself is, of its kind, better than all other human things. For it desires earthly peace for the sake of enjoying earthly goods, and it makes war in order to attain this peace; since, if it has conquered, and there remains no one to resist it, it enjoys a peace which it had not while there were opposing parties to contest it for the enjoyment of those things which were too little to satisfy both.[26]

The order of the city of man, though it is corrupt and fallen in its desires, is structured by divine providence so that it provides the lesser goods of peace and tranquility.

Taken in this light, we can begin to see how Augustine is both a Christian realist and a just warrior. Like Christian realists, he is pessimistic with respect to any attempt on the state's part to obtain those higher goods for which the city of God alone, in his telling, is fit. As Paolucci explains, "Christians cannot, in good faith, constitute a kingdom or *polis* of their own in this world, they cannot, in good faith, claim to have a politics of their own. The only politics possible on earth is that of coercive power used to restrain coercive power, which has always characterized the *civitas terrena*."[27] To read Augustine's endorsement of just war as giving rise to holy war, as do many Anabaptist and Eastern Orthodox scholars, is either to misapprehend Augustinian thought, or to uncritically accept later medieval glosses on

---

[25] Augustine, *City of God*, in *Political Writings*, 13-14.
[26] Augustine, *City of God*, 13-14.
[27] Paolucci, introduction, xviii.

Augustine as authoritative in ways he himself would have rejected. Augustine's critics, in short, are apt to focus on the "good" aspect of his judgment of war, while missing the "lesser" part entirely.

A careful reading of Augustine's most famous quote on just war supports this interpretation:

> The natural order which seeks the peace of mankind, ordains that a monarch should have the power of undertaking war if he thinks it advisable, and that the soldiers should perform their military duties in behalf of the peace and safety of the community. What is the evil in war? Is it the death of some who will soon die in any case, that others may live in peaceful subjection? This is mere cowardly dislike, not any religious feeling. The real evils in war are love of violence, revengeful cruelty, fierce and implacable enmity, wild resistance, and the lust of power, and such like; and it is generally to punish these things, when force is required to inflict the punishment, that, in obedience to God or some lawful authority, good men undertake wars, when they find themselves in such a position as regards the conduct of human affairs, that right conduct requires them to act, or to make others act, in this way.[28]

Those quoting Augustine here most often leave off the first half sentence, in which he attributes war to the "natural order," and begin the quote with his question: "What is the evil in war?" This is to miss the emphasis Augustine places on war as a result of "natural" order.

By extension, we can infer that Augustine recognizes that, like all "natural" goods, a just war is only good in any sense due to divine providence. Earthly powers who in their own strength attempt to fulfill the functions of the city of God by creating a "heaven on earth" will, when all is said and done, come to an idolatrous identification of the city of man with the city of God, and in so doing may corrupt even the lesser goods they can provide.

A Christian realist would certainly agree with Augustine's pessimism regarding the schemes of man. Yet I suspect some might also worry that his establishment of a category of earthly "lesser goods" will do too much to remove the tragic element from our understanding of war.

---

[28] Augustine, *City of God*, 163-64.

REINHOLD NIEBUHR AND MODERN
CHRISTIAN REALISM

Niebuhr in context. It is common for scholars of Christian views of war to claim Reinhold Niebuhr as the inventor of Christian realism. Since the bulk of this essay thus far has demonstrated pre-Niebuhrian roots to the tradition, I need not go much further into my skepticism regarding this claim. It suffices to add that, as Eric Patterson points out, Niebuhr is also only the most identifiable figure associated with a broader mid-twentieth-century Christian realist tendency in the Anglo-American world, which included other thinkers such as Martin Wight, Herbert Butterfield, and John Bennett, and practitioners such as John Foster Dulles.[29]

Still, Niebuhr is critically important to Christian realism as both its most visible representative and the man who perhaps most clearly articulated its theological underpinnings in ways that are distinct from other approaches. I would argue that Niebuhr articulated a previously inchoate tradition, diffusely scattered throughout Christian history, and brought it into dialogue with modern secular thought on war in a way that was both new and extremely important. Wight, Butterfield, and others, to include English school and neoclassical realist international-relations theorists, all drew from this tradition, though I suspect many of them would also fit more comfortably within the just war paradigm than would Niebuhr.

Niebuhr's theology and anthropology. The roots of Niebuhr's distinctive Christian realist theological approach may be found in his understanding of sin, which is far from Augustinian. To quote him directly, "Sin is not so much a consequence of natural impulses, which in animal life do not lead to sin, as of the freedom by which man is able to throw the harmonies of nature out of joint.... Egoism is sin in its quintessential form. It is not a defect of creation but a defect which becomes possible because man has been endowed with a freedom not known in the rest of creation."[30]

Further, Niebuhr explicitly claims that sin is "not so much an inherited corruption as an inevitable taint upon the spirituality of a finite creature, always enslaved to time and place, never completely enslaved and always under the illusion that the measure of his emancipation is greater than it

---

[29]Patterson, introduction, 1.
[30]Niebuhr, *Beyond Tragedy*, 20.

really is."[31] This understanding of sin is much closer to Basil of Caesarea than Augustine. In short, Niebuhr sees sin as rooted in the very thing that makes humanity unique and special: human freedom.

This is the source of the tension between freedom and finitude which is central to Niebuhr's thought. Niebuhr perceives the fall, as Patterson explains, as "symbolic of the historic disjunction of the real and the ideal. However the ideal is known and the purpose of history is pursuit of the ideal, comparing present efforts to the law of love."[32] For Niebuhr, the only resolution to the tension between freedom and finitude is what Robin Lovin calls "a complete trust in God which alleviates all anxiety and thus relieves us of the need to make ourselves the object of our trust."[33]

Here Niebuhr is indebted not to Eastern Orthodoxy but to neo-orthodoxy, a school of philosophical theology that drew on the insights of existentialism. Over against the liberal positivism of the social gospel, the neo-orthodox theologians juxtaposed radical trust in God as almost axiomatic. For Niebuhr, this attitude is not, as Daniel Rice explains, "a capitulation to cynicism or fatalism. Rather, it was an expression of a trust in God that releases us into a life of responsible action in spite of the failures, contradictions and penultimate tragedy of history."[34]

Niebuhr's theological anthropology applied to politics. Niebuhr's understanding of sin, freedom, and finitude led him to reject utopian schemes for human improvement in favor of what Eric Patterson describes as "practical suggestions for advancement, which he readily provided."[35]

Just as the tension between freedom and finitude is resolved by trust in God, so too is the tension between what Niebuhr calls "consistent optimism" and "consistent pessimism."[36] Both of these attitudes are dangerous in Niebuhr's telling:

---

[31]Niebuhr, *Beyond Tragedy*, 39-40.

[32]Eric Patterson, "Niebuhr and His Critics: Realistic Optimism in World Politics," in Patterson, *Christian Realists*, 43.

[33]Lovin, introduction, xv.

[34]Rice, *Reinhold Niebuhr*, 156.

[35]Patterson, "Niebuhr and His Critics," 45.

[36]Reinhold Niebuhr, *The Children of Light and the Children of Darkness: A Vindication of Democracy and a Critique of Its Traditional Defense* (New York: Charles Scribner's Sons, 1944), xxi-xxii.

A consistent pessimism in regard to man's rational capacity for justice invariably leads to absolutistic political theories; for they prompt the conviction
that only preponderant power can coerce the various vitalities of a community
into a working harmony. But a too consistent optimism in regard to man's
ability and inclination to grant justice to his fellows obscures the perils of
chaos which perennially confront every society, including a free society.[37]

Niebuhr's critique of consistent pessimism is ironic, given his debt to Augustine. Indeed, as Rice explains, Niebuhr insisted that

> an analysis of Augustine's and Luther's dualism and consequent "realism" af-
> fecting political communities must yield the negative conclusion that the
> realism was too consistent to give a true picture of either human nature or
> the human community, even before the advent of free governments, and was
> certainly irrelevant to modern democratic governments.[38]

However, Niebuhr saw "consistent pessimism" in modern times as originating from a reaction to the consistent optimism found in democratic
liberalism. In his words,

> The consistent optimism of our liberal culture has prevented modern demo-
> cratic societies both from gauging the perils of freedom accurately and from
> appreciating democracy fully as the only alternative to injustice and op-
> pression. When this optimism is not qualified to accord with the real and
> complex facts of human nature and history, there is always a danger that
> sentimentality will give way to despair and that a too consistent optimism
> will alternate with a too consistent pessimism.[39]

Again, Niebuhr saw the solution as rooted in Christianity: "A Christian view
of human nature is more adequate for the development of a democratic
society than either the optimism with which democracy has become historically associated or the moral cynicism which inclines human communities
to tyrannical political strategies."[40]

Further, Niebuhr believed that Christianity's understanding of original
sin is what makes it so well-suited to a balanced understanding of humanity.
According to Niebuhr, the Christian understanding of sin reminds us that

---

[37]Niebuhr, *Children of Light*, xxi-xxii.
[38]Rice, *Reinhold Niebuhr*, 158-59.
[39]Niebuhr, *Children of Light*, xxiii.
[40]Niebuhr, *Children of Light*, xxiv.

no matter how wide the perspectives which the human mind may reach, how broad the loyalties which the human imagination may conceive, how universal the community which human statecraft may organize, or how pure the aspirations of the saintliest idealists may be, there is no level of human moral or social achievement in which there is not some corruption of inordinate self-love.[41]

As a consequence, Niebuhr, and the Christian realists who followed him, viewed democracy as "the most appropriate form of government for human beings whose self-transcending freedom enables them to anticipate a meaningful history, even though their finitude ensures that they will never achieve it."[42] As Niebuhr said in one of his most famous quotations, "Man's capacity for justice makes democracy possible; but man's inclination to injustice makes democracy necessary."[43]

To be sure, Niebuhr's faith in democracy is not utopian, but as Patterson explains, "Individuals can act for good or evil, and their freedom to follow either path is the perennial dilemma of history. However, better institutions which realistically view the human condition and balance power can approximate justice, moderate power, and continue improving until 'the end of the age.'"[44]

Niebuhr's political theology applied to political order. All of this sets the stage for Niebuhr's conception of a just political order, which is integral to his conception of war. Central to this concept is Niebuhr's belief in what Patterson calls the "geometric growth of the will-to-power within the community, which is far stronger proportionately than an individual's will-to-power."[45] Niebuhr himself roots this in a kind of human group pride that underlies all societies:

Man, being more than a natural creature, is not interested merely in physical survival but in prestige and social approval. Having the intelligence to anticipate the perils in which he stands in nature and history, he invariably seeks to gain security against these perils by enhancing his power, individually and collectively. Possessing a darkly unconscious sense of his insignificance in the

---

[41]Niebuhr, *Children of Light*, 16-17.
[42]Lovin, introduction, xix.
[43]Niebuhr, *Children of Light*, xxii.
[44]Patterson, "Niebuhr and His Critics," 46.
[45]Patterson, "Niebuhr and His Critics," 31.

total scheme of things, he seeks to compensate for his insignificance by pretensions of pride. The conflicts between men ... are conflicts in which each man or group seeks to guard its power and prestige against the peril of competing expressions of power and pride. ... This conflict is by its very nature a more stubborn and difficult one than the mere competition between various survival impulses in nature.[46]

Again, we see reflected here the tragic irony of Niebuhr's thought: it is humanity's innate freedom and capacity for love that gives rise to a dangerous self-love that worsens human conflict. As Patterson explains, this tendency is magnified by the state, which "makes unique demands on the individual, trading a guarantee of security for the minimal insecurity of enhanced government authority, and demanding resources and allegiance from the individual."[47] Just as the demands the state makes are greater, so too is the sense of pride it requires to maintain itself, and the corresponding tendency toward collective egoism and self-love.

In short, Niebuhr's differences with Augustine about the individual capacities of humanity do not lead Niebuhr to an unbounded optimism about the state: his pessimism here is more clearly Augustinian. Nevertheless, Niebuhr seeks to avoid a pessimism that is too consistent. He believes that a "true political morality" is possible, and should be based on "a political policy which will reduce coercive power to the minimum and bring the most effective social check upon conflicting egoistic impulses in society"; generate "moral idealism which will make for a moral and rational adjustment of life to life, and exploit every available resource of altruistic impulse and reason to extend life from selfish to social ends"; and "encourage a religious worldview which will do justice to the ideals of the spirit which reach beyond the possibilities of historic achievement."[48] Niebuhr, in short, agrees with Augustine that the city of man cannot achieve the city of God's ends, but holds out hope that the true religion the heavenly city represents can act as a guiding moral spirit pointing the city of man toward a higher good than the mere restraint of the violently insane envisioned by Augustine.

---

[46]Niebuhr, *Children of Light*, 20.
[47]Patterson, "Niebuhr and His Critics," 32.
[48]Reinhold Niebuhr, *Moral Man and Immoral Society* (New York: Charles Scribner's Sons, 1932), 257.

Political order, then, is "the lowest approximation of political love, for although order falls short of the ideal, it nevertheless provides the primary security and stability necessary for fundamental harmonies between citizens and states to develop."[49]

To achieve these ends, a just political order must avoid the twin terrors of tyranny and anarchy, which result, in Niebuhr's telling, either from liberty at the expense of order or order at the expense of liberty.[50] "True justice," in the Niebuhrian understanding, "personifies both order and freedom, for it provides safe conditions necessary for realized empowerment."[51]

Niebuhr's concept of political order applied to issues of war. This understanding of political order undergirds Niebuhr's approach to war. True justice can never be taken for granted: "International peace, political and economic justice, and every form of social achievement represent precarious constructs in which the egoism of man is checked and yet taken for granted."[52] As a consequence, "Society must strive for justice even if it is forced to use means, such as self-assertion, resistance, coercion . . . which cannot gain the moral sanction of the most sensitive moral spirit."[53]

Thus, pragmatic use of force must come in service to higher ends, which for Niebuhr tended to involve the establishment of institutional checks and balances against abuse of power, capable of limiting the risks of both tyranny and anarchy.[54] In the end, however, Niebuhr understood that power must be met with power, and he condemned the democratic nations for failing to do so in the run-up to World War II.[55] Pacifism, for Niebuhr, was "a large-scale abdication of responsibility," and submission to tyranny was "neither just nor loving."[56] On the contrary, "the state has the responsibility to combat injustice. This logically may result in military response to a belligerent foe, self-defense, or security stratagems, such as containment."[57]

---

[49]Patterson, "Niebuhr and His Critics," 34.
[50]Patterson, "Niebuhr and His Critics," 35.
[51]Patterson, "Niebuhr and His Critics," 35.
[52]Reinhold Niebuhr, *Christianity and Power Politics* (New York: Charles Scribner's Sons, 1953), 38-39.
[53]Niebuhr, *Moral Man and Immoral Society*, 257.
[54]Patterson, "Niebuhr and His Critics," 35.
[55]Patterson, "Niebuhr and His Critics," 39.
[56]Patterson, "Niebuhr and His Critics," 40.
[57]Patterson, "Niebuhr and His Critics," 40.

Even so, Niebuhr retains a deep ambivalence toward the use of force: "The state may use force, but only in fulfilling its responsibility to justice."[58] His argument for the use of force was largely reactive rather than proactive.[59] Furthermore, he accepted that engagement with politics, and the use of force itself, would have deleterious spiritual consequences. At the same time, these consequences must be accepted, because inaction means that others will suffer injustice: "We cannot purge ourselves of the sin and guilt in which we are involved by the moral ambiguities of politics without also disavowing responsibility for the creative possibilities for justice."[60]

Niebuhr saw force as "a form of injustice for it transgresses human freedom, and even in the cause of justice coercion dirties one's hands. War is the extinguishing of human life and breaking the law of love, even in self-defense."[61] At the same time, "a unit with political power has a duty to use it responsibly. Proper utilization might include bettering the socio-economic environment of the country, education, welfare, etc. Internationally this would include pressuring tyrannies to change, supporting constitutionalism, working for international order, and the like."[62] Here Niebuhr echoes Basil of Caesarea on statecraft as a necessity. Niebuhr's ultimate philosophy calls for a "realistic appraisal of affairs and concerted action now based on Niebuhr's doctrine of the responsibility of the powerful."[63]

And so we return to the place where we began: King David, the warrior king who conducted righteous war on God's behalf, who was required to sacrifice his dream of building the temple as a consequence. For Niebuhr, dirty hands are a necessary sacrifice on the part of the soldier or political leader: a duty from which they must not shrink, and at the same time, also something to be avoided unless absolutely necessary.

The ultimate goal is real, tangible improvement toward justice, and a preservation of nations and the world against the tyranny and anarchy that result from individual or collective self-love. Perfection, of course, is

---

[58]Patterson, "Niebuhr and His Critics," 40.
[59]Patterson, "Niebuhr and His Critics," 40.
[60]Reinhold Niebuhr, *The Nature and Destiny of Man* (New York: Charles Scribner's Sons, 1964), 272.
[61]Patterson, "Niebuhr and His Critics," 41.
[62]Patterson, "Niebuhr and His Critics," 42.
[63]Patterson, "Niebuhr and His Critics," 44.

unattainable, but striving is required. As Patterson succinctly summarizes, "The law of love will only be fully realized beyond natural history, the present organizing structures can only aim at approximating it. But the birth and maintenance of such improving order relies on human ingenuity, which can either subvert justice or uplift it."[64]

CONTRASTING NIEBUHR WITH HIS COLLEAGUES, CRITICS, AND CONTEMPORARIES

It is worth briefly concluding this discussion of Niebuhr by both exploring a few similarities and differences between his thought and the classical realpolitik of Morgenthau, and saying a few words about the Christian realists who were contemporaneous with, or came after, Niebuhr.

Niebuhr and Morgenthau. As stated at the outset, there are substantial differences between both Niebuhr and Morgenthau on one side, and the modern neorealist international-relations-theory paradigm on the other. Just as the neorealists rejected classical realism as unscientific, so too Morgenthau and Niebuhr would likely have been deeply skeptical of neorealism's claim to an almost scientific ability to create predictive models. Niebuhr and Morgenthau shared a skepticism about the ability of social science to reliably predict, let alone shape, human behavior.[65]

Niebuhr "saw the usefulness of the scientific method in the domain of human affairs as severely limited by both the complexity of history and the fact that human beings are not disinterested observers relative to the phenomena they are studying."[66] Morgenthau emphatically agreed, affirming that "the intellectual methods which are capable of understanding politics and society in general are bound to be different from the methods which apply to the discovery of the secret of nature."[67]

I believe both men would have been extremely skeptical of the neorealist attempt to universalize a set of generally applicable principles in international relations that do not depend on the historical circumstances of the state or society in question.

---

[64]Patterson, "Niebuhr and His Critics," 46.
[65]Rice, *Reinhold Niebuhr*, 148.
[66]Rice, *Reinhold Niebuhr*, 148.
[67]Rice, *Reinhold Niebuhr*, 148.

Niebuhr and Morgenthau also shared a recognition of the tragic element in history, a skepticism regarding excessive utopianism, and a sense that judgments on matters of war and peace must, of necessity, be moral ones.

For all their similarities and a well-documented personal affinity between the two that lasted decades, there were a few significant differences. In general, Niebuhr found Morgenthau's pessimism, and that of his fellow realists, too consistent, and was more open to real, tangible human improvement and, to a limited degree, altruism. Rice attributes the difference between the two men on this point to Niebuhr's Christian understanding of grace.[68] There was, for Niebuhr, a "beyond tragedy," what Rice calls a "perspective of hope, of faith, of love, and of forgiveness that rendered pessimism penultimate rather than ultimate."[69]

Further, Niebuhr feared that Morgenthau's rigorous exclusion of any motive other than interest in statecraft "may have made the mistake of obscuring the important residual creative factor in human rationality."[70] "In Niebuhr's convictions that love is the law of the self and that self-love is a violation of that law," Rice argues, "we find the wellsprings for his critique of the political realist's assessment of self-interest in political affairs." He insisted that in their reaction to extreme idealism some realists go too far in claiming that the nation should only act on its own self-interest. Because "collective self-interest is so consistent," Niebuhr thought it was "superfluous to advise it."[71] His point was that "a consistent self-interest on the part of a nation will work against its interests because it will fail to do justice to the broader and longer interests, which are involved with the interests of other nations."[72] In short, while Niebuhr agreed with the tragic historical account of Morgenthau, he persistently sought to leaven it with a robust understanding of Christian hope—an ultimate optimism rooted not so much in humanity ourselves but rather in the God in whose image we are made.

Wight, Butterfield, and the Christian realist roots of the English school of international relations. Two of Niebuhr's Christian realist contemporaries in Britain, Martin Wight and Herbert Butterfield, deserve special mention

---

[68]Rice, *Reinhold Niebuhr*, 156.
[69]Rice, *Reinhold Niebuhr*, 156.
[70]Rice, *Reinhold Niebuhr*, 159.
[71]Rice, *Reinhold Niebuhr*, 161.
[72]Rice, *Reinhold Niebuhr*, 161.

in this essay due to the role they played in preserving the Christian realist tradition. Butterfield was a great admirer of the Whig political tradition in England, which stood for

> commitment to ordered liberty, willingness to compromise, a moderate outlook that seeks the middle ground, a distrust of extremes, a recognition of the strengths and virtues of one's political opponents, and an awareness of the limits of politics and of one's own wisdom . . . for a gradual, ordered progress, the kind that is conducted somewhat as opportunity allows or as necessity dictates.[73]

White, likewise, held a position described by Daniel Young as "Whig realism," which was "an outgrowth of his [Wight's] Christian realism as modified by what he called the Whig tradition."[74] For Wight, this meant "the tradition of constitutional government which descends from Aristotle through Aquinas to Locke and the Founding Fathers of the United States."[75]

Both Wight and Butterfield, then, blended a Christian anthropology with a hope for the emergence of just government characterized by ordered liberty. This balanced, modestly optimistic realism is quite Niebuhrian.

While the Niebuhrian perspective—and even the more pessimistic but still historically oriented realism of Morgenthau—was marginalized in the United States, the same did not happen to the views of Butterfield and Wight across the Atlantic. In the United States, as Roger Epp explains,

> the claim for a scientifically-respectable, autonomous academic specialization of international relations in which research could be conducted and grants solicited on the basis of a demarcated expertise, necessarily came into conflict with resistant elements of the Christian realism tradition. In other words, a specialization could only develop to the exclusion of explicit theological categories and of theological-philosophical considerations.[76]

As stated above, Niebuhr in particular, and Christian realists in general, rejected this "new scientism" in the field of international relations, and so

---

[73]Hoskins, "Reinhold Niebuhr and International Society," 68-69.

[74]Daniel Young, "Martin Wight: Politics in the Era of Leviathan" in Patterson, *Christian Realists*, 103.

[75]Martin Wight, "Western Values in International Relations," in *Diplomatic Investigations: Essays in the Theory of International Politics*, ed. Herbert Butterfield and Martin Wight (London: George Allen and Unwin, 1966), 89.

[76]Roger Epp, "The Ironies of Christian Realism: The End of an Augustinian Tradition in International Politics," in Patterson, *Christian Realists*, 202.

were pushed aside by American political scientists like Kenneth Waltz. In Britain, by contrast, "the climate remained more congenial to perspectives and questions grounded in the [Augustinian] tradition."[77]

This difference is attributable, at least in part, to the influence of Wight and Butterfield on what came to be known as the English school of international relations. Wight, whose thought was particularly influential on later English school realists, was critical in preserving the English school's openness to Augustinian thought.

While Niebuhr's relationship with Augustine is marked by both agreement and disagreement, Young argues persuasively that Wight, who profoundly influenced the English school, was more Augustinian than Niebuhr or Butterfield. In particular, Young cites Wight's

> strict separation of earthly and heavenly cities, his comparison of current concentrations of power in "neo-pagan" states with the biblical Babylon, and his warning that Christians should prepare for the catacombs in the coming apocalypse. Wight also cited Augustine's denial of progress in the domain of secular history and the earthly city against latter-day manifestations of "pelagianism" or "liberal optimism," which bore some responsibility for twentieth century cataclysm.[78]

The new Augustinians: Christian realists who are also just warriors. To a Christian audience not directly involved in the academic debates of international relations, this history may seem unimportant, but it is necessary to understand one of the most confusing aspects of contemporary Christian realism—namely, the high number of prominent just war scholars and theorists who also identify with Christian realism. These modern thinkers prominently include Jean Bethke Elshtain, Eric Patterson, and a generation of scholars associated with the new evangelical foreign-policy journal *Providence* (providencemag.com).

I would argue that there are three primary reasons for this dual identification with the just war tradition. First, many of these thinkers, Elshtain in particular, are profoundly influenced by Augustinian thought. Given

---

[77]Epp, "Ironies of Christian Realism," 214.
[78]Roger Epp, "The 'Augustinian Moment' in International Politics: Niebuhr, Butterfield, Wight and the Reclaiming of a Tradition," in *International Politics Research Papers, No. 10* (Aberystwyth, UK: Department of International Politics, University College of Wales, 1991), 3.

Wight's formative influence on this tradition, an Augustinian just war theorist might have a strong affinity for English school realism. Second and related, Christian realism's critique of neorealism's exclusion of any moral, theological, or philosophical judgment from the analysis of international relations is antithetical to any project seeking to bring just war thinking back into the scholarly debate. To a degree, then, any attempt to bring the just war tradition into dialogue with contemporary international issues will necessarily be influenced by English school and probably Christian realism, as this is the only real perspective open to just war thinking within modern international-relations scholarship.

Finally, a Christian realist disposition, which takes tragedy, irony, and the law of love as the starting point for its analysis of war and peace, can be harmonized with the just war tradition. Indeed, perhaps history's most prominent just warrior, Augustine of Hippo, engaged in exactly this kind of harmonization. In short, not all Christian realists are just warriors, and not all just warriors are Christian realists, but one can be both a Christian realist and a just warrior, and an increasing number of modern Christian thinkers on war fall into what I would call this "new Augustinian" camp.

CONCLUSION: THE STRENGTHS AND WEAKNESSES OF CHRISTIAN REALISM

Notwithstanding the overlap between Christian realism and just war theory, there is a diffuse strand of Christian realist thought, found in Origen and Tertullian, the Cappadocian fathers, and Niebuhr, that does not fall into the just war tradition. What separates this strand of Christian realism from both pacifism and just war is its unwillingness to seek to resolve the inherent tension warfare represents for a Christian: a refusal to argue away either war's necessity or war's tragic consequences—dirty hands in particular—for the participants and their societies.

This tension, for the Christian realist, reflects our Christian anthropology as human beings made in the image of God and yet subject to sin. On this basis, this dirty-hands Christian realism critiques each of the two positions on the grounds of the other: just war for its perceived unwillingness to grapple with the tragedy of war, and pacifism for its perceived unwillingness to take the concrete actions necessary for the preservation of one's neighbor.

Strengths and weaknesses of dirty-hands Christian realism. Living into the inherent tension Christian anthropology represents is Christian realism's greatest strength. As Christians, we must affirm the truth of this dual reality. To minimize either the image of God or the effect of the fall is to risk an unbalanced theology of war. Christian realism reminds pacifists of the burden loving our neighbor in the midst of the fall places on Christians toward action. At the same time, it can serve as a reminder to just war theorists about the inherently tragic nature of war, and a caution against any tendency toward minimizing the moral tragedy that accompanies the destruction of human beings who bear the image of God. The additional strengths of Christian realism are the humility of its moral judgments, and a corresponding wariness with respect to any utopian idealist project in the state.

On the other hand, Christian realism—particularly when separated from the just war tradition—has some weaknesses worth considering. First, it tends to be long on critique and short on clear guidance. Compared to the other traditions, it provides little in the way of a framework for the moral decision-making of a statesmen or citizen. As a disposition, rather than a concrete tradition of moral reasoning such as just war or a fixed, unalterable principle of prohibition such as pacifism, Christian realism does more to shape the character of the statesmen than it does to provide a road map as to the moral decisions the statesmen makes regarding war. Christian realism is perhaps too humble at times, particularly when disaggregated from the well-articulated mode of moral reasoning the just war tradition represents.

Then too, in denying war the status of a lesser good, Christian realism may actually be more permissive than just war: if one's hands are dirty in any case, a just warrior might ask, what limiting principle would Christian realism impose to distinguish actions in war that make one's hands too dirty? Christian realism must, of necessity, work harder to avoid a slide into what Niebuhr calls a "too consistent pessimism," and thereby sanctifying cold-blooded realpolitik.

Finally, Christian realism requires a certain willingness to live in tensions, ambivalence, and ambiguities, which in and of itself could be a challenge for a political leader contemplating the question of how to respond to the particular circumstances war always represents.

Case studies in contemporary Christian realist moral reasoning. Examination of some contemporary hard questions Christian ethicists might face will elucidate both the strengths and the limitations of a distinct Christian realist perspective. As my own scholarly interests have gravitated toward political Islam and the Middle East, I will address three issues from that context as examples: the use of drone strikes in counterterrorism, enhanced interrogation techniques used to obtain intelligence from known terrorists, and provision of military support for state or non-state actors involved in civil wars after the Arab Spring. Each of these will be assessed from the perspective of dirty-hands Christian realism, without reference to the just war tradition.

I believe dirty-hands Christian realists would accept the moral necessity of drone warfare. They would applaud the fact that drone warfare opens up the possibility of eliminating dangerous terrorists with the lowest possible loss of life. Since avoiding the destruction of image bearers is central to the moral architecture of Christian realism, at first glance, the benefits would seem obvious.

Yet I believe the Christian realist would add a caveat: notwithstanding the fact that drone strikes are justifiable, Christian realists would still worry about the impact of taking human life. Two concerns would, I think, be particularly relevant. First, pastorally, they might emphasize the drone operator, whose extreme physical separation from the taking of life could lead to a false sense of moral insulation from the act, which could cause long-term psychological or spiritual harm. Penance is not the tool used by modern evangelical Christians to help those who have taken life be reconciled to God, the church, and themselves. However, Christian realists would likely urge churches to play an active and positive role in this personal, pastoral reconciliation, using whatever tools are most theologically appropriate in that church's context.

The second caveat involves the state as a whole. Here, Christian realists might worry that such a sterile, distant means of taking human life might cheapen the overall respect for human life of the state. In particular, reduction of warfare to a utilitarian, technological calculus might, for a Christian realist, raise concerns that both the tragedy of war and the potential of the human being made in the image of God could become abstracted away into a mere cost-benefit analysis. Notwithstanding these caveats, a Christian realist would likely see the use of drones as the best of a bad set of options, and recognize that the moral problems of killing must be accepted.

With respect to enhanced interrogation, the distinctive Christian realist perspective begins with dirty hands. Of course, use of enhanced interrogation techniques that break the will of the person being interrogated would be morally problematic. Force as a means of persuasion is, to a degree, always a source of dirty hands for the Christian realist.

So, what limitations would the distinctive Christian realist perspective place on enhanced interrogation? I believe the primary circumstantial concerns would focus on the desired end state of the interrogation, and based on that end, evaluate acceptable means. In other words, interrogation of a known terrorist believed to have credible information about an impending attack would give both the state and the interrogator a moral duty to use much more severe means than would be employed on, for example, suspected terrorists believed to have useful but not time-sensitive background information on the organization with which they are believed to be connected.

For a Christian realist embracing the understanding that use of force necessarily implies dirty hands, means are justified, first and foremost, by the ends to which force is put. I believe this is a contrast to the just war tradition. Since just war does not view the use of force intrinsically through the lens of dirty hands, certain acts of violence will be out of bounds, pure and simple, from this perspective. While just warriors might disagree about exactly where to draw the line, I believe they would agree that a line must be drawn beyond which the state cannot go, regardless of the desired end. So while a dirty-hands Christian realist and a just warrior might come to the same conclusion about a given form of enhanced interrogation, the moral reasoning that led them to this conclusion might be very different.

Finally, to address the issue of support for state or non-state actors engaged in civil wars—such as those that have raged in several Middle Eastern countries since the Arab Spring—I believe a Christian realist operating outside the just war tradition would, again, view this calculus through the lens of ends: in this case values, interests, and peace.

From a values perspective, modern Christian realists have generally followed Niebuhr's preference for liberal democracy and in that Niebuhrian vein would see thwarting the regional ambitions of powers motivated by an antidemocratic or totalitarian ideology as of paramount importance. Thus, if siding with an actor in a civil war furthered the ends of containing such a revisionist power, some Christian realists might be willing to accept a higher level of moral ambiguity from the actor they support than would just warriors.

On the other hand, Christian realists would certainly also raise questions about what, if any, interest their government actually has in the region. The humility and acceptance of limits found in Christian realism would lead to a question about whether supporting this particular actor fits with the limited capacities of their state, or whether interest dictates that those resources should be used elsewhere.

Finally, similarly to just warriors, Christian realists would assess the likelihood that the actor they are considering supporting can win the civil war quickly, thereby reestablishing peace. Unlike a just warrior, the distinctive Christian realist's recognition of the presence of dirty hands could lead to a diminished concern over the morality of the means this actor uses to win, so long as victory is swift, decisive, and ultimately leads to peace. Just war thinkers such as Eric Patterson have revived interest in the relationship between victory and the just war tradition, so such conversations are not absent from just war thinking. However, with respect to concerns about victory, I believe the relationship between ends and means discussed in the above case on enhanced interrogation might similarly divide just war thinkers from Christian realists with a dirty-hands perspective.

These three cases show the strengths, and weaknesses, of Christian realism when it is separated from the just war tradition. On one hand, Christian realism's recognition of the moral consequences of killing an image bearer produces pastoral and antitechnocratic caveats that enhance Christian moral reasoning regarding drone strikes. On the other hand, without a natural limiting principle, the dirty-hands Christian realist perspective could very easily be used to justify enhanced interrogation practices that would shock the conscience, if only the situation is deemed serious enough. Finally, the distinctive Christian realist approach to the question of supporting actors in civil wars demonstrates the strengths and weaknesses of ambiguity. While Christian realists must balance several different ends in their calculation, the absence of the common criteria and limiting principles imposed by the just war tradition is readily apparent. In almost every recent civil war, Christian realism's arguments might easily be deployed on either side of the argument. It is perhaps unsurprising, then, that so many modern thinkers have blended a Christian realist disposition with the moral reasoning of the just war tradition, in the hope that such a synthesis can maximize the strengths, and minimize the weaknesses, of Christian realism.

A Just War Response

ERIC PATTERSON

A. J. Nolte's excellent chapter on Christian realism is useful in mapping some of the boundaries between various forms of realism, both in the academy and in the Christian-Augustinian tradition. My response largely agrees with Nolte's analysis of the theological roots of contemporary Christian realism, as associated with Reinhold Niebuhr, and Nolte's analysis distinguishing Niebuhrian and just war forms of Christian realism. I will expand on some key points, both of agreement and disagreement.

First, Nolte rightly tries to narrow the field by distinguishing different ways that the term *realism* is used in the social sciences, particularly those whose primary study is war, peace, and security. There are ethical forms of realism (classical realism, Christian realism) as opposed to merely materialistic forms (realpolitik, neorealism, some forms of militarism). Rob Joustra and I have thus distinguished between Christian realisms (including Niebuhrian, just war statecraft, etc.) and pragmatic realisms to delineate the difference.[1] These distinctions are important because without them the lay reader, or the professional from another discipline, walks into the middle of tightly drawn intellectual battle lines without a map through the minefield of terminology and presuppositions.

Nolte is also helpful in centering in on original sin and human anthropology. Christian realisms, of all types, begin with the idea that God created humanity in his image—with great potential and requirements for stewardship in this world—but human sin has disordered the self, relations with

---

[1]Robert Joustra and Eric Patterson, eds., *Christian Realism for Terrifying Times: Three Generations of Christian Realism* (Eugene, OR: Wipf & Stock, 2022).

others, and relations with God. An important point flows from this analysis, one that is implicit but not explicit in Nolte's chapter. International-relations scholars recognize three different domains of political life, or three "levels of analysis": the individual level, the domestic political level, and the international level.[2] This distinction is important because it is too simplistic to say that any given war was the result of one person's, or everyone's, sin. As bad as Hitler was, and as much as he contributed to World War II, it was not Hitler alone, or even the Hitler-Mussolini-Tojo alliance, that caused World War II. They contributed to it, but they were not the sole cause.

Thus we must look at the second and third levels of analysis to help us understand political life, and especially the causes of war. That means we need to look at the role of domestic politics, including cultures of militarism, strong or weak political institutions, the way that coalitions form and compromise on courses of action, and the like. In the case of the Second World War, the weakness of German political institutions, a culture of militarism in some quarters, the inability for the political center and left to stand up to the Nazis—all played roles in Hitler's ascendancy. So, too, we must look to the third level of analysis, the international level, where there is no overarching government to stop conflict. Scholars call this "anarchy," the lack of centralized authority. Hitler played the game of power politics very well as neither the League of Nations nor any individual government (i.e., France, Britain) was willing to stand up to him in 1933–1939.

The reason the three levels of analysis are important is because too much narrow focus on individual human sin misses contributions by both Augustine and Niebuhr. Augustine's two-cities model, and his blessing of political and military leaders (e.g., in *Letter* 189), points to a strand of thinking that emphasizes the good of political institutions: they promote peace and the common good, and restrain evil. This doctrine will be fleshed out later in Christian history in the themes of subsidiarity and sphere sovereignty. At the same time, political institutions can consolidate power in ways that allow one or a few to dominate the many in a way that no individual should. Moreover, a myopic view on individual human sin misses Niebuhr's point that there seems to be a magnification of chauvinism in the collective.

---

[2]The classic statement of the three levels of analysis is Kenneth Waltz, *Man, the State, and War* (New York: Columbia University Press, 1959).

Groups can be more egotistical and more jingoistic than individuals. We see this in mob violence and hypernationalism. Those millions of Germans who were caught up in the Nazi culture of Aryan and Teutonic supremacy were pulled into evil far beyond what they ever would have dreamed of perpetrating, as individuals, against their Jewish doctors or neighbors.

Thinking about the distinctions in the three levels of analysis allows us to look more critically at the New Testament, which is somewhat missing from Nolte's chapter. Then again, such analysis is often missing from Niebuhr's writing, which usually sees the Bible as symbolic rather than literal. Niebuhr consistently emphasized what he called the law of love, which was expressed in an idealized form that stands above and beyond all human efforts. But what does the New Testament actually have to say about collective violence, or those entrusted with the power of the state? It is noteworthy what is *not* said. Although John the Baptist, Jesus and his disciples, and the apostolic church all dealt routinely with soldiers and other public officials, there is not a single injunction to "drop your weapons" and leave one's job. Instead, those in public service are admonished to avoid abusing the vulnerable, not disavow their vocation. Jesus says that a Roman centurion had greater faith than anyone in Israel. Peter's first Gentile convert was a believing Roman centurion named Cornelius. Paul and Peter called on believers to pray for political authorities, and Paul's letters affectionately greet public servants such as a city treasurer and members of Caesar's household.

These people are not just individuals, but as soldiers or public officials they represent that second level of political life. This suggests another limitation of Niebuhrian Christian realism: Niebuhr has very little to say about the doctrines of *stewardship* and *vocation*. Augustine, Luther, Calvin, Wesley, and many contemporary evangelical thinkers recognize that humans have specific callings in various domains of life and that we are all called to various forms of private and collective stewardship. These doctrines are largely missing from Niebuhrian analysis. Niebuhr, like Hans Morgenthau, tends to look over the shoulder of the elite statesman and give policy advice at that level. Hence Niebuhr's ethic of the "dirty hands" of the statesman who must make "tragic" decisions due to the necessity of time and place. The other Christian realist tradition, the one that goes from Augustine through today's just war scholars such as James Turner Johnson, J. Daryl Charles, and Marc LiVecche, recognizes that living out a vocation of law enforcement, military service, or other governmental roles can be a virtuous pursuit based on neighbor love.

Nolte is right that Niebuhrian Christian realism focuses a great deal on power.[3] This is rooted in the fact that Niebuhr, among others, was influenced by Marxism in the 1920s and thus a key to his approach is to "deconstruct" power relations. One sees this particularly in the writings of Niebuhr as he looks at race and class relations as well as the relationships between various political powers. He exposes the power relationships including the subtle ones that most people do not realize are there. Christian realists emphasize security, justice, and equality. This is an interesting point—the notion of equality. Niebuhr reminds us that an overemphasis on individual liberty, or license, usually comes at the expense of someone else. Often individuals, who are radically free, achieve their "freedom" on the backs of others. This is reminiscent of Aristotle's polity where a minority is "self-sufficient" (free) due to the labor of the servant class. Consequently, Niebuhrian Christian realism reminds us that we should care a great deal about equality, because equality is not only a condition under the law; it is a condition in which power balances power. Equal individuals are less likely to coerce one another than one radically free individual, who may have paid for that liberty at the expense of others.

Niebuhrian Christian realism emphasizes limits and restraint. Whereas liberals are typically idealistic revolutionaries willing to radically upset the world in favor of utopian schemes, Christian realists are skeptical about such possibilities. Niebuhr called himself a "realistic optimist," and that is perhaps the best way to think about this. Christian realists, on the one hand, are deeply concerned about unintended consequences. They recognize that in political life, any stone that is thrown into the pond generates thousands of ripples that emanate outward and are difficult to track and account for. More importantly, Christian realists are deeply concerned with the notion

---

[3]Some material in the following paragraphs is adapted from Eric Patterson, "Ronald Reagan's 'A Time for Choosing': A Christian Realist Reading," in *The Reagan Manifesto: "A Time for Choosing" and Its Influence*, ed. Eric D. Patterson and Jeffry H. Morrison (New York: Palgrave Macmillan, 2016), 115-30.

of politics' greatest sin, which is hubris, or self-destructive pride. And over and over, particularly in Niebuhr's most famous book, *The Irony of American History* (1952), he emphasizes how hubris clouds judgment and can lead to tragic results.

Let me conclude by borrowing a critique of Niebuhrian Christian realism from Keith Pavlischek.[4] Pavlischek is an ethicist, just war expert, and a seasoned veteran of the US military and intelligence community. Pavlischek argues that Niebuhr and his contemporaries were pacifistic idealists in the 1920s who were mugged by the grotesque reality of National Socialism. Because they were idealists, they did not lose a sense of the perfect in what political life is supposed to be (e.g., "law of love"), and thus they were extremely critical of government policies and often called for extreme limits on when governments could go to war. But according to Pavlischek, when that threshold was reached, the dirty-hands argument suggested that there were few limits as to how the tragedy of war was to be executed. Once the decision has been made, and because one was going to be morally tainted in any event, anything goes. In other words, just as Nolte has argued, Pavlischek is saying that almost any means (e.g., firebombing civilian centers, using atomic weapons) are allowed under the Niebuhrian model.

In its heyday, Niebuhr's Christian realism of the 1940s–1960s made many contributions in the West: it pushed the Christian church of the 1930s away from pacifism; it provided a moral rationale against fascism and then communism; it provided a social and academic service in deconstructing power relations; and it provided a powerful lens for analyzing all forms of force, be it violence, coercion, or subtle forms of social control, as well as clarified definitions of peace. However, much of this happened in the op-ed pages, in books and lectures, and in foreign-policy journals rather than in the lecture halls of traditional social science academe and, as Nolte demonstrates, this means that the Niebuhrian strand of Christian realism lacked a firm basis for deepening its roots in the academy.

---

[4]Keith Pavlischek, "Reinhold Niebuhr, Christian Realism, and Just War Theory," in *Christianity and Power Politics Today: Christian Realism and Contemporary Political Dilemmas*, ed. Eric Patterson (New York: Palgrave Macmillan, 2008), 78-93.

A Nonviolence Response

MYLES WERNTZ

THE TRAGEDY OF THE TRAGIC

Christian realism presents a unique challenge for Christians exploring questions of war and conflict. As a relative latecomer to this historic conversation, realism positions power as the central consideration rather than fidelity or virtue or justice, and in the process elevates aspects of power that are frequently muted in both just war and pacifist evaluations. How one reads the Christian tradition leading up to the emergence of Reinhold Niebuhr is up for debate: Nolte's interpretations of Augustine and Gregory of Nazianzus are highly contested.[1] But Nolte raises important questions about how Christians negotiate the practical difficulties of conflict.

The approach that emerges, around both what is natural and how war appears as a tragedy of temporal life, requires further examination, as it greatly affects how Christians understand war and its relationship to the Christian life. In what follows, I will lay out the ways in which tragedy takes central stage in Nolte's explication of Christian realism, and what effects this has on understanding the nature of the Christian life with respect to suffering, power, and war.

THE EMERGENCE OF THE TRAGIC

In his reading of Augustine and the Cappadocians, Nolte contends that the conversation around Christian involvement in war when it first emerged oriented around notions of purity and impurity. It was, Nolte contends, the

---

[1]On the difficulties of the realist reading of Augustine, see Michael J. S. Bruno, *Political Augustinianism: Modern Interpretations of Augustine's Political Thought* (Minneapolis: Fortress, 2014), 64-120.

primary responsibility of the church to make sure that in their discussions "Christians kept themselves pure of all defilement" (p. 122). And so, as the church grew, more pastoral attention was given to soldiers returning from war. Whereas in early days it could be assumed that a Christian would be martyred rather than participate in violence, by the time of the Cappadocians, more practical considerations were emerging. This does not, it seems, obviate the seriousness of the question: as Nolte observes, in one case Saint Basil the Great says that the one who has killed in war must refrain from the Eucharist for three years. There are reasons to name this as something other than "pragmatic," as Nolte does (pp. 100-102). Prior to the Cappadocians, canons had begun emphasizing that clergy were not to take life, not as an abandonment of an ideal but a tightening of it. The priest, the exemplar of the congregation, sets before the church the ideal of the moral life, to which all are to aspire.

Likewise, we see this seriousness in Nolte's citation of Augustine on the Sermon on the Mount: war produces all manner of injustice and vice, and the restriction of those who have participated in it from the Eucharist for three years was in order that these persons might properly be able to distance themselves from the vices therein. Basil's comments, in other words, are not so much a concession to soldiering as they are a recognition that soldiering does in fact do real spiritual damage, proportionately less than premeditated murder, but real damage nonetheless. These developments are best characterized, thus, not as pragmatic concessions, but as a principled approach to penance, a position that is consistent with the earlier writers. For even in the early church there were those who converted from the military to Christianity, with corresponding questions of participation in war emerging as they converted.

Naming the moves made by Basil and Augustine as "pragmatic" is important, because it characterizes engagement in war a matter of necessary practical deliberation rather than what it is: a grave moral concern for which penance must still be made. This all matters then for how we name participation in violence: whether as that which is normatively to be avoided (and named as sin when engaged in) as held in the nonviolence view; or how realism will name it, as a tragic reality of living in a complex society in which Christians have a public presence. Nolte is right to question whether Augustine's schema gives too much credence to the notion of war as a "lesser good" (p. 50), trying to make lemonade out of rocks. But the alternate description

here—that war is not a "lesser good," but a matter of tragedy and inevitability in a world of sin—opens up a different problem. For in naming war
as "tragic," war emerges as an activity that creation produces, and that people
are caught up in not as a matter of volition but as a matter of *necessity*.

The key move here is when Nolte names war, following his reading of
Augustine, as a matter of "natural" order (p. 128). When we participate in
war, then, because war is part of life in the natural world, we do so not as an
ideal, but as tragedy, the collision of one ideal against another. War as "natural"
emerges as a facet of public life that enables realism to avoid the conversation
of whether war implicates one in *sin* (a conversation primarily had between
pacifists and just warriors), and to replace these discussions with ones about
whether war is *necessary*, as a check against egoism. From the pacifist and just
war perspectives, this description of war as intrinsic to the natural world and
thus inseparable from creaturely life is troubling, not least because it natu-
ralizes something that, for hundreds of years, was viewed not as an act of
nature but as a feature of *fallen* nature. To say that something happens in a
broken world is not to say that it is naturalized, but to say that it is pervasive
and yet not appropriate to the nature we have been given by God.

Viewing war from the viewpoint of necessity and tragedy rather than sin
opens up a second question: What is the benefit of such a definition? In the
case of Reinhold Niebuhr, realism offers an account that hews more closely
to the human condition than other political alternatives: it makes sense of
the finitude of human society while also viewing religious ideals as things
worth striving for. War serves to preserve the best approximations of justice,
all while fully acknowledging the limits of human action. As Nolte acknowledges of Niebuhr—realism and its treatment of war lead us to support
democracy as the appropriate and defensible form of human life capable of
checking egos. But again, this is to naturalize an agonism that is alien to our
ordering as creatures and, ironically, to present a democratic polity which is
alien to the Scriptures as worth defending by the people of the book.

THE PEDAGOGY OF THE TRAGIC

It is here—in naturalizing war as a limited action ordered toward the preservation of a proximately just society—that realism's treatment of power
comes in. The "dirty hands" that all creatures in history bear is a call to

embrace our finitude and to use constrained forms of power toward the proximate good of the world. Emphasizing the ways in which Christian realism contributes to "living in tension" and "shaping character," Nolte argues that the realism tradition is equipped better than "a fixed, unalterable principle" like pacifism to address the dirty hands of the world (p. 141). Setting aside the fact that realism has its own unalterable principles—such as the tragedy of the world, the necessity of force, and the natural necessity of democracy—I want to interrogate specifically what it would mean for Christian realism to "shape character" around issues of power and violence.

Nolte argues to the contrary, saying that in the use of force, "means are justified, first and foremost, by the ends to which force is put" (p. 143), so that power (a morally neutral form of agency) is made good or bad by the ends toward which it is used. But, as I have laid it out, questions of war are naturalized, better understood as practical necessity and not first issues of sin or innocence. And so the use of force cannot be understood as "better" or "worse" in a moral sense, only in a statecraft sense: that which preserves a democratic society, that which preserves society, that which preserves the lives of the innocent (how this last category might be determined apart from the language of morals, I do not know).

Nolte assumes that the morality of the conflict will mitigate the use of force, even if war is treated as a prudential action rather than a theological one. But again, as already discussed, if war is a matter of tragic necessity as opposed to sin or fidelity, it is unclear what metric can be employed to name whether the conflict is good (or whether social stability is itself a desirable reason for the use of force). The problem this yields for assuming that war can then be *morally* restrained is that power is taught to be put into service toward ends we cannot name morally, and only those ends that can be named practically: what perpetuates stability and reduces tyranny. Put more sharply, realism makes power and the exercise of war into an amoral form of human agency, put into service toward the preservation of an end that we can only name in terms of its practicability.

At this point, we are very far from a traditional Christian grammar that speaks in terms of sin and guilt, culpability and innocence, grace and truthfulness: the language of personal agency and thus of moral obligations that accrue to us. But once war is conceived of as an event embedded within a tragic but *necessary* framework, it is unclear to me how anything that governs how we get into war, why we might desire or not desire war, or prevent war can be spoken of in anything other than the language of—as Nolte rightly worries—realpolitik, actions governed not by moral evaluation but by what works. To be sure, realism will always appeal to moral reasons for refraining from war or not, but my concern is that those reasons will be naturalized, articulated only in political terms of necessity that ultimately have no need for the language of Christianity, with Christianity now the handmaiden of statecraft.

POWER, SUFFERING, AND WAR

The pedagogy of the necessary offers a very different description of power from the language of Scripture, which Nolte describes as giving it roots. For in Scripture, power is not described in terms of doing what is necessary but doing that which is good—not in terms of what helps a state to survive but in terms of that which directs a people to God. In Philippians 2, for example, we find that Christ's service and servitude are what the power of God looks like; in 2 Corinthians, Paul describes the power God gives as taking the form of weakness; in Revelation, the Lamb who conquers is one who speaks words from a neck that has been cut. In none of these situations are Christians depicted as those who save the world by taking up the reins of historical necessity, but by being the people of Christ in a suffering world.

While realism might also value the role of suffering for the good, because war emerges as a matter of historical necessity, it does not logically have a way to account for how these sacrifices might come to be. Realism has a place for the necessity of sacrifices and for the defense of that which is valued, but where do such impulses for protection come from? How are we able to name what is worth protecting, and more importantly, when our means for protecting it are inconsistent with the thing protected? For the pacifist, consistent witness to the person of Christ and to Christ's love for the enemy means that there are limits to our means of preservation; preserving a good thing in a way that dishonors why we preserve it means that all has been for nothing. The kind of suffering presumed by Philippians, Corinthians, and Revelation remains for realism a laudable ideal, but there is no reason I would offer myself as a sacrifice in that way if the ultimate goal is not the preservation of the enemy, but of the rational goods of a society and of my own life.

In treating war as tragedy, realism unintentionally gives up the game—not just for treating war within the framework of Christian teaching, but for being able to speak morally about war at all. It does so with the intent of practically addressing violence in the world, and in this way it speaks the same language as both pacifism and the just war. But insofar as it proposes to offer an account of war that goes beyond the limits of both pacifism and just war thinking, it comes up short. For neither pacifism nor just war nor realism can propose truthfully to end violence in the world. One need not, as Niebuhr does, point to the inevitably egoistic forms of human sociality to see that.[2] One can agree with Niebuhr that people are fallen without saying that theological thinking is limited to interpersonal conflicts and not political ones, but it requires unhooking—as Niebuhr does not—concepts of engaging with conflict from defending particular forms of human sociality. In the end, what Christians can and should promise is to live lives that mirror the God who has already acted on behalf of the just and unjust, to break the bow, take away the warhorses, and to proclaim peace to the nations—not to be able to save the world at the cost of leaving the frame of that faith to the side (Zech 9:9-10).

---

[2]For Reinhold Niebuhr's treatment of this theme, see his *Moral Man and Immoral Society* (1932; repr., Louisville, KY: Westminster John Knox, 2013).

A Church Historical Response

MEIC PEARSE

"It has been argued," says A. J. Nolte, "that the difference between just war and Christian realism is that the former sees war as a lesser good, while the latter sees it as a lesser evil" (p. 118). (Though he contends for Christian realism, he nevertheless distances himself from the latter evaluation.) Yet it is the contention of my own essay that war is neither of these things—that, in itself, it is radical evil, such that it neither allows evasion nor suffers its participants to "stand firm" (so to speak) morally. Rather, it drags them down ever more deeply into the pit, weaponizing the very "rules" or well-meaning interlopers (e.g., peacekeeping forces) designed to constrain it, in a race to the bottom that is resistible, if at all, only by a party possessed of greatly superior force.

However, Nolte's insight that the self-love interjected into human action by sin is "a tendency only intensified by the state" is profound. His quotation of Eric Patterson—"geometric growth of the will-to-power within the community, which is far stronger proportionately than an individual's will-to-power" (p. 132)—is illuminating, as is his reference to Reinhold Niebuhr's observation about "human group pride that underlies all societies" (p. 132). The state greatly amplifies the exertion of power in the service of selfish ends beyond what any individual or group could exert. Moreover, it lends such exertions a patina, or simulacrum, of morality: to fight for "my nation" and its interests stakes a far higher claim than fighting for my own personal property. Religion can be appended to the claims of the state—if only as a cultural flag—in a way that is hardly possible when contending for oneself alone (though perhaps jihadist terrorists in our own time might be said to have managed this feat). Furthermore, when things go wrong, whether morally or at the level of implementation, blame can more easily be diffused when the complexities of government or the state are involved.

Nolte's Christian realism shares with my own view that it "is less a fixed principle, such as pacifism, or a tradition of moral reasoning, such as the just war tradition, and more a disposition toward war, history, state power, and international relations" (p. 119)—and, I would add, toward the nature of Christian discipleship and of the church.

What he rightly calls "the biblical tradition of ambivalence and contradiction toward war and violence . . . that extends through the Old to the New Testament and beyond" (pp. 120-121) has been pointed out in my own contribution. As I mention there, the Old Testament can be squared neither with pacifism nor with the just war tradition, while the New Testament merely "tilts in a pacifist direction" (p. 195); both testaments have their difficulties for those who wish to claim them for a cut-and-dried view.

The ambivalence continues, as Nolte rightly points out, into some of the early church fathers. He gives contrasting quotations from Tertullian, and also from Origen, though in all honesty, it should be mentioned that the preponderance of statements on the question during this period tilts strongly against militarism, and even against participation in war for the Christian.

This tilt begins to change quite swiftly during the fourth century. Nolte is quite correct to point out that Augustine, though the most prominent theorist of the new, militarist perspective, is not the first proponent. He points to Basil of Caesarea's rather convoluted sanctions on the topic of military service. Perhaps, though, these convolutions are analogous to those Nolte notes in the Old Testament concerning the invidious position of King David. As I point out in my own essay, Basil's sanction of military service is framed in terms that make clear he was pushing back on his readers' expectations—and so, by strong surmise, on what earlier Christians had known to be the traditional Christian stance on the matter of warfare.

Yet in Basil's shifting position, and in the dealings between Ambrose and Theodosius concerning penance for a massacre, so ably expounded on by Nolte, we see the inevitable result of a church that has ceased to be (in sociological terms) a minority or sectarian movement. It has become a civic religion, a sacralization of a particular state and its necessary workings

—including war. As I have argued in this book and elsewhere, it is precisely the connection with state structures that the teachings of Jesus were designed to render impossible—and it is no accident that it is the fourth century that witnessed a great hermeneutical shift, in the form of the relationship between the testaments, to bring it about anyway.[1] All Augustine was doing, in his later writings, was standardizing and schematizing what had become, by his late career, an established revolution in theology. Those of us who reject that revolution, and the religio-political synthesis that it created, must of necessity appeal back, beyond it, to those earlier church fathers whose vision remained that of Jesus and the apostles.

Nolte's stress on Augustine's realistic assessment of political life, its contamination by human sinfulness, and so on is entirely fair; these are realities with which it would be difficult to quarrel. My rejection of just war and Christian realist positions rests not on some idealistic assessment of politics and its possibilities but on a refusal to sacralize, as a part of Christian theology, the necessarily grubby workings of politics, including military force. One need not be a purist Anabaptist on the point; it is certainly possible, *where circumstances permit* (which, historically, they mostly do not), for the Christian to participate. But we must reject going a step further: invoking the name of Christ over one's political and military choices. For once we make *that* move, we make the political and military clash between Christians-invoking-the-name-of-Christ inevitable. And even if, by some miracle, we avoid that for a while, we nevertheless identify some political order, some military campaign, with that of Christ—which is blasphemous, and for which we have no warrant whatsoever.

Sadly, we need look no further than our own day to see precisely this happening, along with all of the predictable results: implacable hostility to the faith by those who oppose the projects thereby "sanctified"; serious spiritual decline among those whose "faith" turns out to be nine parts political; and the virtual impossibility of evangelism in societies exposed to such prolonged shame and disgrace brought on the gospel.

Of course, it is perfectly true, as Nolte points out, that Augustine's endorsement of just war does not leave him guilty of the holy wars of the

---

[1]See Meic Pearse, *The Gods of War: Is Religion the Primary Cause of Violent Conflict?* (Downers Grove, IL: InterVarsity Press, 2007), chap. 9.

Crusades—phenomena he could hardly have envisaged—as some of his critics have insisted. Even so, once we have given Christian sanction to uses of lethal force—*not* in the highly generalized terms of Paul in Romans 13:1-7, which amount to the merest observation as to why rulers exist—then it is hardly surprising if the just war criteria are extended to encompass the kind of legitimation that its protagonists will designate holy war. For that is what war does: it seizes hold of everything, including the categories of legitimation and delimitation, and weaponizes them. Some wars are "just" if fought for *x*, *y*, and *z*? Very well, we will show that the thing for which we desire to fight meets those criteria. And in the end, we will show that the religious permissions are, in fact, religious commands: *Deus vult!* God wills it!

Of course, one cannot willy-nilly make such arguments as I have just done. Almost any precept or idea is capable of infinite extension, or of perversion. Almost any principle can be taken to an absurd or grotesque conclusion. Augustine, as Nolte rightly insists, is hardly guilty of the Crusades. Yet the later perversion or debasement often indicates that something was wrong in the first place. What that something was in this case has been sufficiently rehearsed by me here to require no further restatement.

Much of the later part of Nolte's essay is given over to a consideration of Reinhold Niebuhr. He was a refreshingly original thinker who has been the favorite theologian of many modern political figures—not all of whom are known as conspicuously religious. His careful balancing between the poles of optimism and pessimism led him to a rather-too-unequivocal support for democracy, though it was a critical support that recognized democracy's inherent fragility—a propensity to devour itself, which we continue to observe in our own day.

I am inclined to agree with Niebuhr that pacifism is an abdication of responsibility—a conclusion he had come to after disavowing his own youthful beliefs in that direction. Yet Niebuhr quite rightly confronted head-on the reality that war, even in a good cause, inevitably perpetrates injustice and breaks the law of love. In this, Niebuhr directly contradicts Augustine, who had insisted that, when the good use violence against the wicked, they are "serving the interests of love."[2] As Nolte rightly says, the

---

[2] Augustine of Hippo, *Letters of St. Augustine* 93.2.8 (*NPNF*[1] 1:385).

soldier's or politician's "dirty hands" are "a necessary sacrifice on the part of the soldier or political leader: a duty from which they must not shrink, and at the same time, also something to be avoided unless absolutely necessary" (p. 135). Because "human beings are not disinterested observers relative to the phenomena they are studying" (p. 136), the warrior, even in (for the sake of argument) a righteous cause, is inevitably enmeshed in the sinfulness against which he or she is fighting.

Even though Niebuhr disagreed with the notion that states should always act in their own self-interest, experience shows that, almost invariably, they *will* do so. (Even the Marshall Plan was, in part, a hedging against communism, given at a moment when the United States accounted for an eye-popping 50 percent of global GNP.) This is why recent clamor in the United States and Britain about the need for "an ethical foreign policy" rings so hollow. For reasons analogous to the diabolical dynamic of warfare, non-self-interested foreign policies will merely be preyed on by hostile powers or local officeholders. (Just think of the fate of much foreign aid!) Given that reality, "enlightened self-interest"—where that is attainable—may be the best that can be hoped for.

In conclusion, it is worth quoting part of Nolte's summary, in order to observe the slippery path down which even his, generally illusion-free, approach leads:

> From a values perspective, modern Christian realists have generally followed Niebuhr's preference for liberal democracy and in that Niebuhrian vein would see thwarting the regional ambitions of powers motivated by an antidemo-cratic or totalitarian ideology as of paramount importance. Thus, if siding with an actor in a civil war furthered the ends of containing such a revisionist power, some Christian realists might be willing to accept a higher level of moral ambiguity from the actor they support than would just warriors. (p. 144)

I, too, am a modern Westerner, with all the predilections for the benefits of a democratic society and abhorrence of totalitarianism that might be expected from such a person. Yet, as a historian and a theologian, I am all too aware of how recent and exceptional those conditions are—of the immorality to which, in the long term, they lead (and have led), and of their utter inappropriateness and unacceptability to populations not already some way down the road toward modern creature comforts and away from patriarchal, hierarchical social structures. Simply as an ordinary observer, I have witnessed the catastrophe that results from following the precepts of the preceding paragraph in, say, Iraq—and the utter collapse of the Christian minority that followed there in the wake of Western-democratic intervention. Those failures are *not* at the level of mere implementation; they stem from the most basic misunderstandings of the societies concerned.

Niebuhr's outlook, then, for all its attractiveness and (theologically, at least) gritty realism, turns out to be one more projection of "our" political order onto the mandate of Christ. And so we are back to square one.

I find myself in agreement with what Nolte considers the strengths of his own position—namely, "the humility of its moral judgments, and a corresponding wariness with respect to any utopian idealist project in the state" (p. 141). Nevertheless, I would wish to disentangle, more radically than he seems willing to do, the label "Christian" from theories of warfare of any kind.

Christian Realist Rejoinder

A. J. NOLTE

Rather than providing a point-by-point commentary on each of the excellent responses by Patterson, Pearse, and Werntz, I would like to use this space to expand on the critique of this approach common to all three responses. This is in part because, as the end of my chapter indicates, it is a critique I in fact share. In different ways, Pearse, Werntz, and Patterson all raise concerns regarding the lack of a limiting principle in a Niebuhrian or "dirty-hands" perspective.

For Werntz, the critique stems from what he sees as a realist shift of the discussion of war's ethics from sin to pragmatism. Pearse shares this concern in part, and is also generally uncomfortable with the application of the term "Christian" to Niebuhrian realism. Pearse also develops the notion that war has an insatiable appetite for destruction—in this case, the destruction of any limiting principle that might be placed on it. Pearse, then, seems to see the problem in terms that are not quite as theological as Werntz, but more the kind of inevitable slippery slope war will create for any ethicist. Finally, Patterson levels a related critique from Keith Pavlischek regarding Niebuhrian idealism. In this view, Niebuhr may have lost the categorical idealism of his early pacifism, but retains an undue optimism about the capacity of human nature for self-limitation, thereby leading him away from the imposition of any fixed limiting principle on statecraft. All of these critiques share in common a sense that, unchecked, the lack of a limiting principle in this Niebuhrian strand of Christian realism will lead to some form of sacralizing atrocity. On a personal note, my coauthors in this venture have rather effectively hit on the aspect of Niebuhrian thought that I find most unpersuasive. In Niebuhr's own terms, I find his optimism too consistent. Indeed, even within Niebuhr's own writings, there is ample reason for skepticism regarding humankind's tendency to self-justification, and the role egoism plays in the state. Given this, the lack of a consistent limiting principle in Niebuhr's thought is indeed troubling.

First, a few words on each of the three specific critiques. Werntz suggests that sin has been replaced by pragmatic necessity as the hermeneutic lens of the realists. On this point, I agree in part, but mostly disagree. Niebuhr had a very real sense of sin's presence and reality, as did the pre-Niebuhrian thinkers I consider Christian realists. The apparent pragmatism of the dirty-hands Christian realists is not a rejection of sin as a category so much as a result of their tendency to approach issues of war pastorally and contextually. Where Werntz is partially correct is in his recognition that concepts of moral guilt loom less large for a Niebuhrian Christian realist than they do in either the just war or pacifist traditions. I have discussed the Niebuhrian and Eastern Orthodox conceptions of sin—both of which are, in my view, less juridical than either Augustine or Anabaptist understandings—elsewhere in this volume, but suffice it to say that this difference is real, significant, and has some explanatory power with respect to the dirty-hands Christian realist's lack of limits. A juridical approach to sin has the effect of putting more types of conduct categorically out of bounds than a less juridical one. Likewise, Niebuhr's optimism could lead him to discount sin's effect on war more than either an Augustinian just warrior or a pacifist. The combination of bottom-up, situation-oriented ethical reasoning and relative optimism about human nature could indeed crack open doors best left closed, where the ethics of war is concerned.

I think Pearse's general point about the self-justificatory tendency of the state, and the historical pattern whereby atrocity could be sacralized, is well taken, yet I'm not sure how the logic of war differs, in Pearse's estimation, from the logic of any other form of politics. A state, after all, is defined by its ability to engage in two forms of coercion: waging war and collecting taxes. Or, to put things in international-relations terms, for a state to be a state, it must have a monopoly of force within the territory it claims, and such monopolies are not maintained without coercion. Indeed, Pearse's discussion of the self-interested corruption of foreign aid hints at a move to broaden this critique of war to all statecraft. If this is the case, then the inescapable logic is that any participation in political life will necessarily lead to the same slippery slope as war itself. After all, everything from domestic taxation to sanctions involves forcible coercion by the state, either of its own people or of other nations. War is an escalation of force, to be sure, but by Pearse's logic, such escalation is inevitable, and radical evil is the necessary result. If war, and by extension all statecraft, is a radical evil, yet pacifism is not a tenable alternative, Christians are left with no concrete guidance whatsoever, a vacuum that the self-interested egoism Pearse rightly describes is likely to fill in rather unpleasant ways.

I believe the critique Patterson—along with Pavlischek—levels against Niebuhr himself is largely accurate. The combination of his tragic understanding of war, largely owing to his pacifist roots, and a somewhat optimistic belief in the goodness of the state stemming from his socialism opens the door to a Niebuhrian embrace of ideological total war. I do not think figures like Basil are quite as sanguine about state power. After all, Basil and his compatriots wrote in the time after Constantine, when imperial power was held by heretics and apostates at least as often as it was by orthodox defenders of the faith. Of course, Basil was undoubtedly idealistic in some ways—few late antique figures who entered the monastic life lacked at least a streak of idealism—but I think the Cappadocians and other proto-Christian-realists remained cognizant of the basic untrustworthiness of state power. However, they believed the institutionalized power of the church would impose any necessary limits on a Christianized empire. The subsequent historical record demonstrates mixed success in this regard, but that history was, of course, not available to the Cappadocians. Nevertheless, it could be argued that even the modest successes the institutional church once had in constraining state behavior are unattainable in the twenty-first century, since no church possesses the institutional power today of the late antique or medieval church.

Ultimately, if we are to fashion a limiting principle from within the dirty-hands perspective, it must be based on the theological concept behind its optimism: the idea of the *imago Dei*. We might propose the following limiting principle: any act of state coercion ought to be done with as little damage to the image of God as possible in those affected by it. Both the ends for which coercive force is to be pursued and the means of force used in that pursuit ought to be judged by this principle. This approximates Niebuhr's "law of love" but, properly understood, builds on it substantially. The fixed principle is that coercive force has a corrosive effect on the human dignity of image bearers, with that effect intensifying as greater degrees of coercive force are applied. On the other hand, true anarchy, in which no coercive force is applied, is equally corrosive to human dignity, as lack of order allows free rein to human sin. Thus, coercive force is necessary to preserve that order which allows for the fullest expression of the *imago Dei*, and the greatest degree of human dignity possible, within a given set of circumstances. Yet, since the application of coercive force can itself undermine human dignity, its application must not exceed that which is necessary to that preservation. This approach retains an element of prudent pragmatism, but a pragmatism rooted in the need to provide the maximum protection possible to those who bear the image of God, through the minimum amount of coercive force commensurate with achieving that objective.

My concern with such an approach is that it may replicate Chesterton's fictional journey in his book *Orthodoxy*, in which a British man, after coming to a strange and wondrous new country, realizes he's in Brighton after all. In seeking to elaborate a limiting principle on this basis, would we merely re-create the just war tradition by another name? Patterson's critique of Niebuhr's relatively absent theology of vocation also comes into play here. Romans 13 strongly implies that the preservation of such an order is a vocation ordained under God's authority. If so, can one acting in this capacity be deemed guilty or sinful? If not, is the dirty-hands tradition's contribution limited to the necessary and important caveat that fulfilling such a vocation will cause spiritual harm that must be pastorally addressed? Still, even if the ultimate contributions are limited, I believe it is worth exploring what insights we might gain through an attempt to substantiate the *imago Dei* as a limiting principle for the dirty-hands perspective.

4

A CHURCH
HISTORICAL VIEW

A Church Historical View
War as Radical Evil

MEIC PEARSE

It is the 1990s in Sierra Leone. And tonight you are keeping watch on the edge of a village, for the country is in the middle of a complex and brutal civil war. Out there, you are pretty sure, are the child soldiers of the Revolutionary United Front (RUF). Repeatedly raped and brutalized, they have been both terrorized by their commanders and utterly inured to horrific violence.

And here they come now, through the gloom. As well as guns, they are wielding machetes, which they use to hack off the hands and feet, or whole limbs, of men, women, and children alike. High on drugs, they cut open pregnant women in grotesque games to bet on the sex of the unborn child.[1] And you have a gun.

Here's what I want to ask you: Will you use it? Because, if you do, you will be gunning down children, boys and girls alike, who have themselves been recruited only by capture and ongoing terror—and, as experience since has shown what could have been predicted in any case, have been permanently traumatized by all they have suffered. These children are victims of horrifying abuse. Combatants they may be, but not in any of the usual senses of that word. To gun them down scarcely meets the criteria of a just war.

And if you don't fire—and keep firing to lethal effect—you will be allowing an appalling fate, far worse than mere death, to overtake the sleeping men, women, and children behind you. For a pacifist, the all-too-foreseeable consequences constitute a nightmare.

---

[1] For a full exposition of the use of child soldiers in the Sierra Leone Civil War of 1991–2002, see Myriam Denov, "Child Soldiers in Sierra Leone: Experiences, Implications and Strategies for Rehabilitation and Community Reintegration," August 2005, https://riselearningnetwork.org/wp-content/uploads/2015/09/Child-soldiers-in-Sierra-Leone-Experiences-implications-and-strategies-for-rehabilitation-and-community-reintegration.-Myriam-Denov-2006.pdf.

You might say that one should hasten to waken the villagers and tell them to flee. But old men, pregnant women, toddlers—and sleepy people of any age, sex, or condition—cannot run fast. And the attackers are eighty yards away. It is your gun or nothing.

You might say that you could shoot over the attackers' heads and hope that they will run. But they won't. To deter, an aggressor has to believe that the deterrent will be used in good earnest. In any case, the children are too terrified of their commanders, and too battle-hardened to flee. And they are on drugs.

* * *

Now it is mid-September 2001. A week ago, the Western world was living its accustomed way of life with little that could count as existential fear: the media were obsessed with the usual round of sporting events, new movies, scandals, and political cheap shots and point-scoring. And then, on September 11, all that was suddenly moved to the back burner. Stock markets crashed; airlines stopped flying; security forces around the world were on the highest alert.

A hard-line Islamist group, al-Qaeda, has hijacked four airliners, killing all on board and, in New York and Washington, large numbers of people on the ground. The attacks on the Twin Towers of the World Trade Center have killed almost three thousand people—but it is believed, at the time, that up to ten thousand have perished. Osama bin Laden is exultant. "We love death. The U.S. loves life. That is the big difference between us"—so *National Geographic* quoted him—though a variant on the saying was a common refrain of other terrorists from the same stable.[2]

What we know in mid-September 2001 is that more such attacks are planned—perhaps on the monstrous scale of a few days ago. Many suspects have been arrested and are under interrogation. In many cases, we know for a certainty that they are part of terrorist groups.

---

[2]Usama bin Laden, "We Love Death, the US Loves Life," posted by ecorporate, YouTube, October 27, 2007, www.youtube.com/watch?v=V_VOjGXpyIU; *Suhail Khan Exposed* (blog), "We Love Death More Than You Love Life," February 1, 2011, www.suhailkhanexposed.com/2011/02/01/we-love-death-more-than-you-love-life/.

And here we are—in the interrogation room. And the wretch is brought in for questioning. He is not compliant; he will tell us nothing.

You know full well what I am about to ask you next. Just how far are you prepared to go in extracting information—not a confession, since we already know he's up to his neck, but information that will enable us to forestall what's coming next? Because if we don't get that information, thousands more civilians may die. He intends it, and his group is planning it.

Torture is bestial. Confessions extracted as a result of it, so it has been demonstrated times without number, are almost worthless. If the pain is excruciating enough, most people will admit to anything suggested, just to make it stop—even if the result leads to the merciful release of death. But is it still morally impermissible if the commodity required is not a confession, but information? And if the person under interrogation is known to possess information that, once given, is at least somewhat verifiable? If such methods save lives, either by fending off an attack, or else by helping in the liquidation of the plotters, many might reconcile themselves even to such horrid procedures.

For pacifists, such dilemmas already presuppose something that they would consider inadmissible—for a terrorist could hardly have been apprehended in the first place by methods consistent with pacifism. But, although neither Cicero's nor Augustine's just war criteria mention torture specifically, it has generally been considered inadmissible in such terms.

So, what to do? Al-Qaeda was bent on making good its promise that similar outrages were planned. During the following years, a wave of attacks against prominent targets were in fact attempted: the US Bank Tower in Los Angeles; the Brooklyn Bridge; the IMF and World Bank buildings and the New York Stock Exchange; as well as shopping malls, airports, international flights, and other targets.

The United States was fortunate in that, thanks to aggressive gathering of intelligence, all were thwarted until 2009, when two attacks, in Little Rock and Fort Hood, killed one person and thirteen people respectively. Four years after that came the Boston Marathon attack, resulting in the deaths of three participants and injuries to 200 more. But Madrid and London suffered more grievously: on March 11, 2004, ten explosions on four commuter trains in the Spanish capital claimed 193 lives and injured a massive 2,050 people. And the following year, on July 7, 2005, coordinated attacks on the transport system of the British capital killed fifty-six people and injured 784.

* * *

This book compares and contrasts Christian pacifism, the Augustinian just war tradition, and skepticism about both of these—that skepticism being the position I shall be arguing in this chapter.

To be sure, I have a healthy respect, not only for my opponents in this debate but also for the bodies of opinion that they represent. For the arguments in their favor are formidable indeed. Pacifism, in particular, would seem to have the New Testament largely on its side, and as a church historian I am acutely aware that the balance of evidence shows the early Christians, certainly until the fourth century, to have taken a very negative view of warfare. Such statements as we have from them are either explicitly pacifist or at least suggestive of a pacifist interpretation. Certainly none of them endorses any justification for participation in armed conflict.

The just war tradition, by contrast, is weak on Scripture (it relies heavily on dubious arguments from the Old Testament—the nature of which we shall consider anon) but much stronger on practicality. The world is a violent place. All social order is attained by threats of violence; if the order is sufficiently long-standing such that those threats become merely implied and then, with the long passage of time, subsumed into the background behind laws, bureaucracies, and diplomacy, then so much the better—and we shall all have nicer, more civilized lives. But as every foreign threat and civil disturbance makes plain, the veneer of civilization is thin, and so the threats can never entirely disappear. And threats, as every parent of small children knows, have no value unless, in extremis, they are implemented. Even the New Testament admits as much in Romans 13:1-7.

Nevertheless, the objections to both these bodies of thought seem to me to be overwhelming, and I shall contend that both positions are finally untenable. War, I shall argue, is a radical evil that cannot be constrained by rules and conventions; indeed, embattled armies weaponize such conventions—and, in the modern era, utilize peacekeepers themselves—to pursue their war aims.

I do not, on account of all this skepticism, advocate an anything-goes policy. Far from it. (My pacifist alter ego is far too close to the surface for that.) But I do want to insist that we look clearly at the presuppositions behind each of the historic contending views, add in a realistic view of human nature, and recognize war for the ultimate horror that it is.

KEY DEFINITIONS: WHAT CHRISTIANITY IS— AND IS NOT

When Christians disagree about things, they tend to deploy biblical texts to justify their own view and to undermine the position of those with whom they are arguing. That is fair enough, in a way; if the doctrine or practice or view that I hold cannot stand up under biblical scrutiny, then it needs to be abandoned in favor of something that does. Certainly I shall be referring to Scripture a lot in the pages that follow.

Nevertheless, there is a key weakness in this approach, which I intend to address at the outset. The Bible, as non-Christians seldom fail to point out, is a very large book, and almost anything can be "proved" from it if we are sufficiently determined. The evidence of that is all around us, in multiple churches and denominations, innumerable contested theologies, and the need for books such as this one.

What is the status of Deuteronomy 20:16-17 ("In the cities of the nations the LORD your God is giving you as an inheritance, do not leave alive anything that breathes. Completely destroy them . . . as the LORD your God has commanded you")—both absolutely and relative to Matthew 5:39 ("Do not resist an evil person. If anyone slaps you on the right cheek, turn to them the other cheek also")?[3] Either course of action might be upheld by some testy expositor as "biblical" or "what the Bible says." And since there is an abundance of both kinds of verse, how are we to adjudicate between them? Many attempts end up straining the sense of either kind, or of both. One does not need to be a religious skeptic to sense this.

So we need to address the question of hermeneutics at an early point. This term refers to the principles by which we expound or interpret a text—in this case the Bible. And the commonest distinction made is that posed,

---

[3]Unless otherwise indicated, Scripture quotations in this chapter are from the New International Version (NIV).

in broadly similar terms, by both Augustine in the fifth century and by Martin Luther in the sixteenth. The former speaks of two "cities" (the earthly city and the city of God); the latter, of two "kingdoms," the earthly and the heavenly. The belligerent texts of Scripture relate to our political or public lives: when government commands us to fight, we are constrained to obey as a matter of duty and obedience to authority—or, as Luther would have said, to "the law." The texts commanding peace relate to our personal and private relations—or, as Luther would have said, they are "the gospel."

The principal objection to this two-kingdoms or two-cities approach, however, is that it confuses the more important, strictly biblical issue— namely, the distinction between the Old Testament and the New. It is no accident that protagonists of just war draw most of their favorite supportive Scriptures from the Old Testament, while Christian pacifists lean more heavily on the New Testament—and in particular on the precepts of Jesus. For it is more than the transition from "law" to "gospel" that is entailed: the two testaments operate at entirely different levels.

As well as giving us absolutely crucial information about the nature of God and of human beings, about the relation between God and his creation, and prophecies of a coming Messiah, the bulk of the Old Testament is the story of a people who become a political entity: Israel. The commands in the Torah are about how to govern such a society "God's way." Of course, Israel is faithless, and the story becomes hopelessly complex—but the failures and the complexity do not concern us here. The point is that there can be no such thing as a pacifist state. (Or perhaps there can be—but only for about twenty minutes.) A political entity of any description exists on the basis of force, whether actual or merely threatened, whether past or present. Every state that exists came into existence as a result of violence—usually its own, but occasionally somebody else's. And only the ability to exercise lethal force (or that of other parties prepared to do so on their behalf) keeps them in existence.

It would be an astonishing surprise, therefore, if the people of Israel did not exercise violence or participate in war. Since God willed their state to come into existence, he gave commands for them to fight.[4] And the laws

---

[4] Of course, the drastic nature of these commands raises weighty questions about the character of God. However, such issues do not belong in this book. See Greg Boyd, *Crucifixion of the*

given to Israel provided for harsh punishments, including death. All states keep internal order only by retaining the option of such a recourse. For that is what it means to be a state.

The New Testament, however, offers no such program. On the one hand, the gospel proclaimed by Jesus is universal, in that it appeals to all people everywhere. On the other hand, it is a transcendent calling to discipleship of individuals by Jesus; the controlling assumption is that only a minority will choose to follow: "Wide is the gate and broad is the road that leads to destruction, and many enter through it. But small is the gate and narrow the road that leads to life, and only a few find it" (Mt 7:13-14). Jesus tells his disciples, "If you belonged to the world, it would love you as its own. As it is, you do not belong to the world, but I have chosen you out of the world" (Jn 15:19). Peter exhorted his listeners to "save yourselves from this corrupt generation" (Acts 2:40)—the implication being that the mass of the "corrupt generation" would remain exactly where they were.

And the church became exactly what one might expect from such teachings: in sociological terms, it was a sectarian movement. It not only lacked power to run society as a whole, it had no aspirations to do so. It was never part of the plan. Indeed, the very foundational teachings of Jesus in the Sermon on the Mount were designed precisely to make such a thing impossible. There, he cites one command of Moses after another, only to add "But I say to you. . . ." Murderers, for example, can be punished by public authorities and, when they can be apprehended, they invariably are. But Jesus tells us that "anyone who is angry with a brother or sister will be subject to judgment" (Mt 5:22). Yet what mechanism could possibly punish us—or even detect us—for the crime of anger? Clearly, the reference to judgment is to no earthly court, but to one in heaven. Again, public authorities can punish adulterers; in the past most governments did so, and some still do. Yet how could this apply to "anyone who looks at a woman lustfully" (Mt 5:28)? States can mandate financial help to the poor (say, through taxes), or at least encourage it by public approval. Yet how does one reward those who, when they give to the needy, "do not let [their] left hand know what

---

Warrior God (Minneapolis: Fortress, 2017), chaps. 7-11, 19, for a treatment of the subject as a whole; A. L. Thompson, *Who's Afraid of the Old Testament God?* (Grand Rapids, MI: Zondervan, 1989), chap. 6, for a tilt at Judg 19–21.

[their] right hand is doing" (Mt 6:3)? Finally, states can impose a compulsory religion and mandate attendance at its ceremonies and services. But Jesus tells his followers, "When you pray, go into your room, close the door and pray to your Father, who is unseen. Then your Father, who sees what is done in secret, will reward you" (Mt 6:6).

Examples could be multiplied at length. But the central point of them all is that Christian faith is no program for government, since its core precepts are not susceptible either to legislation or to enforcement. The Ten Commandments ("Moses said") were so susceptible—but Jesus says to us something different. That being so, there is no such thing as a "Christian" economic or educational policy, nor a "Christian" legal system, nor a "Christian" social ideal. Christians, from the very beginning, had their own ways of organizing *themselves*—but not for organizing wider society as a whole. It is for this reason that modern critics of Christianity, who regularly castigate the New Testament for "supporting" slavery (it doesn't) or at least for condoning it, are entirely missing the point. Christians no more condoned slavery than they condoned abortion and infanticide—though Christians' behavior in respect of all of these issues was far out of line with Roman standards and expectations.[5] Indeed, it was their very separatism and outlandishness that constituted a principal reason for Roman persecution when it finally came during the 60s of the first century.

This being so, any and all Christian discussions about warfare were, by the nature of the case, about whether Christians might participate in it and under what circumstances. They were not about whether a war might be "just." The very idea of a "just war" did not arise, because Christians were not pulling the levers of power, nor did they ever expect to. That was not what Christianity was about. (And, we might add, it was not, before modern times, what politics was about, either. Politics was not about "principles" or "policy"; it was about personal power. That was why private individuals, whether Christians or otherwise, had no place in it.) Christian faith was entirely about how to live in this world as disciples—as a people being *in* that world but not *of* it.

---

[5] Briefly stated, Christians recognized slave marriages among themselves, and allowed slaves and ex-slaves to lead churches. They condemned infanticide and abortion, and rescued abandoned babies from rubbish heaps where they had been left to die.

To summarize: the Old Testament is (largely) about running a particular country or nation—namely, Israel. The New Testament is about being disciples of Jesus in a world where "we do not have an enduring city, but we are looking for the city that is to come" (Heb 13:14). Christians are called to live by the latter. They do not offer sacrifices for sin in the temples; they do not follow Old Testament dietary laws; and they do not seek to establish a theocracy. That being so, there can be no question of laying down principles for a just war. The only question is whether, war being declared, we as Christians may participate—or whether this is one of those many occasions where we are called on to show our defiance of human laws and suffer the consequences.

THE WAR OVER SCRIPTURE

War in the Old Testament. The Old Testament is generally understood as sanctioning war. We think of all the brutal conflicts in the Torah or in the books of Samuel and Kings, at least some of which are explicitly sanctioned by God. Indeed, some of those raise unique problems that lie (to the relief of all three of my coauthors, I suspect!) well beyond the scope of this book. Even so, they do illustrate the general truth that *all* political entities come into existence as the result of violence—whether enacted in the distant past or more recently; and whether as a result of conquest, massacre, and displacement, or of some reconfiguration caused by political upheaval or war.

But beyond the rather large issue of divinely sanctioned "taking the land," even the Old Testament is at least a little ambiguous on the topic of warfare. On the one hand, Ecclesiastes notes wistfully that "wisdom is better than weapons of war" (Eccles 9:18). And Isaiah prophesies that

[God] will judge between the nations
  and will settle disputes for many peoples.
They will beat their swords into plowshares
  and their spears into pruning hooks.
Nation will not take up sword against nation,
  nor will they train for war any more. (Is 2:4)

(Judging by progress so far, though, that one may definitely be for the eschaton.)

On the other hand, the psalmist praises

The LORD my Rock,
Who trains my hands for war,
And my fingers for battle. (Ps 144:1 NKJV)

This psalm is generally attributed to David, and the Septuagint (a Greek translation produced centuries later, between ca. 250 and 132 BC) insists that it refers specifically to his battle against Goliath.

Further, God proclaims of Babylon that

You are my war club,
    my weapon for battle—
with you I shatter nations,
    with you I destroy kingdoms. (Jer 51:20)

Is God underwriting the wars even of heathen nations? Does this validate the "God is on our side" discourses of almost all countries going to war— leaving the central question, not of *whether* God can be on anyone's side, but of *whose* side he is on? (And how will we ever resolve those questions to everyone's satisfaction?) Or should we listen instead to the pacifist, who will say that God is not validating the actions of the Babylonians or of any other combatants, that war remains impermissible, that he is merely letting us know that he instrumentalizes even human wickedness for his purposes?

How can we reconcile the Sermon on the Mount with Romans 13? The New Testament has its own difficulties. "Blessed are the gentle," said Jesus, "for they will inherit the earth. . . . Blessed are the peacemakers, for they will be called sons of God" (Mt 5:5, 9 NASB). Again, "Do not resist an evil person. If anyone slaps you on the right cheek, turn to them the other cheek also. . . . I tell you, love your enemies and pray for those who persecute you" (Mt 5:39, 44). These texts, cited so often by Christian pacifists, certainly do seem to make it clear that Christians are to be both peaceful and peaceable.

In that context, Jesus' troublesome saying "Don't imagine that I came to bring peace to the earth! I came not to bring peace, but a sword" can persuasively be interpreted as metaphorical (Mt 10:34 NLT).[6] Far from calling

---

[6]The more troublesome saying in Lk 22:36 ("But now let the one who has a moneybag take it, and likewise a knapsack. And let the one who has no sword sell his cloak and buy one" [ESV]) is less amenable to such glossing. Certainly, it is hard to see how this "fits" with the general picture emerging from the Gospels.

for violence, he was merely pointing out that the spread of the gospel would be accompanied by uproar—as it frequently continues to be to this day.

And yet Paul in Romans insists that rulers "do not bear the sword for no reason. They are God's servants, agents of wrath to bring punishment on the wrongdoer" (Rom 13:4). How can this be squared with Jesus' instructions?

It is generally explained by most expositors that the gospel references are to private violence (which is forbidden[7]), while Paul is speaking of "the sword" being used to maintain public order by the state—which is a "minister of God." This seems an eminently sensible distinction; as I have pointed out, pacifism can never, by its very nature, be a public policy. That reality is implicitly recognized by Jesus when telling Pilate that his kingdom is "not of this world" and that "if My kingdom were of this world, My servants would be fighting" because that's how this-worldly kingdoms come into existence, and how they maintain themselves (Jn 18:36 AMP). They *would* be fighting. *But they're not.*[8]

That distinction established, however, raises the crucial question: Can a Christian, committed to nonviolence both in private life and in the service of Jesus' kingdom, serve as a magistrate, or as a soldier—thereby acting as an instrument of "wrath" on internal enemies (rebels and criminals) and external foes (in a war) of the public, this-worldly kingdom in which he happens to live?

The answers seem confusing. When John the Baptist encountered soldiers who asked, "What should we do?" (by way of repentance), John replied, "Don't extort money or make false accusations. And be content with your pay" (Lk 3:14 NLT). The glaring absence of the command to actually "stop being soldiers" implies a permission to remain in military service.

Does it count that this is John the Baptist speaking, and not Jesus? Did the Messiah's commands contradict those of the one who prepared the way? What kind of hermeneutical tangle does *that* open up?

---

[7]Indeed, Paul himself had condemned private violence just a few sentences earlier: "Never take revenge. Leave that to the righteous anger of God" (Rom 12:19 NLT).

[8]Actually, when the soldiers had come to arrest him, one of Jesus' followers had drawn a sword and cut off the ear of the high priest's slave (illustrating, as usual, that violence tends to hurt and kill those inconsequential to the conflict rather than the principal aggressors). And Jesus reproved him: "Put your sword back into its place. For all who take the sword will perish by the sword" (Mt 26:52 ESV).

Or should we conclude that the gospel line is: If you are a soldier when you become converted, it's okay to stick with it, but if you're not, then don't enlist? If so, what happens when the now-converted soldier is called on to kill people?

Or should we instead point to the distinction between private and public violence, and conclude that the latter is sanctioned for the kinds of reasons Paul gives in Romans 13? So, the Bible says . . . ?

These are the conundrums that continue to occupy protagonists of both pacifism and just war theory. Both positions require hermeneutical stretches and exegetical handstands that strain credulity (mine, at least) to the breaking point.

Unspiritual though it may sound, therefore, it seems wisest to confine myself to the generalizations I made in the previous section—where we are on far more certain ground:

1. The Old Testament legitimizes warfare, because it is the story of the creation and maintenance (very bad maintenance, as with all states) of a political entity. Creating it required conquest; maintaining it required lethal force against murderers within and against enemies without.

2. The New Testament, by contrast, eschews any program for running society or creating nations, whether Christian or otherwise. Accordingly, it stresses peace, while allowing for the observation (not commandment) that public authorities "do not bear the sword for no reason" (Rom 13:4).

Whether Christians as individuals may participate in the structures of government and the state is the decisive question. The New Testament generally presupposes that they would not, though Acts gives us examples of a converted centurion and a strong evangelistic appeal made to King Agrippa. But political participation for private individuals is a luxury of liberal Western states in the modern era. For most of Christian history, believers have actually been persecuted, and in many places still are, rendering such questions almost redundant.

Almost all readers of this book, however, live—historically speaking—in extraordinary circumstances. They may be Christians *and* take public participation for granted. And therein lies our *real* dilemma.

PACIFISM IN THE EARLY CENTURIES?

It is one of the central conditions of my church historical position that pacifism is only viable, consistent, and actually Christian if it is part of a complete refusal to participate in public life, especially politics. Yet outside of the Amish and at least some Mennonites, this view is almost nowhere visible among contemporary Christians. So it is worth considering how believers in the post–New Testament period dealt with this issue.

Indeed, after a consideration of the biblical texts themselves, we come to the question of what the earliest Christians made of them. Put simply, to know what a text means, we need to know what it meant to its original audience—or else the biases of our own age and the shortcomings of our own understanding will constantly mislead us. And this brings us to the writings of the church fathers—by which I mean the more important earliest Christian leaders and teachers whose writings have come down to us. What did they understand Jesus and the apostles to have taught about questions of war and peace?

This is no mere abstract history lesson: a very great deal is at stake. For Catholics and Orthodox, the writings of the church fathers have—not individually but collectively—a real authority in establishing tradition. Understandably, many evangelicals may bristle at this idea; "tradition" can be a cloak under the cover of which the actual statements of Scripture can be lost sight of or even reversed. Yet the tendency of some evangelicals—to insist that they can leap across two millennia and grasp "what the Bible says" without any context, or as though we were also living in first-century Palestine, and that the experience of the centuries since is but a catalog of errors we can safely ignore—is hardly better. For in almost every case, "what the Bible says" turns out to mirror the central political and social conceits and the reflexive thought forms of the modern evangelical expositors in question; it also turns out to be identical with the unacknowledged traditions (often quite recent) of the expositors' particular group or denomination. Treated this way, the Word of God becomes less a light to our path than a mirror to our own faces, less a rebuke to our frailties than a crutch to support them and an excuse to vindicate them.

The church fathers should matter to us, *not* because they are (quite) "authoritative," but because, collectively, they have evidential value. And the closer a given Christian teacher is to the time of Jesus and the apostles then, all other things being equal, the greater the evidential value of his writings. What do I mean by "evidential value"? Simply that the first disciples of Jesus and the apostles were in a far better position than those who came later to be clear about what Jesus, the apostles, and the New Testament writings *mean* on any given topic. The later a person comes along, the more he or she will be swayed by the same tendency as we ourselves are: to "read back" into Scripture some understanding that was not intended, to assemble texts alongside one another in ways that the apostles themselves would not have done. Where the early church fathers speak with one voice (which is not always the case), then it is strong evidence that *that* was the sense intended by the New Testament writings.

This is not so very hard to understand. We see the same tendency at work in our own times. Many contemporary preachers in almost all denominations are "guilty" of departing quite considerably from the doctrines of their founders—and sometimes even reversing them. (Whether or how far this is a good thing is quite a different matter.) But the same tale could be told of Methodists concerning Wesley, Lutherans concerning Luther, Presbyterians and Reformed concerning Calvin, and Mennonites concerning Menno Simons. All end up either tolerating or even propounding things their founders would not have countenanced.

If we have the advantage in being able to see (if we are attentive to such things) where different strands of thought lead over time, that is more than outbalanced by the proximity of the early church fathers to the direct teaching of the apostles, in its context—and so to appreciate what was meant by it.

This brings us by a short route to the question of what the earliest post–New Testament Christians thought about issues of war and peace. As with the New Testament writings themselves, the pacifist case is strong, though less than conclusive.

It should be said that the conditions for pacifism in the early church were favorable: Christianity was, in sociological terms, a sect—it neither had, nor sought, governmental responsibility. Hence, there was no need to consider whether a particular conflict was "just" or, in some political sense, needful. Indeed, Christians were being actively persecuted from AD 64 onward, and would remain under sporadic persecution for two and a half centuries. That fact in itself, quite apart from the teachings of Jesus, was quite enough for Christians not to carry the geopolitical needs of their persecutors very close to their hearts.

But in fact we do see many pacifist or near-pacifist statements consistently from Christian leaders during this period—and, most importantly, *no statements* pointing in the opposite direction.[9] For example, Justin Martyr (100–165) was a notable Christian apologist who made it clear that the turn away from violence was a key characteristic of believers: "We who used to kill one another, do not make war on our enemies"; and "We who were filled with war and mutual slaughter and all wickedness, have each and all throughout the earth changed our instruments of war, our swords into ploughshares, and our spears into farming tools."[10]

Given that the "our" before "enemies" is unlikely to refer to the population of the Roman Empire as a whole (ordinary people did not identify themselves with the population of the state in which they happened to live until much more recent times), is this really a renunciation of any and all participation in the Roman Empire's wars? Or is this merely a forswearing of personal and group violence? Although a pacifist understanding of Justin looks likely, a less categorical reading is at least possible.

However, when Hippolytus (ca. 170–235), the leader of the church in Rome, made similar statements, he related them specifically to nonparticipation in the political order. He did so in the context of what kinds of catechumens (people who had studied the basics of the faith and wished to be baptized) should be allowed to proceed to baptism. Hippolytus's strictures were harsh, and there is more than a hint of legalism about some of them. Still, he says,

> A military man in authority must not execute men. If he is ordered, he must not carry it out. Nor must he take a military oath. If he refuses, he shall be rejected [by the church, and from baptism]. If someone is a military governor, or the ruler of a city who wears the purple, he shall cease or he shall be

---

[9]Pacifist and pseudo-pacifist quotations from the early church fathers could be multiplied at length. Those interested in garnering the full harvest should type "pacifism," "early church," and "quotes" into a search engine.

[10]Justin Martyr, *First Apology* 39; *Dialogue with Trypho* 110 (*ANF* 1:176, 254).

rejected. The catechumen or faithful who wants to become a soldier is to be rejected, for he has despised God.[11]

If you are a soldier, you must refuse the military oath (which was pagan, and so impermissible to Christians) and must refuse orders to kill anyone. These requirements were presumably impossible; no army could accept such "conditional" obedience—least of all the Roman. So they were tantamount to a requirement that you resign. And if you were not yet a soldier but sought to become one, you were also rejected from baptism. Not only that, but political leaders, whether military or civil, were not eligible to join the church either.

Whatever we think of all this, Hippolytus's pacifism is at least consistent: nonparticipation in officially sanctioned killing demands nonparticipation in officialdom. That is because states and kingdoms necessarily come into existence by violence and subsist by threatening it for the future—both to fend off external enemies and to maintain internal order. Christ's kingdom, by contrast, is not of this world, and his people are to refuse to fight—not only "for Christ" but for anything else.

Just over a decade after Hippolytus's martyrdom in 235, his near-contemporary Cyprian of Carthage (ca. 200/210–258) scathingly denounced warfare in categorical terms: "Murder, which in the case of an individual is admitted to be a crime, is called a virtue when it is committed wholesale. Impunity is claimed for the wicked deeds, not on the plea that they are guiltless, but because the cruelty is perpetrated on a grand scale."[12] It is very difficult to interpret this statement as anything other than unambiguous pacifism. But perhaps the strongest statement of this kind came a couple of generations later, from Lactantius (ca. 250–ca. 325), a teacher and scholar who became a Christian sometime around 300—just as Christians were about to endure the last and worst of the great Roman persecutions. He wrote, "It will not be lawful for a just man to engage in warfare. . . . It is the act of putting to death itself which is prohibited. Therefore, with regard to this precept of God, there ought to be no exception at all, but that it is always unlawful to kill a man, whom God willed to be a saved creature."[13] Yet he himself wrote just a few years later that "bravery, if you fight in

---

[11]Hippolytus of Rome, *Apostolic Tradition*, 16, in Roberts and Donaldson, *Ante-Nicene Fathers*, vol. 5.
[12]Cyprian of Carthage, *Epistles* 1.6 (*ANF* 5:277). This was written probably in 246 or 247.
[13]Lactantius, *Epitome of the Divine Institutes*, 6.20 (*ANF* 7:187).

defense of your country, is a good, if against your country . . . an evil."[14]
Needless to say, no such sentiment can be found in the New Testament.

So whence the huge change of mind? Lactantius had taken a position as
tutor to the son of Constantine, who in 312 became Roman emperor,
bringing the persecution of Christians to an end—and, during the following
decades, showering the church with privileges and marks of imperial favor.
And pacifism, as I have indicated, is not a doctrine consonant with politics
and state power.

We can deride Lactantius as a sellout if we wish. Or praise him as a realist.
Certainly he was a harbinger of a gigantic shift that would take place in
Christian teachings and practices of all kinds during the course of the fourth
and early fifth centuries, as Christianity moved from being a persecuted sect
to favored religion—and then, from the 380s onward, to being the de facto
official religion of the Roman Empire and persecutor of non-Christians.
Not the least of these dramatic shifts in doctrine would be a reversal of the
relationship between the two testaments. Instead of reading the Old Testament in the light of the New (or of "the Christ event," as modern scholars
put the matter)—which had been the procedure of the New Testament
writers themselves, and of their successors during the first three centuries—
the Old Testament now became normative.[15] For it was the latter that
provides the instructions and examples needed to run a state or a country.
First among these is the legitimation of warfare. As we are about to see,
Christians during this period would often go much further than Lactantius's tentative, revised position about fighting in defense of one's country.

JUST WAR—A CHURCH HISTORICAL APPROACH?

Pacifism, as I have noted, is not consonant with holding political power.
Yet during the course of the fourth century, Christianity was transformed
from being a persecuted outcast to being the recipient of ever more

---

[14]Lactantius, *Epitome*, 61 (*ANF* 7:248). It is ironic, perhaps, that Lactantius's patron Constantine
had fought for the imperial title over six years (306–312)—during which time his actions might
well have counted as "fighting against his country." Legitimacy, it has often been noted, tends to
be conferred retrospectively.

[15]The end result of this process speaks for itself. But the interested reader can easily look up to see
the far greater prominence of the Old Testament in the writings and argumentation of post-
Nicene church fathers (i.e., post-325) compared to their predecessors.

political favor, until finally, by century's end, it was the ostensible rationale for government itself. Unsurprisingly, at least some Christians—and, by the close of the fourth century, almost all of them—began to change their tune concerning the essential mechanism for upholding political power: organized violence.

Lactantius, as we have seen, distanced himself from his earlier vehement pacifism to suggesting that defense of one's country was a moral good. Later in the century, Basil of Caesarea (330–379) related that "I have become acquainted with a man who demonstrates that it is possible even in the military profession to maintain perfect love for God and that a Christian ought to be characterised not by the clothes he wears but by the disposition of his soul."[16]

This language betrays what Basil knew—and clearly expected his readers would know—had been the Christian position in the past: "It is possible"— "*even* in the military"; "the clothes he wears" (i.e., military uniform) had clearly been considered disreputable in themselves, but now Basil insists that it was the inner person that counted for more. Basil evidently knew that he was pushing back on his readers' expectations.

Athanasius of Alexandria (ca. 297–373) struck a more confident note when he stated, "One is not supposed to kill, but killing the enemy in battle is both lawful and praiseworthy."[17] If the lawfulness might reasonably be deduced from Romans 13:4 ("Rulers do not bear the sword for no reason. They are God's servants, agents of wrath to bring punishment on the wrongdoer"), the praiseworthiness would be harder to find. Such terminology belongs rather to the civic and imperial ethos of classical Rome than to anything in the New Testament.

This reassertion, in Christian guise, of traditional Roman martial virtues is even more marked in the most important of the new type of Christian thinker: Augustine of Hippo (354–430). Augustine's influence in reshaping Christian thought in the West is vast: even today, most Western Christians, Protestant and Catholic alike, find it hard to distinguish between "what the early Christians thought" and "the Augustinian

---

[16]Basil of Cappadocia, *Letters* 106 (*NPNF*[2] 8:186).
[17]Athanasius of Alexandria, *Letter* 48 (*NPNF*[2] 4:557).

tradition," on a wide range of matters. Yet the two categories are *far from identical!*

Augustine asks, "What is it about war, after all, that is blameworthy? Is it that people who will someday die anyway are killed in order that the victors might live in peace? That kind of objection is appropriate to a timid man, not a religious one."[18]

That all modern readers will be appalled by the drift of his questions we can take for granted. But it is the content of his adjectives "timid" and "religious" that betrays the fact that his argument owes everything to traditional Roman military and civic values, and nothing (except formally) to Christianity. To be "timid" was a serious fault for traditional Romans. It was unmanly. And to be "religious" was to show devotion to the Roman gods—and thereby to Rome itself. Of course, Augustine was not exhorting loyalty to the Roman gods, but his use of "religious" echoed the old pagan civic and imperial loyalty, rather than the Christian ethos of taking up one's cross.

Even more damning, perhaps, was his claim, immediately after this passage, that "a righteous man, who happens to be serving under an ungodly sovereign, can rightfully protect the public peace by engaging in combat at the latter's command when he receives an order that is either not contrary to God's law or is a matter of doubt (in which case it may be that the sinful command involves the sovereign in guilt, whereas the soldier's subordinate role makes him innocent)."[19] This, surely, is the plea of the concentration camp guard: "I was only following orders!"

Yet—and here is the real sting—who, once they have taken up arms in a cause insufficiently dubious (given their limited state of knowledge of politics, and their total ignorance of what might transpire next), is in any position to refuse orders? One *might* do it, of course, if one is commanded to perpetrate a massacre. But, short of that, almost no one *will* do it. How many Allied aircrew in the Second World War saw themselves as guilty of breaching the just war criteria by bombing civilians? Did any of them bomb military targets with a good conscience but then refuse the mission to create the Dresden firestorm in which tens of thousands of civilians were

---

[18] Augustine of Hippo, *Against Faustus* 22.74 (*NPNF*[1] 4:301).
[19] Augustine of Hippo, *Against Faustus* 22.75 (*NPNF*[1] 4:301).

carbonized? Even one airman? Of course not. To accept enlistment is to agree to do what will happen next.

And yet it is Augustine who is credited as the creator of the just war criteria. In point of fact, he took the theory devised over four centuries earlier by Cicero (106–43 BC), the Roman politician and orator, and gave it a Christian gloss for his own age. By Augustine's mature years, it was axiomatic that the Roman Empire—or what was left of it (it was fast crumbling to barbarian invasions)—was a Christian empire. Consequently, there needed to be some religious guidelines concerning warfare. A particular conflict might be considered morally defensible if it was declared for a just cause (*jus ad bellum*) and conducted in a just fashion (*jus in bello*).[20]

The great historian of the twentieth century A. J. P. Taylor has commented on this development. War in Europe, he noted, was endemic for many centuries, and the realization that this was likely to continue "produced . . . attempts to eliminate war altogether, or, if these failed, to lessen its horrific consequences. [This] lay behind the medieval pursuit of 'the just war,' a pursuit as elusive as that of the Holy Grail. For it is almost universally true that in war each side thinks itself in the right, and there is no arbiter except victory to decide between them."[21]

The point is well taken. Just war theory is about restraining hypothetical conflicts. In all *actual* wars, however, both sides claim to be vindicated by the theory. And so the wars play themselves out, with each weaponizing moral arguments about the injustice of the other, as part of the conflict itself—both while it is going on and in retrospect.

The Crusades were accounted not merely just but actually holy—though few would think them such nowadays. And yet we need not doubt that the participants thought of themselves as just at the time even as, in Jerusalem in 1099, their horses "waded in blood up to their knees, nay up to the bridle. It was a just and wonderful judgement of God that the same place should receive the blood of those whose blasphemies it had so long

---

[20]Many books spell out this theory and its ramifications. For simplicity and brevity, the reader could do worse than to consult my *Gods of War: Is Religion the Primary Cause of Violent Conflict?* (Downers Grove IL: InterVarsity, 2007), chap. 10.

[21]A. J. P. Taylor, "War and Peace," *London Review of Books*, October 2, 1980, www.lrb.co.uk/the -paper/v02/n19/a.j.p.-taylor/war-and-peace.

carried up to God."[22] Yet we recoil in horror at the seventy thousand Muslims killed and the Jews burned alive in their synagogues during the capture of the city.

If all combatants, even those who perpetrate such atrocities, see themselves as justified by moral criteria—and each of the stipulations mentioned by Augustine and Cicero turns out to be very elastic indeed—it is because the protagonists (mostly) see everything in very different terms. (That is almost a tautology: no difference, no war.) This is the precise opposite of the dreamy-eyed idealist who insists that, if people just understood each other better, fighting would be averted. For the dynamic runs in precisely the opposite direction: the deepening of conflict generates an inability to see. One need look no further than the purblind nature of current American domestic politics to see that process at work: neither side is, psychologically, very far from "just" violence against the "insane" other.

If that is too painful for us, let us consider three Russian appeals to "just war" or "just" preparations for war, and then measure our own responses to them. My calculation is that they will strike the Western reader (and I am here assuming that my readers are, for the most part, Westerners), including supporters of just war theory, as strained. And that might give us pause to wonder if our own justifications look equally strained when viewed from a cultural or temporal distance.

In 1925, Ivan Alexandrovych Ilyin, a White exile from Bolshevism, wrote *On Resistance to Evil by Force*. Penned in response to Leo Tolstoy's religious pacifism, his book is, to my Anglophone sensibilities, almost unreadable, even in translation, with its strange, cloying fusion of philosophical logic-chopping and mystic sentimentality.[23] The point of the exercise was to persuade all Christian Orthodox Russians to return to the battle against the godless Bolsheviks who had just defeated them in the Russian Civil War. And in that cause, he wrote, "White warriors, bearers of the Orthodox sword . . . ! In you there is an Orthodox knightly tradition, . . . you have

---

[22]The chronicler Raymond of Aguilers, *History of the Franks Who Captured Jerusalem*, as cited in N. Cohn, *The Pursuit of the Millennium* (Oxford: Oxford University Press, 1970), 67-68.

[23]In fairness, his long-suffering translator explains that at least one aspect of this—namely, his "tendency to use awkward compound words"—is "a habit he picked up from his forays into German philosophy." I. A. Ilyin, *On Resistance to Evil by Force*, trans. K. Benois (Zvolen, Slovakia: Taxiarch Press, 2018), xiii.

maintained the banners of the Russian warriors of Christian favor.... Let your sword be a prayer, and your prayer be a sword!"[24]

If the language grates a little, we might remind ourselves that it was a cry to resist the bloodthirsty, godless wickedness of the Communists. Quite true, but there is a problem: the actual record of the White forces in the civil war was fully as atrocious as that of the Reds; their propensity to antisemitic massacre, worse.[25] Yet this was the battle Ilyin was calling on the same people to fight once again.

More recently, in 2013, as Mikhail Kalashnikov neared death at the age of ninety-four, his conscience was stricken: "The pain in my soul is unbearable." Why? He was the inventor of the world's most successful rifle. Even today, large areas of the Global South are awash with AK-47s, which can be bought for just a few dollars and have killed countless numbers. But Patriarch Kirill of Moscow assured him that he was "an example of patriotism and a correct attitude toward the country.... When the weapon is in defense of the Fatherland, the Church supports its creators and the military, which use it."[26]

And in 2020, the online magazine *Orthodoxy in Dialogue* reported that Russia is building a new cathedral "dedicated to the Armed Forces [which] will be decorated with the faces of President Vladimir Putin, Defense Minister Sergei Shoigu and Soviet leader Josef Stalin ... at a sprawling military-themed park near Moscow."[27] As well as celebrating victory in World War II (universally called the Great Patriotic War in Russia), the 2014 annexation of Crimea is depicted.

---

[24]Ilyin, *On Resistance to Evil by Force*, 1.

[25]"The officers and men of the [White] Army laid practically all the blame for their country's troubles on the Hebrew. They held that the whole cataclysm had been engineered by some great and mysterious society of international Jews.... Among Denikin's officers this idea was an obsession.... When I told them that I and most of my best friends were Freemasons, and that England owed a great deal to its loyal Jews, they stared at me askance and sadly shook their heads in fear for England's credulity.... When America showed herself decidedly against any kind of interference in Russia, the idea soon gained wide credence that President Woodrow Wilson was a Jew." John Ernest Hodgson, *With Denikin's Armies: Being a Description of the Cossack Counter-Revolution in South Russia, 1918–1920* (London: Temple Bar Publishing, 1932), 54-56.

[26]See CBS News, "AK-47 Designer Kalashnikov Wrote Penitent Letter," January 14, 2014, www .cbsnews.com/news/ak-47-designer-kalashnikov-wrote-penitent-letter/.

[27]*Orthodoxy in Dialogue*, "Russia's New War Cathedral Glorifies Stalin, Putin, and the 2014 Theft of Crimea from Ukraine," April 26, 2020, https://orthodoxyindialogue.com/2020/04/26 /russias-new-war-cathedral-glorifies-stalin-putin-and-the-2014-theft-of-crimea-from-ukraine.

Why will Western readers look at all of these "blessed war" claims with some degree of revulsion? It will be because they do not—cannot—identify with Russia and its history and its priorities.

But that's the point. "Holy justice" in conflict, claimed by enemies or rivals—or merely those, like the crusaders, very distant from us in time— will strike us as hollow, not as just, still less as holy. Yet arguments for bombing the civilians of Nazi Germany will seem to some, at least (and, in 1943, to most) as plausible, or even compelling. As Ilyin said of the White Russian cause, it was "not only permissible, but . . . a knightly duty."

That being so, we might expect theories designed to constrain war to fail in that endeavor, and to be used instead as legitimations of "our" cause and condemnations of "theirs." In practice, that is exactly what always happens.

NEW ISSUES THAT CONFOUND
THE OLD CATEGORIES

War, so far as prehistorians can make out, has been with us since human beings first settled down in agrarian societies and claimed particular pieces of land (and the crops that grew on it, and the animals that grazed on it) as "property." Techniques of warfare may have changed over the centuries, and the technology for waging it may have become ever more fearful. But the moral issues that surround it have remained, in principle at least, broadly the same until relatively recently in human history.

I have argued here that war is a radical evil, dragging everybody engaged in it, or merely unfortunate enough to be located in its vicinity, ever deeper into the moral abyss. Pacifists may refuse it, but their stance delivers up not only themselves but also their loved ones and their neighbors into the hands of whoever is strongest, to do with as he will. Protagonists of just war may attempt to delimit it, but the process has a satanic way of both rendering any "rules" meaningless and weaponizing the codes themselves, along with their would-be enforcers. In recent centuries, the process has become even messier and yet more insusceptible of moral regulation.

At the "top" end of warfare, we have seen the creation and proliferation of weapons of mass destruction: atomic weapons, of course, but also chemical and biological ones. Because of them, the whole dynamic of warfare has gone through one of its periodic shifts. Back during the First World War, the technology of defense was far ahead of that of attack: that was why trench warfare produced such prolonged deadlock. Later, with the development of rapid tanks capable of moving at thirty or forty miles per hour, and of fast fighter and bomber aircraft, the advantage swung back toward attack. But the advent of nuclear weapons—and after them, chemical and biological weapons capable of being used as vehicles of mass destruction—has given attack a decisive advantage: put bluntly, there is very little that can be done to defend against them, except to deter their use in the first place. This scheme during the Cold War was appropriately called "mutually assured destruction." And, paradoxically, that grim assurance kept the peace.

There is no way that the actual use of such weapons could be consistent with just war theory: the incineration of hundreds of thousands—and, in a full-scale exchange, of hundreds of millions—of men, women, and children, and the reduction of much of the planet to a radioactive wasteland is not remotely compatible with the Augustinian criteria. And yet the state that renounces their use is effectively disarmed—and so defeated in advance—in the face of an enemy prepared to use them. The argument is all of a piece with that of pacifism itself.

Thirty years after the end of the Cold War, the dilemma of head-on rivalry between nuclear-armed superpowers has not entirely evaporated. Indeed, it appears to be edging back. But now the danger has been enhanced by the fact of nuclear proliferation. It remains likely that even the rogue states that have acquired or are acquiring such weapons can be deterred. The biggest threat comes from those to whom they will leak such technologies. If and when a nuclear attack really occurs, it is very unlikely that it will be delivered by intercontinental ballistic missiles over the polar ice caps; it will more likely detonate in a lift shaft in a skyscraper, placed there by suicide bombers acting on behalf of an undiscoverable proxy of a proxy—for a non-state actor that cannot be deterred, and against whom it is impracticable to retaliate in kind. What then?

This brings us to the "bottom" end of warfare. The word *terrorism* was first used to describe the "terror" inflicted by the French revolutionary government of the 1790s against its enemies, both real and imagined. But even that was a description of the actions of what we might now call a "rogue state." In more recent times, the term has been used to describe the calculated violence, short of revolution or civil war, perpetrated by non-state actors—namely, terrorist groups of all kinds. In the nineteenth century, they generally confined themselves to the assassination of political figures. In the early twentieth century, the scope was widened in some places to attacks against soldiers, policemen, and public functionaries. But in recent generations members of the public have come under attack—most vividly on 9/11—from bombers, hijackers, gunmen, kidnappers, and so on in pursuit of a wide range of political causes. It is another example of the deepening moral abyss that is war. But it also raises the question of how to counter it—and the moral constraints on doing so.

For pacifists, the answer is clear. They will use no forceful means to counter terrorism. As a moral exemplar this may be excellent, but it does nothing to rescue the people living in fear of attack. As we have seen, it might be argued to be the most faithful expression of Christian discipleship, but it entails a forswearing of all civic engagement. For all civil society, from the most trivial level to the tables of government, rests on deterrence underpinned by force: "Little Johnny, if you hit your sister again, you'll be in your room until dinner, and grounded for a week!" "Disrupt this class one more time, and you'll be in detention." "Rob the gas station, and you'll be cooling your heels in jail." "Violate our coastal waters, Mr. President, and we'll send in our air force." The maintenance of any civil peace absolutely demands the credible threat of force against those who disrupt it.

Yet how does one fight the terrorist? He is not in uniform. So can we use violence against him only once he has already struck? And if not—if we give ourselves permission to kill those we know to be plotting—how do we obtain that information? Is it "Christian" to use a network of informers (i.e., of liars)? And what of the heightened risk posed by the suicide bombers who emerged first with the Hindu Tamil Tigers in the Sri Lankan Civil War of 1983–2009, and were quickly followed by a variety of Islamist groups? May we deploy torture? Is that compatible with a Christian conscience and with the just war criteria? It seems to me that squaring it with those criteria would require an exposition and argumentation so abstruse as to amount to transparently self-serving pedantry. I contend that no Christian criteria can resolve these problems for us—*not* because the faith is inadequate, but because that it is not what Christianity is for.

We have already noticed the appalling dilemma posed by child soldiers. But what of the young teenagers—mostly girls—brainwashed to be used as suicide bombers in places like northeastern Nigeria? Some have extricated themselves at the last moment, but many more have not. Should they be shot down before they can detonate themselves (or *be detonated* by their handlers)?

Finally, we come to the most recent field of warfare: the new vistas opened up by the internet and cybernetics. Military analyst David Kilcullen points out that, in the face of overwhelming Western (especially American) military might, the danger of future conflict is moving toward "liminal warfare"—"a vertical series of increasingly more energetic and observable actions, from clandestine activity at the bottom to open conflict at the top"; and "conceptual envelopment"—"a horizontal spectrum of small challenges . . . that expand beyond an adversary's ability or even inclination to respond. The purpose of each is to apply pressure while sowing disinformation, leaving the West in doubt about whether it is experiencing a conflict at all until it is too late to do anything about it."[28]

The Russian seizure of Crimea in 2014 is a classic example. Another example of nonstandard warfare is the use of bots to sow seeds of online disinformation, to undermine confidence in public institutions (especially electoral processes), and to stir up civil conflict. The acquisition or use of economic assets to place a financial chokehold on an adversary or to bring down their economy: this is yet another avenue into which future conflict is drifting.

It is easy to envisage the use of massive cyberattacks on opponents. Indeed, they have already begun. At what stage would their escalation count as war, justifying a response in kind? Or justifying a conventional military strike? Or even a preemptive attack—whether in cyberspace or by high explosives? After all, the kind of cyberattack that closes down all of a country's public utilities (electricity, water, gas) would certainly lead to the deaths

---

[28]This is a summary of Kilcullen by Michael Puttré, "Winning on the Battlefield Is Not Enough," *Discourse*, May 13, 2020, www.discoursemagazine.com/politics/2020/05/13/winning-on-the -battlefield-is-not-enough/. Puttré also briefly mentions Qiao Liang and Wang Xiangsui, *Unrestricted Warfare* (Brattleboro VT: Echo Point, 2015). Will Selber, review of *The Dragons and the Snakes: How the Rest Learned to Fight the West*, by David Kilcullen, *The Strategy Bridge*, May 27, 2020, https://thestrategybridge.org/the-bridge/2020/5/27/reviewing-the-dragons-and-the -snakes, gives an excellent survey of the arguments of Kilcullen's book.

of many people. Yet it would all be over in a few minutes—so whoever struck first would likely win. Again, it is far from clear how such mind-boggling calculations could or would fit into the logic of the just war criteria. As so often in human affairs, the sheer multiplicity of factors and the rapidly changing nature of both society and technology render even the possibility of applying the Augustinian categories (or of the Geneva Convention) ever more tenuous. But then, this merely illustrates the unrealistic nature of the enterprise in the first place.

CONCLUSION

In this section, I outline five propositions that summarize my position:

1. The Old and New Testaments operate at two different levels: the former providing examples and instructions for running a polity "God's way"; the latter transcends that and provides an ethic that is for all people anywhere, who are called *out of* "the world" to follow Christ—and from which no political principles can therefore (legitimately) be drawn.

2. Accordingly, the Old Testament is hard to square with pacifism (or, for that matter, with just war theory!), whereas the New Testament tilts in a pacifist direction, *precisely because* it forswears attempts to direct society as a whole; Jesus' kingdom is "not of this world" (Jn 18:36), and its citizens are to be *in* the world, but not *of* it (Jn 17:14-16).

3. Pacifism, though it has strong arguments in its favor, demands (if one is not to be a hypocrite) disengagement from political society—because, as Romans 13 makes plain, the credible threat of violence is an intrinsic prerogative of the state and necessary for maintaining it.

4. Although attempts may be made to contain war, they will rarely succeed—principally because participants typically weaponize whatever comes to hand, *including* the persons, institutions, and supposed laws that are intended to contain violence. This can be seen easily in the fact that, in almost all conflicts, *both* sides claim to be justified by just war criteria.

5. Modern developments in warfare—weapons of mass destruction, suicide terrorism by non-state actors, brutalized child soldiers, and cyber-warfare—have rendered just war criteria more nonsensical than ever, and

attempts to make the new developments fit the old categories risk reducing the entire approach to the merest casuistry.

Warfare, I contend, is radical evil. It drags its participants down into ever lower moral depths. Intrinsic to that evil is that it does not—unless one wishes to abandon the defenseless to their fate—even allow us the opportunity of refusing to participate and of submitting to whichever monster wins.

Christians are by all means to be peacemakers. But that work comes in three stages:

1. Moral suasion needs to happen when conflict seems possible but still some way from being actualized.

2. After conflict is over, peacemaking—whose practitioners Jesus calls "blessed" (Mt 5:9)—consists in the binding up of wounds: literal/physical, social, psychic, and political.

3. But during conflict itself, the peacemaker is confined largely to persuading parties of the futility of pursuing war—that is, of pragmatics—along with holding individuals back from atrocities.

Given all of this, I contend that neither pacifism nor just war theory is consonant with the frightful world of war in reality. And given the exegetical gymnastics needed by both positions, I conclude that neither has the unambiguous support of Scripture.

A Just War Response

ERIC PATTERSON

Pearse's church historical view is a polemical essay that cites almost no historians, ignores the best historians on the ethics of warfare or seminal just war scholars, does not mention the pacifist Schleitheim Confession or other key evidence, and neglects certain critical distinctions.[1] Perhaps the best way to get at the bones of this essay is to go to the very last page of the church historical position, which provides a summary. I will utilize that outline as the start for my remarks, and I'll conclude with an area where I am in some agreement with the author. Although we agree on many points, we strongly disagree on their implications.

The author begins,

> The Old and New Testaments operate at two different levels: the former providing examples and instructions for running a polity "God's way"; the latter transcends that and provides an ethic that is for all people anywhere, who are called *out of* "the world" to follow Christ—and from which no political principles can therefore (legitimately) be drawn. (p. 195)

This statement is partially accurate. It is true that the Old Testament history largely, but not exclusively, focuses on the Hebraic polity. However, we should not assume that principles of good governance in ancient Israel are somehow different from the principles of order and justice for good governance today. The Wisdom literature has a lot to say about leaders listening

---

[1]Two of the best are Frederick H. Russell, *The Just War in the Middle Ages* (Cambridge: Cambridge University Press, 1975); and James Turner Johnson, *The Just War Tradition and the Restraint of War* (Princeton, NJ: Princeton University Press, 1981). A recent application is Nigel Biggar, *In Defence of War* (Oxford, Oxford University Press, 2014).

to wise counsel, counting the cost before building or going to war, and up-holding justice. These are universal, timeless truths that did not expire at the end of the Old Testament. Moreover, the examples of David and Moses are reported alongside the public servants of Egypt and Babylon (Joseph, Nehemiah, Daniel). Their examples are similarly timeless for the public servants of the New Testament era, whether it be Erastus (a city treasurer or public works official mentioned by Paul) or British member of Parliament and antislavery advocate William Wilberforce.

As I have argued elsewhere in this book, what is lacking here and for so many evangelicals is an accounting of the biblical doctrines of *stewardship* and *vocation*. Biblical figures such as Moses, Hezekiah, and Cornelius are not just individuals but also public servants in their roles as soldiers or gov-ernment officials. Augustine, Luther, Calvin, Wesley, and many contem-porary evangelical thinkers, such as Paul Helm,[2] recognize that humans have specific callings in various domains of life and we are all called to various forms of private and collective stewardship. These doctrines are largely missing from Pearse's essay. Christian thinking, from Augustine through today's just war scholars such as James Turner Johnson, J. Daryl Charles, and Marc LiVecche, recognizes that living out a vocation of law enforcement, military service, or other governmental roles can be a divine calling like all other forms of work.

A second fundamental problem in this essay is a lack of understanding of the difference between *force* and *violence*. The author argues, "The threat of violence is an intrinsic prerogative of the state and necessary for main-taining it" (p. 195).

This is a simplistic reading of a more complicated set of issues.[3] Force is lawful, restrained, under authority, and motivated toward the end of peace. Violence, in contrast, is unlawful, unrestrained, often perpetrated by those without authority, and motivated by something other than love. The Bible and the Christian tradition teach that legitimate political authorities have a moral duty to vigilantly employ restrained force to counter lawlessness in

---

[2]Paul Helm's work is among the most influential in evangelical circles. See his widely cited *The Callings: The Gospel in the World* (Edinburgh: Banner of Truth Trust, 1987).

[3]Material in the following two paragraphs is adapted from Eric Patterson, "Just War: 20 Years Since 9/11," Wheaton College, 2021, www.wheaton.edu/academics/academic-centers/wheaton-center -for-faith-politics-and-economics/resource-center/articles/2021/just-war/.

domestic and international society. The key, therefore, lies in motivation and how force is employed. We can tell the difference between firm but loving parental discipline: it is quite different from anger-induced, unrestrained child-beating. So, too, we can tell the difference between law enforcement killing a murderous kidnapper to save a child as contrasted with unlawful police brutality. C. S. Lewis famously paraphrased Martin Luther, "Does anyone suppose that our Lord's hearers understood him to mean that if a homicidal maniac, attempting to murder a third party, tried to knock me out of the way, I must stand aside and let him get his victim?"[4]

In short, violence is different from sheer force: it is illegitimate, unrestrained, beyond the law, motivated by an anger verging on hatred, and dehumanizing. The same holds true with the application of military force in which there is a difference between lawful, restrained, morally guided fighting on the battlefield and immoral, unrestrained violence. The distinction between force and violence is lost in Pearse's chapter. That is unfortunate because it has ramifications for law enforcement, the armed forces, and political leaders who make decisions about national security. Fortunately, this type of moral distinction is in tune with what the Bible has to say, both in the Old Testament, which routinely condemns lawlessness, and in the New (e.g., Rom 13).

Thus far I have challenged two of the author's suppositions, both having to do with key biblical themes that are apparent in both the Old and the New Testaments and that require more sophisticated frames of reference. A third, somewhat histrionic problem can be found here:

> Modern developments in warfare—weapons of mass destruction, suicide terrorism by non-state actors, brutalized child soldiers, and cyberwarfare—have rendered just war criteria more nonsensical than ever, and attempts to make the new developments fit the old categories risk reducing the entire approach to the merest casuistry. (pp. 195-96)

I offer two points for the reader's consideration. The first is historical. The second is moral. First, the reality of human history, such as that of the Roman Empire, the Muslim-era conquests, the Crusades, or later wars, is that war can

---

[4]C. S. Lewis, "Why I Am Not a Pacifist," in *The Weight of Glory and Other Addresses*, ed. Walter Hooper (1949; repr., San Francisco: HarperOne, 2006), 86.

be disastrous and brutal. We have records of ethnic cleansing and barbarism from the Mongols, Romans, and many other peoples. Genghis Khan exterminated entire cities. All of this violence occurred face-to-face: it was total destruction and brutality. Hence, the author's argument that there is something new today in suicide terrorism, child soldiers, and attacks on civilians ultimately fails; these are simply more efficient ways of doing old harms. It is only the scale of modern explosives, not the antagonists or the victims, that is new.

From a moral perspective, how do we even know these things are wrong? How are such distinctions made? We know these things are wrong due to thoughtful Christian just war thinking. It is nonsensical not to be able to make right distinctions between using force to protect the innocent as opposed to rape, pillage, and plunder. It is nonsensical to assume that any conflict between nuclear powers must escalate to full nuclear annihilation: somehow the US-Soviet rivalry avoided this for a half century. It is nonsensical to suggest that sophisticated analyses of a moral and restrained approach to collective self-defense is mere sophistry.

The author writes,

> Although attempts may be made to contain war, they will rarely succeed—
> principally because participants typically weaponize whatever comes to hand,
> *including* the persons, institutions, and supposed laws that are intended to
> contain violence. This can be seen easily in the fact that, in almost all conflicts,
> *both* sides claim to be justified by just war criteria. (p. 195)

I do not dispute that in any conflict, to paraphrase Abraham Lincoln, both sides see their cause as just. But that does not make it so. One of the easiest ways to see the fallacy on this point is the fact that the massive communist armies of the twentieth century, as well as those of other totalitarian regimes, typically must rely on forced conscription. The armies of modern despots typically did not volunteer to protect their flag and fellow citizens: they are not motivated by neighbor love and love of country but are compelled to the trenches. What a difference from the modern volunteer army, such as those in Canada, Australia, the United States, the United Kingdom, and elsewhere! A variety of tangible and intangible benefits are provided to the citizen volunteers of democracies, but when they think a war is immoral, as some did with regard to Vietnam, they push back.

But the larger point made by the author—that attempts to contain war "will rarely succeed"—is inaccurate. For centuries there has been a set of unwritten but widely accepted taboos, such as not assassinating the enemy's monarch. Over the past 150 years there have been deliberate and important efforts to limit the destructiveness of war: the 1863 Lieber Code (which became the Uniform Code of Military Justice of the United States and many other countries), the 1868 St. Petersburg Declaration, the 1907 Hague Convention, the 1949 Geneva Conventions and Genocide Convention, the 1977 Additional Protocols, and various covenants on chemical weapons, nuclear proliferation, conventional weapons, and so on. If "anything goes," the United States would have used its vast power unrestrainedly in Vietnam, Afghanistan, and Iraq. In addition to moral restraint, there are also practical limitations, such as prudence in not retaliating in ways that cause mutually assured destruction. It is groups such as the Islamic State (ISIS) that demonstrate abnormal, unrestrained violence.

In conclusion, let me largely agree, but modify and extend, a point that the author makes. He says,

> Christians are by all means to be peacemakers. But that work comes in three stages:
>
> 1. Moral suasion needs to happen when conflict seems possible but still some way from being actualized.
>
> 2. After conflict is over, peacemaking—whose practitioners Jesus calls "blessed" (Mt 5:9)—consists in the binding up of wounds: literal/physical, social, psychic, and political.
>
> 3. But during conflict itself, the peacemaker is confined largely to persuading parties of the futility of pursuing war—that is, of pragmatics— along with holding individuals back from atrocities. (p. 196)

Yes, the Bible teaches that all Christians are called to be peacemakers. In our daily lives, in all of our relationships, we are to be peacemakers. That is true at home, at work, at church, in our neighborhood, and everywhere we go: we are to be at peace, as much as is possible, with everyone. Some people, such as police and military personnel, are also called to keep the peace. In other words, when it comes to life in society, there are different ways that Christians may be preserve or advance peace.

The US military as well as humanitarian agencies provide a helpful framework here by delineating five phases of conflict. Experts in these arenas understand that there is a long prewar phase before bullets fly in any conventional sort of conflict as when countries plan and prepare for contingencies (phase 0) and when formal diplomacy, led by ambassadors and representatives from the US Department of State or the British Foreign and Commonwealth Office, for example, are at work (phase 1). At the same time, members of civil society engage in innumerable activities designed to advance peace and the common good, including, for example, "track two diplomacy," which refers to nongovernmental actors who advance peace and dispel misunderstanding by engaging one another and/or government agencies outside of traditional government-to-government channels.

Clearly, when it comes to the prewar phases of international relations, there is much space in which Christians might be engaged. For instance, Christians (and other faith-based groups) are often the ones who attempt to ameliorate the conditions of poverty and instability that might make some believe that war is necessary in the first place. Often there are Christians, based on their clerical authority as bishops or priests or due to their leadership of faith-based NGOs (e.g., the president of World Vision or Catholic Relief Services), who have private channels of communication that can be utilized for the purposes of communication and safe meetings. This track two diplomacy can also bring belligerents into a safe space for dialogue to end war. The Catholic Church provided such relationships and space for the end of Mozambique's civil war in 1992; similarly, in 2019, the pope and the archbishop of Canterbury worked to bring South Sudan's warring factions to the Vatican for a retreat to advance peace. As has been documented elsewhere, such individuals and organizations can play a similar role in providing a sanctuary for negotiations to end other conflicts.[5]

When political instability goes beyond tension to outright conflict (phases 2–3), Christians are also needed on the battlefield, from the highest

---

[5]See Eric Patterson, "Religion, War, and Peace: Leavening the Levels of Analysis," in *Handbook of Religion and Security*, ed. Chris Seiple, Dennis R. Hoover, and Pauletta Otis (London: Routledge, 2012), and Eric Patterson, *Politics in a Religious World: Building a Religiously Informed US Foreign Policy* (New York: Continuum, 2011).

leadership posts down to army privates in the trenches. This is where I obviously disagree with Pearse. We want such individuals to be motivated by neighbor love and a commitment to justice, which will translate into not only love of one's family at home and love of one's country but also love of one's comrades and love of those who need protecting or defending, based on a commitment to restrained force in pursuit of a better security. At war's end (phase 4), we need Christians to be serving in law enforcement and in the justice system to punish wrongdoing, restrain future wrong, and help establish a just and enduring order. We also want Christians in the medical and mental health services to provide succor and treatment.

It is noteworthy that the first to leave are the UN peacekeepers or the invading forces, leaving many local people behind in situations of injury, destitution, and loss. Often Christians and other faith-based actors commit to demonstrate true long-term charity by caring for the needs of average citizens affected by war in places such as Africa, central Asia, Latin America, and the Far East.

Sadly, it is rare to hear pastors and priests laud the work of such professionals and equally rare for congregations to join in prayer for warriors, politicians, diplomats, and aid workers who are responding—at their own peril—to the geopolitical hazards of fallen humanity. We live in a sinful and insecure world. Some Christians are called to work in situations of violence and instability to help their fellow human beings. This is why Christian thinking and action are needed in times of war and peace.

A Nonviolence Response

MYLES WERNTZ

Meic Pearse's argument for the church historical view turns on two intertwining theses. It may be the case that (1) pacifism and just war do in fact have much to commend themselves each within Scripture, but (2) because war is a "radical evil," neither one is applicable as a coherent moral position. Pearse's essay opens with two grotesque scenes, one from Sierra Leone and one from September 11, 2001—worst-case scenarios for a pacifist—meant to display the limits of moral thinking to real-world instances (pp. 169-72). And though Pearse's intent is not to argue against only pacifists, these scenes of catastrophic violence present an intoxicating possibility: perhaps whatever scriptural ethic there is surrounding violence is not only impossible but inapplicable as well. In what follows, I will argue that not only does Pearse's hermeneutic for the relationship between Scripture and the moral life have difficulties, but it fails to see that purity is not the aim for a scriptural ethic, but fidelity.

THE LIMITS OF A BIBLICIST HERMENEUTIC

Pearse's argument offers one and a half cheers for both pacifism and the just war, offering that pacifism has the stronger historical and scriptural case because of the New Testament evidence and the witness of the earliest Christian writings. But, on the practical front, pacifism does not stand up to the test of such horror, not because the position is without warrant, but because "war is a radical evil" that confounds the moral framework which constrains the exercise of both pacifism and just war (p. 58). The emergence of new forms of violence, such as cyberwarfare, terrorism, and nuclear arms, demarks a new boundary that is "more insusceptible of moral regulation" (p. 191). Whether with respect to terrorism, which does not openly identify itself as an enemy, or cyberwarfare, which does violence but without bloodshed, the old frames cannot match the modern challenges.

While Pearse is, in my view, correct about how to read the scriptural witness on this question, his position emerges at a high cost: the wisdom of Scripture with respect to conflict is no longer applicable in our complex modern world. Pearse, then, offers an old criticism: whatever might have been applicable of the Scriptures or in the second and third centuries no longer obtains in practice today because of the shift in the culture of war. Curiously, Pearse does not hold the same position on other aspects of Scripture, calling the gospel "universal," in that it "appeals to all people everywhere" (p. 175). The question that is left unanswered here is this: On what basis is it the case that Jesus' proclamation of the kingdom of God—proclaimed in a first-century tongue that has gone extinct, and to an agrarian audience that no longer exists—"universal," while the nonviolence teachings and practices that are derived from Jesus and of the New Testament are not?

To follow this logic consistently, one of two things would have to be true:

Either (1) "gospel" (a linguistically proclaimed and culturally laden concept) logically befalls the same fate as other similarly conceived elements (i.e., the moral teachings) of the New Testament, and is irretrievable from the past, or (2) the gospel is able to move in and through cultures in a way that is malleable and intelligible across cultures—while the moral frameworks dependent on Scripture are not.

Neither one is desirable.

In the first case, the Scriptures—including the gospel—are simply artifacts, cultural products that would require a very specific world for them be intelligible. "Gospel" would be simply a sociocultural word in a particularly Palestinian context, which requires that linguistic world in order to be intelligible. In the second case, while the gospel is rescued from the recesses of the first-century world, the ethics, metaphors, cultural forms, forms of witness, and practices of the Bible are all left within layers inaccessible to the modern world: the idea of the gospel escapes its historical epoch, but only as an idea, not an embodied reality. Likewise, this seems to defy the way in which gospel operates in Scripture, not as an idea, but intertwined with particular practices of gathering, sharing resources, eating, worshiping, and the like.

The culprit for this dilemma is not Pearse's vision of "gospel"—transcultural, binding, available to all persons in all times. The culprit here is that, in his reading of Scripture, "gospel" functions in one way (unrestricted by time), while the ethics that make theological realities visible within Scripture are treated as time-bound. Insofar as we find "gospel" maintaining a central core within the preaching and teaching of the New Testament, so too we find the ethics of the New Testament functioning; for without practices, our reading of the Scripture becomes simply a set of ideas apart from the transfiguration of bodies, churches, and worlds. More specifically, Christian moral approaches to war are treated as immovable relics that have not in fact developed and, as such, must be left in the ancient cultures in which they were first articulated.

I will limit my comments to his treatment of the pacifist position to show this. In his explication of the scriptural roots of pacifism, Pearse offers a common objection—that pacifism is apolitical, restricted to the personal. Delineating between Romans 12 and Romans 13, Pearse offers the common reading that Jesus—in commending nonviolence—is referencing a kingdom "not of this world" (i.e., one apart from the realm of public politics): the specter of the Anabaptist Schleitheim Confession looms large here in Pearse's assumptions. He then draws the conclusion that the "New Testament . . . eschews any program for running society or creating nations" (p. 180), with the assumption that any commitment to pacifism necessarily means either abdicating public life or leaving pacifism behind as a relic of a primitive age in which Christians did not have the complications of public participation.

In his description of nonviolence, Pearse binds nonviolence to a specific (and arguably dubious) apolitical ethic derived from Romans 12, while leaving off other avenues developed by later Christians. For example, the teaching of Jesus in Matthew 5 regarding love of enemy and of nonretaliation is deployed by Jesus as a way to challenge the violence of the guards, to deflate the power of Pilate, and to negate the retributive actions of his own disciples. In each instance, the nonviolence exercised did far more than mend interpersonal fences, but enacted a very public vision of a political world in which violence was not the law. Likewise, in Colossians 1:24, Paul's reference to suffering for the Colossians—embracing the physical suffering given him by his enemies—is for the sake of extending the gospel mission into the far reaches of the empire: Paul's willingness to turn the other cheek literally extends the physical mission of a gospel that converts the empire.

Aside from being something other than an apolitical and interpersonal ethic, incapable of infiltrating the complex public square of governance and the common good, what we find in Scripture is a complex refusal to enact violence that is already *within Scripture* improvising to meet the complexity of violence. It is not as if "violence" was understood to mean simply one thing in the first four centuries of Scripture and somehow becomes unruly in the twenty-first century. Both within Scripture and within the patristic era, defenders of this ethic rooted it in various reasons, ranging from its association with blood to its incompatibility with the liturgy to the idolatry embedded within the Roman imperium: violence is manifold and requires a manifold response.

It is possible to take the approach, which Pearse does not, that scriptural ethics can be carried forth as *principles*: that nonviolence is an ethos not bound to particular cultural logics, but—like "gospel"—deployable in multiple times and places. Such an approach has been taken by others, but it too carries the cost of rescuing Scripture from the iron cage of history as a set of ideas. Christianity and the gospel message are a matter of apprenticeship and improvisation: disciples are sent by apostles, learning the saving faith of the gospel at the hands of others, and then going out into new worlds and new contexts to make that faith known. Over and over again, we find this to be true in church history, that gospel expands in its meaning and scope, much like reflections on various moral questions within the Christian life.

Mark Douglas's recent work on Christian pacifism in an environmental age is instructive here.[1] By examining the ways in which Christian pacifism has become pluriform (a movement already seen within Scripture), he demonstrates how Christian pacifism's development is not a departure from some original purity. Rather, because the Scripture is already embedded within the world, the ethic of Scripture—consistent with gospel—develops not only to meet the evolutions of violence but also because traditions within the world are not static. Carried forth by the living body of the church, nonviolence has gone through various iterations—from the peace

---

[1] Mark Douglas, *Christian Pacifism for an Environmental Age* (Cambridge: Cambridge University Press, 2019).

of God of the Middle Ages to the more dramatic forms of the Franciscans to the Anabaptists to the more secularized statecraft versions of the eighteenth century and beyond. Joined by the common presumption, which Pearse rightly affirms, that pacifism is consistent with the Scripture, these various versions continued to bear witness to cultures very different from the one of Scripture.

THE RETRIEVAL OF SCRIPTURE AND THE RECOVERY OF THE WORLD

Locking pacifism (or just war) into the originating cultural framework is not a new move, but it comes with a real danger, not only for moral thinking, but also for how we understand Scripture. Naming war as a "radical evil" is dangerous, for in describing war as a moral activity that falls beyond the purview of Scripture's framework, he also makes war into an activity that is irredeemable and that Scripture cannot speak into in a morally cohesive way. War, in its modern permutations, becomes an abyss from which the participants are unable to be saved, and one into which the Scriptures and their God cannot reach. But nothing could be further from the truth. It is true, to the point of being almost banal, that the world of Scripture is not the modern world, but that is far different from saying that the Scriptures have no connection to the questions of the modern world.

In recognizing the ways in which Scripture's ethics—as part of the very gospel being spread from the Jews to the Gentiles—are part of a living tradition, we are freed not only from seeing Scripture as unable to speak to war's modern form but also from limiting Scripture's reach into the world as well. Part of the legacy of early Christian pacifism is the ways in which early interpreters like Origen typologically read the Old Testament in ways that not only took the teeth from attempts to reenact the violence of the Old Testament but also gave new tools to the ethics of Jesus. Because the Old Testament anticipates its fulfillment, the violence of Joshua is not simply a relic to be tossed away, but speaks to the ways in which Christians continue to wrestle against sin. It is put to new service, given new breath, and set free to address not only the body of violence but also the soul.[2] What

---

[2]Origen, *Homilies on Joshua*, trans. Barbara J. Bruce, ed. Cynthia White, Fathers of the Church (Washington, DC: Catholic University Press of America, 2002).

is needed here is to follow the example of Scripture and of Scripture's earliest interpreters and to remember that the Scriptures continue to speak long after their cultural world has died. Pearse, in dividing the Scriptures from the modern world of war, does so to keep us from making wooden applications of Scripture to complex modern questions, but inadvertently consigns the world to answering theo-ethical quandaries without recourse to the Scriptures.

"The world" was never singular, even within Scripture, but this was no difficulty even then. As the apostles traveled the Roman world with the gospel, there were commonalities that persisted, most centrally the resurrection of Jesus from the dead. But the gospel presentation, or elements of Paul's teaching, were not the same every time: as Paul traveled, his reasoning in the synagogues wound through the law en route to Christ, while appealing to pagan poets and reason when with the Gentiles. And so it is with the ethics of the gospel as well. The Christian ethics of pacifism have expanded since the age of Scripture, and now play in ten thousand fields, bringing peace to various faces of violence.[3] But it is always in expansion and imitation of the same Jesus who disarmed Peter, taught his disciples to turn the other cheek, and forgave the soldiers who murdered him.

---

[3]See Myles Werntz and David C. Cramer, *A Field Guide to Christian Nonviolence: Key Thinkers, Activists, and Movements for the Gospel of Peace* (Grand Rapids, MI: Baker Academic, 2022).

A Christian Realist Response

A. J. NOLTE

Given that Meic Pearse's thought-provoking essay rejects both pacifism and just war based on his reading of church history, it is appropriate to focus the bulk of my response on these issues. I will also freely confess that most of what follows is my (nonspecialist) interpretation of that history, drawn from personal and professional studies in both Christian political thought and, separately, preparation for Anglican holy orders.

In his essay, Pearse argues against what he describes as "the tendency of some evangelicals—to insist that they can leap across two millennia and grasp 'what the Bible says' without any context" (p. 181). I heartily agree with this condemnation, and would extend it also to church history. Yet, where ante-Nicene perspectives on war are concerned, I think many church historians default to this text-without-context approach. This is, I suspect, because the modern evangelical supposition that one Christian's interpretation is as good as any other is too deeply ingrained to do otherwise. This was decidedly not the way the early church saw things. Local councils, episcopal pronouncements, canons, and so on had much more weight than individual theological opinion.

While Augustine was the first theologian to develop the "two cities" metaphor in a systematically theological way, the reality is that, institutionally, it was more than a metaphor. Just as it borrowed philosophy from the Greeks, the church assiduously copied Rome's municipal institutions, notably the idea of the urban diocese overseen by an *episkopos*, or bishop. Whatever one's own ecclesiological assumptions, it is a pretty clear matter of history that the authority of bishops over local churches and, theoretically at least, bishops in council over a wider swath of the church depending on the council, was well-established by the time of Justin Martyr. (The speculated holdouts were Alexandria and, ironically, Rome, and Rome at least had regular bishops by then.) Thus, if we are to mine the church fathers for "evidential value," we must put this evidence in the context of a church hierarchy that, by as early as 150 and probably earlier, had authoritative mechanisms for resolving intra-Christian disputes. This is not to say that vast theological diversity didn't exist—it did—but rather that the absence of any official pronouncement on a contentious issue meant an absence of consensus in a local area, let alone the church as a whole.

In this context, it is significant that there is no evidence of any conciliar decree or canon or authoritative episcopal pronouncement regarding Christian participation in war before 314—the year after Constantine's ascension to the West, ten years before his ascension to rule over the whole empire, and eleven years before Nicaea, the first of the ecumenical councils. In 314, there was one such pronouncement at the Council of Arles, called by Constantine, which called for the excommunication of conscientious objectors. While this was almost certainly done under pressure from Constantine, it is hard to imagine bishops who had just suffered extreme persecution under Diocletian meekly overturning a widely held three-hundred-year consensus against participation in war, if it existed, just because Constantine asked them to do so and promised future benefits if they did. The evidence of Arles is far from conclusive, but it tends to cut against the idea of a universal or near-universal pre-Constantinian pacifist consensus.

At the same time, a council in Ancyra (modern-day Ankara), in territory held by Constantine's pagan co-emperor Licinius, provided penitential canons for both involuntary homicide and willful murder, but was silent on the question of Christian soldiers who had killed in war. Aside from these very late and, in different ways, inconclusive local councils, there is basically nothing. Pearse does cite a statement by Cyprian, bishop of Carthage, which is the closest we have to a bishop taking a position critical of Christian participation in war. Even so, Cyprian, who was noted as a strict disciplinarian, issued no canons forbidding Christians from participating in war, requiring them to abstain from sacraments if they did. Hippolytus, whom Pearse also cites, did issue such prohibitions. But Hippolytus was an antipope, who specifically rejected the authority of his bishop because he considered that bishop not rigorous enough. This rejection of his bishop's authority placed Hippolytus well out of the mainstream by Christians at the time he wrote, and so while we can learn something from his liturgical works, he probably ought to be taken with a grain of salt where matters of the rigors of Christian discipline and practice are concerned.

This absence of evidence is significant because we do have ample evidence that Christians served as soldiers and fought in Rome's wars. Two examples suffice to make the point clear. First, there is archaeological evidence. As Philip Wynn explains, "The recent archaeological find of a Christian place of worship within the fort of Dura Europos in Roman Mesopotamia indicates that by the early third century not only were there significant numbers of Christians in the army, but that to some extent their presence had received at least tacit 'official' recognition."[1] This permission was sometimes more than tacit. "Julius Africanus was probably born ca. 160 in Jerusalem," Destina Iosif explains. "He regarded himself as a Christian, took part in the expedition of emperor Septimius Severus (193–211) against the Osrhoenes in 195, established a library in the Pantheon in Rome for Severus Alexander (222–235), was an ambassador of the colony of veterans at Emmaus-Nicopolis, composed works on Christianity and works on military topics, and still was regarded as a Christian and respected by significant Christian theologians like Origen, Eusebius and Jerome."[2] If there was a Christian place of worship at a Roman fort near the Persian border—an area that, given the endemic hostilities between Rome and Persia, may well have seen combat—and a well-known Christian figure who served as a close military associate of a Roman emperor, then the issue cannot have been a generally settled one. Indeed, the fact that men like Tertullian and Hippolytus felt the need to criticize fellow Christians for serving in the Roman military proves that they were, in fact, doing so in sufficient numbers that attempts to make them stop were deemed necessary. In short, Christians were serving in the Roman military before Constantine, other Christians were seeking to forbid

---

[1]Philip Wynn, "War and Military Service in Early Western Christian Thought, 200–850" (PhD diss., University of Notre Dame, 2011), Umi Dissertation number 3492609 (2012), 68.
[2]Destina Iosif, *Early Christian Attitudes to War, Violence and Military Service* (Piscataway, NJ: Gorgias Press, 2013), 2.

them from doing so, and none of the extant records of local councils we have indicate that the church felt the need to clarify the dispute.

How can we make sense of this absence of evidence? I suggest that, once again, contextualizing those thinkers most identified with a strongly oppositional stance toward Christian participation in war is useful. Tertullian, Hippolytus, and to a lesser extent Origen and Cyprian all fell on one side of the most intense ante-Nicene argument in pastoral theology: that between the rigorists and the laxists. In general, this debate revolved around two related issues: what accommodations, if any, could be made with pagan culture, and what was to be done with those Christians who lapsed from their faith in the face of persecution? Rigorists, unsurprisingly, took a more uncompromising position on both issues, while laxists were more accommodating. Hippolytus was something of an ultra-rigorist, going into schism against the bishop of Rome due to the latter's laxist sympathies. Tertullian was also a known rigorist, before his rigorism eventually led him to an association with the heretical Montanist sect that believed their founder, Montanus, was the incarnation of the Holy Spirit. Cyprian, regarded as orthodox by subsequent generations in the East and West, followed somewhat after the pattern of his North African predecessor Tertullian, taking a more rigorist position than the bishop of Rome at the time, though not so staunchly as Tertullian or Hippolytus. Eventually, after the great persecution under Diocletian, North African rigorism would become so extreme as to largely cut itself off from the church entirely during the Donatist schism—a schism so enduring that it persisted into Augustine's day.

Insofar as there is any evidence of early Christian conflict over soldiers participating in war, I believe it was most likely subsumed into this broader conflict. The divide was only intensified by the great persecution under Diocletian, from which Constantine, by any fair reckoning, delivered the church. A common impression of Constantine is that he imposed a kind of heavy-handed coercion or co-optation on the Christian church—a narrative that, it must be admitted, the Council of Arles reinforces. Yet, when it came to matters of theology and intra-church disputes, Constantine's clear preference was for the various factions to stop fighting one another—a state of affairs he was never able to achieve. Yet, as more and more pagans became

Christian, rigorism either diminished or, in some cases, transformed itself, as monks replaced martyrs as the idealized holy men of late antiquity.

It should be noted that I described men like Tertullian and Hippolytus as strongly opposed to Christian participation in war, and not as pacifists. This is because it is not entirely clear to me that the opposition to war expressed by ante-Nicene rigorists is actually pacifism. There is Tertullian's ambiguity, revealed in his assertion that Christians pray for the bravery of Roman armies, and expanded on by Origen's claim that Rome won its military victories due to Christian prayers. Wynn argues that this perspective is far from an outlier: "Christian writers repeatedly expressed for centuries thereafter, both in the action of historical narratives and in explicit statements, the idea that prayer, though increasingly only that of the clergy, could actually effect divine intervention in matters of war, and that in the end prayers were more effective in battle than weapons."[3]

The conception of the church here is not that of the distinctly separate city envisioned by Augustine and institutionalized by bishops and diocese, but rather analogous to the relationship contemporary pagan, Christian, and Jewish thinkers imagined between the body (the world) and the soul (the church). As the very early but anonymous Epistle to Diognetus states,

> The distinction between Christians and other men is neither in country nor language nor customs. For they do not dwell in cities in some place of their own, nor do they use any strange variety of dialect, nor practise an extraordinary kind of life. . . . Yet while living in Greek and barbarian cities, according as each obtained his lot, and following the local customs both in clothing and food and in the rest of life, they show forth the wonderful and confessedly strange character of the constitution of their own citizenship. . . . To put it shortly, what the soul is in the body, that the Christians are in the world.[4]

Just as the soul must be kept clean, the rigorists argued, so too must the church be kept clean. Yet, as society became Christianized, that need for purity, while not eliminated, necessarily had to shift. Thus, the burden of preserving the purity of society's soul moved from the general Christian laity to the clergy, and the monastic clergy in particular. If what we have,

---

[3]Wynn, "War and Military Service," 66.
[4]*Letter to Diognetus*, in *From Irenaeus to Grotius: A Sourcebook in Christian Political Thought*, ed. Oliver O'Donovan and Joan Lockwood O'Donovan (Grand Rapids, MI: Eerdmans, 1999), 12.

then, is a less than universal sense that participation in war is impermissible because of the need for Christians to maintain purity as they approach God to pray for military victory, can we actually describe this pre-Constantinian rigorism as pacifist? I would argue that it leads just as naturally to either just war or a Niebuhrian-style Christian realism as it does to pacifism.

Let me make a final point specific to a more modern exponent of the "dirty-hands" Christian realist perspective: Reinhold Niebuhr. Niebuhr's answer to the question Pearse poses at the beginning of his essay is, I think, relatively clear: pick up the gun and defend your village from the child soldiers. To stand aside and allow others to suffer, or to allow others to sin in your place, would have been inconsistent with Niebuhr's ethic. I believe the Cappadocian fathers and many Orthodox thinkers who, in my view, share a Christian realist perspective that we call Niebuhrian today, would have agreed with him on this point. In fact, there is much in Pearse's perspective that comes close to Niebuhrian Christian realism: a sense that pacifists and just warriors alike are too neatly resolving the paradoxes of Scripture where war is concerned; a recognition of the evil in war; and a further recognition that war is, short of the eschaton, endemic to the human condition. Yet Niebuhr would, I think, differ from Pearse practically. For Niebuhr, the law of love led to what I'd call a bias toward action. Weighing the evil of war and the evil of totalitarianism in the balance, Niebuhr at times found war the less tragic of the two. This is not to diminish his concept of the tragedy of war, but rather to emphasize what he saw as the greater tragedy Nazi and Soviet tyranny would impose. At other times, such as the Vietnam War for example, Niebuhr came to different conclusions. From the Cappadocians to Niebuhr, proponents of the dirty-hands strand of Christian realism have been content to call war evil—yet they also argue that the realities of the fallen world mean that, under certain circumstances, Christians must engage in it nonetheless.

Church Historical Rejoinder

MEIC PEARSE

It is, of course, impossible to contribute to a volume such as this one without straining at least a little at the bounds of Christian charity by treading on the toes of one's fellow authors—and being stomped on in one's turn. Still more challenging is the fact that disagreements over the particular issue in question—in this case, war and peace—stem from a veritable mountain of disagreement entailing entire theologies, ecclesiologies, and hermeneutics. To lock horns on issue x is, without the utmost restraint by all parties, to drag in fundamental presuppositions about what it means to be a Christian. This difficulty is barely assuaged by the fact that all of us own to being evangelical. Still, we try.

Concerning Eric Patterson's opening broadside, I certainly plead guilty to having read different books from those he has read himself—and am sorry that we might differ as to who counts as the "best historians," or that his choices in that regard are weightier than my own references to the church fathers. Neither am I ignorant of the Schleitheim Confession—which, by unfortunate coincidence, I refer to in my reply to Werntz (and not, as Patterson rightly points out, in my main contribution).

But precisely this awkward coincidence illustrates one of the principal differences between my own approach and Patterson's. His case relies—excessively, in my mind—on authority—a magisterium, if you will. The theologians of Christendom ("Christian states") and their latter-day successors who have, by the nature of the case, dominated Christendom's institutions, and whose dicta—like their underlying assumptions—are repeated by one another, have an accumulated authority. I am very far from wanting to scrap all of this on the basis of some spurious "first principles" reasoning, like Thomas Paine's woefully unprophetic tilting against Edmund Burke.[1] (For, as modernism has borne out, almost anything could then be justified.) Nevertheless, we cannot ignore the contexts in which Christian leaders write. And, in general, the closer early church fathers were to the period of the New Testament, the closer they were (not uniformly, but in their general tenor) to its central ethos and emphases. Hence my repeated citations of *early* church fathers—whereas people of Patterson's persuasion are generally reduced to general references to the later Augustine (if fighting shy of quoting some of his rather distasteful arguments for just war). From Augustine, the line of descent through Patterson's chosen authorities is clear.

In his response to me, Patterson perpetuates a tendency notable in his principal essay: an overwhelming emphasis on modern Western (and especially US) examples. The obvious rejoinder to that observation is that this book is designed for an audience of the living and the Western. But I would respond that, outside of that context, the generalized theory would seem to most readers abhorrent. We have, then, an all too neat fit between a particular theology and his (and, mostly, our) political preferences. Any remaining Marxists (whose worldview is largely nonsense, of course) can afford the rare luxury of laughing up their sleeves; for them, all appeals to religion are cloaked (or self-delusional) appeals to the mundane (or, as they would say, "real") interests of the party in question.

Where I would concede to Patterson is in his criticism of my incautious use of the word *violence* when *force* would have been more circumspect. I was using the term in a loose or generic sense, and was not thereby implying that such uses of force were ipso facto illegitimate. On that, at least, I retract.

Concerning Myles Werntz's critique from the perspective of nonviolence, it appears either that he has misunderstood my position to some extent or

---

[1]The literary clash between these titans in the early 1790s concerned the significance of the French Revolution. Paine was the more "arresting" writer—but it was Burke's fears that were borne out by events in the form of the Terror (mass executions of royals, priests, and anti-revolutionaries) of 1793. Paine was certain that tradition was so much hokum that could be swept away by the abstract principles of the revolutionaries: "Every generation is, and must be, competent to all the purposes which its occasions require. It is the living, and not the dead, that are to be accommodated." Thomas Paine, *Rights of Man*, ed. Henry Collins (Harmondsworth, UK: Penguin, 1977), 63-64.

that I have failed to make myself quite clear. He summarizes my view as being that "the wisdom of Scripture with respect to conflict is no longer applicable in our complex modern world" (p. 205). This is a point on which he expatiates at some length. It is a misunderstanding to which, I fear, I may have contributed.

My actual view is that the New Testament evidence is at least somewhat ambiguous—which is, of course, why both pacifists and protagonists of just war can both appeal to its authority (though, to be sure, generally to different texts). In point of fact, I maintain that there is no simple New Testament view on this topic, for reasons I have already rehearsed. Certainly, I do *not* maintain that the gospel or any of its teachings are redundant, whether in modern or any other circumstances. Nor do I separate out "gospel" and "ethics" as he implies.

Werntz's accusation that I think "any commitment to pacifism necessarily means . . . abdicating public life" (p. 206) or that "pacifism [can be left] behind as a relic of a primitive age in which Christians did not have the complications of public participation" (p. 206) is, however, nearer the mark. As I have said in my principal essay, modern social conditions in which ordinary people, including Christians, can participate freely in public life raise new questions that did not exist in the early centuries. But new circumstances in themselves could never allow us to override original New Testament principles: my point is that it is questionable whether pacifism is an unambiguous principle of the early church.

I am not sure I understand what kind of world is in Werntz's mind when he claims that Matthew 5 "enacted a very public vision of a political world in which violence was not the law" (p. 206). Of course, I think that Matthew 5 does nothing of the sort. If he means that the renunciation of force can be a "public vision of a political world," then he has forgone the principal admirable quality of Christian pacifism and, in seeking to disarm the persuadable, would deliver the world into the hands of the darkest forces of the world. Suddenly, the protagonists of just war have a point after all!

It seems a little unjust to point at my highlighting of the modern complexities of war as if I were thereby formulating an argument for changing our ethics. I point to those complexities merely in order to highlight the impossibility, in its starkest guise, of the just war criteria.

Werntz is on firmer ground, however, when he argues that "in describing war as a moral activity that falls beyond the purview of Scripture's framework, [Pearse] also makes war into an activity . . . that Scripture cannot speak into in a morally cohesive way. War . . . becomes an abyss . . . into which the Scriptures and their God cannot reach" (p. 208). That is a stark way of putting the matter. And, of course, I do not quite mean what he describes. With Dietrich Bonhoeffer, I would want to say that there will be occasions when we cannot but be tainted by sin. And that war throws up such occasions more frequently than any other human activity. That, in choosing the lesser evil, we are nevertheless choosing evil. "To make non-resistance a principle for secular life," says Bonhoeffer, "is to deny God, by undermining his gracious ordinance for the preservation of the world. But Jesus is no draughtsman of political blueprints."[2]

A. J. Nolte's critique is perhaps the gentlest of the three. Perhaps this is due to the fact that he and I both eschew the more formulaic answers of the two traditional schools of thought; both of us are keenly aware of how every historical occasion of conflict, much though it may have in common with its predecessors, is also unique in the dilemmas it poses for those who wish to act rightly in the world.

I heartily agree also with his warning that what I have called "the tendency of some evangelicals—to insist that they can leap across two millennia and grasp 'what the Bible says' without any context" should be extended to church history. I shall be mightily disheartened, however, if I am guilty of the reproof implied; I have spent my entire career seeking to let the dead speak to us in terms that they themselves would have recognized!

Nolte's slightly disingenuous self-description as a "nonspecialist" in church history made me smile—for he proceeds to give us a master class in that discipline (albeit from rather more of a "high" ecclesiological perspective than my own). Indeed, I find little to reply to in the bulk of his response. His treatment of the early church fathers is exemplary in seeking to account for their positions in terms that they themselves would have recognized and assented to (though his remarks about Tertullian are a little unfair).

---

[2]Dietrich Bonhoeffer, *The Cost of Discipleship* (New York: Macmillan, 1979), 161.

He highlights the ongoing pastoral debates in the early centuries between rigorists and their opponents, and concludes, "Insofar as there is any evidence of early Christian conflict over soldiers participating in war, I believe it was most likely subsumed into this broader conflict" (p. 213). Well, precisely! Did Christians take a negative view of warfare in a society inclined to glorify it? Yes. Was this negativity absolute, to the point that there were no soldiers in the churches? No. Were there other issues, apart from the use of force, dissuading Christians from being in the military? Yes.

I do part ways with Nolte, of course, in the conclusions he draws from this mixed picture. His hero, Niebuhr—like mine, Bonhoeffer—sees that the Christian acting in the world will have "dirty hands." But for Niebuhr, this seems to be a relatively dispassionate, or "rational" conclusion; for Bonhoeffer, the dirty hands are acquired amid weeping and wailing. There is an analogy here between the standard Protestant doctrine of "justification by faith" and Bonhoeffer's. For the former, it is a proposition, "a spiritual principle"—a part of systematic doctrine; for the latter, it is bound up with discipleship: "The only man who has the right to say that he is justified by grace alone is the man who has left all to follow Christ."[3] The difference is a recognition of the enormity of what is happening.

In the same way, I was a little horrified at Nolte's assured reply to what I had intended as a purely rhetorical question: "Pick up the gun and defend your village from the child soldiers" (p. 215). For me, at least, the dilemma I had posed was "rhetorical" in the sense that there could be no answer that is not horrific, that is not undertaken with fear and trembling. Both Nolte and I reject the formulaic, straightforward answers of just war and pacifism; I would have been glad if he could have joined me at this point also.

---

[3] Bonhoeffer, *Cost of Discipleship*, 55.

Concluding Remarks

PAUL COPAN

In his work on Scripture and violence, biblical scholar
L. Daniel Hawk notes two prominent threads of interpretation. One "seeks
to recover and live out the pristine, pre-Constantinian commitment to nonviolence that prevailed among Christians when they occupied the outskirts
of power."[1] The other thread "sees a shift but not a radical break, nor a turn
from biblical teachings."[2] From this perspective, Hawk notes,

> God adapts as God has always done in concert with human partners and
> within human systems throughout the ages. Christians are to work within
> the system because God continues to be present within the system. Ethical
> reflection takes place within a complex of factors that require those at the
> center to make hard decisions that affect thousands of lives.[3]

He continues,

> Though this dichotomy is overdrawn and there are nuanced perspectives be-
> tween the poles, the point is to engage in conversation with believers who are
> equally faithful, thoughtful, and sincere. Each can sharpen the other's po-
> sition: challenging, holding accountable, considering the alternatives, how
> both sides can engage in peacemaking, etc.[4]

This four-views volume embraces this type of conversation between
"equally faithful, thoughtful, and sincere" Christian scholars who

[1] L. Daniel Hawk, *The Violence of the Biblical God: Canonical Narrative and Christian Faith* (Grand
Rapids, MI: Eerdmans 2019), 208.
[2] Hawk, *Violence of the Biblical God*, 208.
[3] Hawk, *Violence of the Biblical God*, 208.
[4] Hawk, *Violence of the Biblical God*, 208.

sharpen and challenge each other to refine, enrich, and illuminate the discussion.

In this spirit, I offer some concluding remarks by drawing some strands together by making certain observations as well as reflecting on the Scriptures as they speak to the two positions on the spectrum: *morally permissible killing* (just war) at the one end and *no killing ever permitted* (nonviolence/pacifism) at the other—and the other two located between them (Christian realism and church historical). Technically, one could extend the end of the spectrum to include *jihad/holy war*, and doing so would position just war *between* jihad and nonviolence. But we here are talking about a range of normative *Christian* alternatives.

In all of this interaction, I trust that readers will likewise be sharpened and challenged by this engaging interaction.

OBSERVATIONS ABOUT THE CONVERSATION

As with similar Christian multi-views books, each contributor begins with particular theological starting points. In addition to focusing on specific biblical texts, contributors may draw on this or that strand of a particular Christian tradition, and they will appeal to specific moral intuitions and certain attendant lines of argumentation. Although philosophical and theological perspectives may often assist us with matters of integration or clarification on a certain topic, evangelicals recognize that the Scriptures are the Christian's ultimate authority and guide, and that tradition—theological, philosophical, or otherwise—is subordinate to Scripture (e.g., Mt 15:1-11; Col 2:8).[5] These Scriptures reveal to us who Jesus is and how we are to live out our earthly lives while imitating him and following in his steps.

Another observation is that these contributors share the same Christ-centered concern for neighbor love and for peace and peacemaking. The second greatest commandment is to love our neighbor as ourselves. But what are the entailments of this love? Could it also include the attempt to protect the innocent—lethally, if necessary—from evil persons intending to harm and exterminate?

---

[5]See Kevin J. Vanhoozer, *Biblical Authority After Babel* (Grand Rapids, MI: Brazos, 2016), as well as Vanhoozer's response to Matthew Levering in *Was the Reformation a Mistake?* (Grand Rapids, MI: Zondervan, 2017).

As for peace(making), the contributors recognize that through Christ, God has made peace with us (Rom 5:1), and he calls us to the blessing and responsibility of being peacemakers (Mt 5:9; 1 Pet 3:11). Now, no contributor would agree to a "peace at any price" idea. For example, peace with God does not come without repentance, and peace with others does not ignore the violation of justice. But what does Christian peacemaking encompass, and what are its limits? With peace (and justice) as its end, could war or policing be justly conducted?

A third observation follows from the second. All parties would agree that every reasonable effort should be made to avoid violence before it erupts. The inherent stance of Christian pacifism serves as an ongoing reminder and a helpful check that we first seek out pathways of reconciliation and also of promoting the gospel with its transforming message of peace. On the other hand, peace-loving just warriors would argue that a strong military may serve as deterrent against saber-rattling nations, geopolitical bullies, or potential terrorist groups who would otherwise do their worst; such a deterrence could be secured without firing a single shot ("peace through strength").

Another consideration is this: if the just warrior is correct that the taking of non-innocent life may be morally permissible through policing or soldiering, it seems that the church and Christian theologians could play an important role in cooperation with local police or the military leadership of a nation. In a book chapter subtitled, "Why the Army Needs the Church," Scottish theologian and emeritus professor at Princeton Seminary Iain Torrance writes of the importance of the church as a moral community to serve as an ethical guide for the military.[6]

Another matter along these lines is, Would it ever be appropriate for Christians within a nation to *pray* for their army? Two pacifistic early church fathers believed that Christians had a role to play here. In his *Apology*, Tertullian wrote, "We pray for life prolonged; for security to the empire; for protection to the imperial house; for brave armies."[7] Origen likewise wrote about praying "to God on behalf of those who are fighting in a righteous

---

[6]Iain Torrance, *Ethics and the Military Community*, Occasional Paper 34 (Strategic and Combat Studies Institute, 1998).

[7]Tertullian, *Apology* 30 (*ANF* 3:42), available at ccel.org/ccel/schaff/anf03.iv.iii.xxx.html.

cause, and for the king who reigns righteously, that whatever is opposed to those who act righteously may be destroyed!" He adds that "none fight better for the king than we do" as "an army of piety."[8]

Fourth, a variety of nuanced perspectives may fit within a particular "camp." While the just war position may have a fairly stable, agreed-on tradition and criteria, Myles Werntz notes that a range of nonviolence (pacifist) positions exist and that we ought not treat such a view in a flattened or monochromatic fashion. Furthermore, Christian pacifism has not been static, but over the centuries it has developed, taken different pathways, and adopted different emphases. Of course, A. J. Nolte and Meic Pearse take a more nuanced position in between the respective ends of the spectrum—just war and pacifism. But it is crucial to take such developments and nuances seriously rather than painting with too broad a brush.

Fifth, no position represented here offers a tidy solution in a messy world. Each contributor acknowledges that sin, violence, and brokenness characterize our earthly human condition. And we also live in the tension of an already-not-yet kingdom. Christ has inaugurated a new creation, but the results of the fall have not yet been eradicated. Because of this dynamic, it seems that each of the four positions comes with attendant difficulties. For example, the just warrior must consider what the soldier or police officer is to do when superiors issue orders that challenge or compromise his conscience. For the pacifist, could our basic, moral, God-given instinct to protect our innocent neighbor justify physically harming or—if necessary— even killing her attacker? Should nations with military resources attempt to protect weaker nations from despotic, tyrannical nations to save multitudes of innocent human lives? Are we culpable for not acting to rescue and protect (Prov 24:11-12)?

Sixth, the use of coercive power is inescapable even for Christians. The pacifistic Quakers undertook a "holy experiment" to establish a "peaceable kingdom" in the "Quaker state" of Pennsylvania (1680–1750)—without the use of coercive force. Eventually, because they did not want to dirty their own hands, Quaker legislators hired fighting men to keep peace and protect citizens.

---

[8]Origen of Alexandria, *Reply to Celsus* 8.73 (*ANF* 4:668), https://ccel.org/ccel/origen/against_celsus/anf04.vi.ix.viii.lxxiii.html.

The key point here—one on which our contributors agree—is that power is not inherently evil. Indeed, the appropriation of power and various forms of coercion are inescapable. Of course, Jesus himself uses coercive force to drive out moneychangers from the temple and to prevent their reentry (Mk 11:15-17). To one degree or another, coercive power is part of life: training up children, church discipline, firing someone from a job, taxation and the specter of a visit from the Internal Revenue Service, armored trucks with armed guards to protect the life savings of pacifist and nonpacifist alike, policing, imprisonment, the exercise of just war (assuming there is such a thing).[9]

THE PRAXIS OF WAR

In the above points I took note of commonalities and basic agreement about war and peace, even if the contributors' respective applications of those views may differ. However, here and in the next section I note some of the messiness that comes with these discussions.

While Werntz and Pearse point out the merits of Christian pacifism, Pearse qualifies his view by noting the merits of the just war view as well. For example, *not* killing a would-be murderer to save innocent lives strikes him as a gross, preventable injustice. But he points out—and here the Christian pacifist view makes an important point—that the actual practice of war brings with it slippery slopes and an array of potentially conscience-defiling acts. However adequate the just war position appears "on paper," numerous practical challenges arise.

Consider the following difficulties: weighing the risks and probabilities in a drone strike; responding to a commanding officer who issues orders that would be conscience-defiling; fighting against child soldiers who have themselves been kidnapped or "recruited" against their will; participating in a war whose cause the soldier considers unjust; the merits of "enhanced interrogation methods"; the limits of engaging in espionage.

On the surface, it might appear that at least some "just war" scenarios run the risk of dirtying the hands of the most virtuous and well-meaning participants. And some might charge that Nolte's argument—the dirty-hands view of Christian realism—is more pragmatic than principled. Indeed,

---

[9]See J. Daryl Charles, "Just War as Deterrence Against Terrorism—Options from Theological Ethics: A Response," *Philosophia Christi* 18, no. 1 (2016): 147-64.

critics like Keith Pavlischek have criticized Niebuhr's realism, which, even when Niebuhr's qualifications have been met concerning *jus ad bellum* (before war is waged), how war is actually waged (*jus in bellum*) is fairly open-ended. However, Nolte lays out a more qualified picture of Christian realism, offering this guiding principle: "any act of state coercion ought to be done with as little damage to the image of God as possible in those affected by it" (p. 165).

In pointing out these things, I am not saying that a just war view would be incapable of responding to the aforementioned challenges.[10] However, one may readily draw on various warfare, terrorist, or policing scenarios to reveal just how complicated and gut-wrenching human moral judgments turn out to be.

SEARCHING THE SCRIPTURES

Reading canonically. Werntz reminds us of the importance of reading the Scriptures canonically—not merely constructing a pastiche of related texts to justify a position pertaining to war and peace—or any other topic. In my estimation, more work needs to be done here. As I've wrestled with these issues over the years, it seems that the Scriptures themselves do not present a tidy and clear-cut picture concerning the use of coercive force.

Here I come back to Hawk's important work on Scripture and violence. He summarizes the canonical movement concerning divine involvement in the messiness of a violent world. In the Old Testament Scriptures, God identifies and aligns himself with the concerns of his covenant people—the nation of Israel, the instrument of blessing to bring redemption to the nations through the Messiah. In doing so, the Lord, who is a warrior (Ex 15:3), exerts his power by siding with and defending Israel against tyrants like Pharaoh—ruler of the superpower in the ancient Near East during that time—and God regularly delivers Israel in battle. But he brings judgment on disobedient Israel as well.

When we come to the Gospels, a shift takes place. God in Christ enters into the world in a different manner: not into the vortex of political and military power structures, as before, but at the margins, away from centers

---

[10]For example, Nigel Biggar, *In Defence of War* (Oxford: Oxford University Press, 2013).

of political power. But even though this is the case, the use of divine coercive force is not completely abandoned.

Jesus and coercive force. Of course, Jesus himself exerts coercive force with the moneychangers as well as any seeking to enter the temple area (Mk 11:15-17). (It will not do to say that no animals were killed in the making of this pericope.) And if Jesus had plainly banned the use of coercive or even lethal force, what were his disciples doing with "two swords" toward the end of Jesus' ministry (Lk 22:38)? Further, Jude 5 gives a clear christological affirmation of Jesus' activity earlier in Israel's history. According to our best Greek manuscripts—following the most recent Greek critical edition of the New Testament (Nestle-Aland 28)—the text reads, "*Jesus*, who saved a people out of the land of Egypt, afterward *destroyed* those who did not believe" (ESV).

Later, in Revelation 2:20-23, Jesus casts the Thyatiran false prophetess Jezebel on a bed of sickness and threatens to "strike" her followers "dead" (Rev 2:23 ESV). Even Jesus' threat to "wage war" against the Nicolaitans (Rev 2:16 NASB) is another temporal judgment, and the language parallels the later reference to the beast who will "make war" against the saints to "kill them" (Rev 11:7 ESV).

Coercive force in the book of Acts. When we come to the book of Acts, Jesus himself strikes Saul blind on the road to Damascus and he is thrown from his horse. And we see other similar smitings by the "angel of the Lord" (Acts 12:23 ESV) and the "hand of the Lord" (e.g., Acts 13:11 ESV). That very same hand of the Lord and angel of the Lord are involved in conversions to Christ (Acts 11:21) and deliverances from prison (Acts 12:7, 11). And what do we make of the apostle Paul's appeal—via his nephew—to a Roman centurion for protection from a mob poised to take his life such that he receives a full military escort out of Jerusalem to Caesarea in Acts 23? Such a scenario appears to reflect Paul's statements in Romans 13—that when the government is carrying out its God-given task as "God's servant," it will protect its citizens, lethally—by "the sword"—if necessary (Rom 13:4 ESV).

Violence in the Old Testament. The Old Testament does not attribute "violence" (*hamas*) to God or to his appointed messengers and prophets. Technically speaking, "divine violence" is an oxymoron. Indeed, Moses' commands and Joshua's military actions against the Canaanites are not termed "violent." "Violence" specifically refers to the deeds *wicked* people engage in—lawbreaking,

acts of wickedness, the oppression of the righteous.[11] So instances like the
Noahic flood, the slaying of Egypt's firstborn, or the command concerning the
Canaanites do not qualify as "violence," biblically speaking. (I have noted elsewhere that, though deaths occurred, much of this language in Israel's warfare
texts is hyperbolic.[12])

Furthermore, the New Testament does not distinguish between a "textual
God" of the fallen, violence-prone ancient Near Eastern narrator or prophet
and the "actual God" of love and forgiveness ("Note then the kindness and
the severity of God" [Rom 11:22 NASB]).[13] Rather, New Testament nar-
rators give *God* the credit for removing the Canaanites from the land and
for victory in battle (Acts 7:45; 13:19; Heb 11:29-34). As John Goldingay
observes, "If there is a contradiction between loving your enemies and being
peacemakers, on one hand, and Joshua's undertaking this task at God's
command, on the other, the New Testament does not see it."[14] We could add
that New Testament authorities considered national Israel's laws on capital
punishment as *divinely* mandated (Mt 15:1-6; Acts 3:23; Heb 2:1-3; 10:28-29;
cf. Heb 12:18-29) and that these do not qualify as "violent" acts.

As with certain warfare scenarios, so biblical texts on war and peace—
even when read canonically—may prove less tidy and more complex than
one may first have imagined. And so conversations such as the one in this
book prove to be immensely valuable and mutually informative. Each perspective can help refine and enrich the others, yielding fresh insight and
creative pathways to understanding the relationship between the use of
power and peacemaking for believers who are citizens of God's kingdom
but who must live out their mortal lives within earthly kingdoms.[15]

---

[11]Jerry Shepherd, personal correspondence, July 26, 2021. Only in Lam 2:6 do we see God's action
against the temple as *violent*.

[12]Paul Copan, *Is God a Moral Monster?* (Grand Rapids, MI: Baker Books, 2010); Copan and Matthew Flannagan, *Did God Really Command Genocide?* (Grand Rapids, MI: Baker Books, 2014);
and Copan, *Is God a Vindictive Bully? Reconciling Portrayals of God in the Old and New Testaments*
(Grand Rapids, MI: Baker Academic, 2022).

[13]For a critique of this distinction, see Paul Copan, "Greg Boyd's Misunderstandings of the Warrior
God," Gospel Coalition, January 26, 2018, www.thegospelcoalition.org/reviews/crucifixion-warrior
-god-greg-boyd/; and especially Copan, *Is God a Vindictive Bully?*

[14]John Goldingay, *Joshua, Judges & Ruth for Everyone* (Louisville, KY: Westminster John Knox,
2011), 3.

[15]Thanks to Eric Patterson, Meic Pearse, and A. J. Nolte for their input on these concluding
remarks.

Contributors

EDITOR

Paul Copan (PhD, philosophy, Marquette University) is the Pledger Family Chair of Philosophy and Ethics at Palm Beach Atlantic University (Florida) and professor in its Master of Arts in Philosophy of Religion program. He is author or editor of approximately forty books, including *An Introduction to Biblical Ethics* (IVP Academic), *Is God a Moral Monster?* (Baker Books), and *Is God a Vindictive Bully?* (Baker Academic). He has been a visiting scholar at Oxford University and president of the Evangelical Philosophical Society. He lives with his wife, Jacqueline, in West Palm Beach. His website is paulcopan.com.

CONTRIBUTORS

A. J. Nolte is assistant professor of politics and chair of the new Master of Arts in International Development program at Regent University's Robertson School of Government. In addition to his work at Regent, Nolte was appointed as canon for governmental affairs to Bishop Derek Jones in the (Anglican) Jurisdiction of the Armed Forces and Chaplaincy in February 2021, and was ordained a priest in January 2022. He lives in Virginia Beach with his wife, Tisa, daughter, Reagan, and son, Jude.

Eric Patterson (PhD) is scholar at large and past dean of the School of Government at Regent University. His government experience includes two stints at the US State Department's Bureau of Political-Military Affairs, two decades as a commander in the Air National Guard, and service as a

White House Fellow. He is the author or editor of fifteen books, including *Just American Wars: Ethical Dilemmas in U.S. Military History, Ending Wars Well, Ethics Beyond War's End*, and *Just War Thinking.*

Meic Pearse, originally from Britain, gained his MPhil and DPhil in ecclesiastical history at Oxford. He led a degree program at the London School of Theology and was for fifteen years professor of history at Houghton College in New York. His best-known book is *Why the Rest Hates the West* (InterVarsity Press, 2004). He currently lives in Osijek, Croatia.

Myles Werntz is associate professor of theology and the director of Baptist Studies at Abilene Christian University. He is the author or editor of multiple books, including *A Field Guide to Christian Nonviolence* (with David Cramer; Baker Academic), *Bodies of Peace: Nonviolence, Ecclesiology, and Witness* (Fortress), and *Sports and Violence: History, Theory, and Practice* (with Craig Hovey and John B. White; Cambridge Scholars Publishing). He teaches and writes broadly in the areas of Christian social ethics and contemporary theology. He lives in Abilene, Texas, with his family.

Name Index

Subject Index

238

Subject Index

Sri Lankan Civil War, 193
state/statecraft, 4, 24-25, 46, 48, 76, 84, 88, 94,
99, 107, 109-10, 117-18, 127, 132-37, 142-44,
155, 157-58, 163-65, 174-76, 184-85, 195, 198
Christian, 56, 107, 121, 124, 216
postwar, 6, 39
prewar, 39
"rogue," 192
St. Petersburg Declaration (1868), 201
stewardship, 15-16, 18, 34, 44, 92, 94, 148, 198
subsidiarity, 20
suffering, 39, 46, 73, 76, 85, 87-88, 151, 155,
206-7
surveillance, 67, 88, 91
enhanced, 83
targets, lawful, 16
targets, nonmilitary, 36
targets, unlawful, 16
technology, 114, 192, 195
temple (of Jerusalem), 120-21
Ten Commandments, 176
terrorism, 3, 7, 18, 67, 83-88, 96, 98, 109, 114,
157, 170-72, 192-94, 200, 204-5, 226
theft, 98
theology, 159, 213
Christian, 8, 57, 97, 109, 159
Hauerwasian, 92
of vocation, 166
of war 122, 141
torture. _See_ enhanced interrogation
techniques
totalitarianism. _See_ authoritarianism
tradition, 107, 207-8
in Christianity, 4, 7, 15, 30, 43, 55, 70, 151,
181, 198, 222
theological, 42, 44
Trinity, 36
Truth and Reconciliation Commission, 30
tyranny, 74, 101, 104, 134, 154, 215
Uniform Code of Military Justice. _See_ Lieber
Code
United Nations, 26, 39, 203

United States of America, 108, 138, 161, 170-71,
200-201
utopianism, 137
Vatican II, 71
vengeance. _See_ revenge
Vietnam, 200-201, 215
violence, 2-4, 8-9, 16, 24, 27, 29, 35-36, 42, 44,
46, 68, 70, 72-80, 82, 84-86, 90-91, 93, 96-97,
101, 103, 106, 109, 111-14, 121, 127, 150, 152,
154, 156, 158, 160, 169, 172, 174-75, 177, 179,
183-84, 189, 193, 195, 198-201, 204, 206-8,
217-18, 221, 223-24, 226-28
mob, 148
organized, 186
virtue, 6, 81, 92, 114
Christian, 43-44
civic, 54
secular, 44
vocation, 15, 18-20, 26, 32, 38, 41-44, 46, 50,
59-61, 92-93, 148-49, 166, 198
war/warfare, 2-3, 5-9, 14, 18, 21, 23, 25, 27-30,
32, 35, 38-40, 44-47, 49, 51-53, 58, 67-70,
72-77, 82-86, 88, 90-93, 99, 101, 106, 110-11,
114, 118-25, 127-28, 132, 137, 140-42, 146-47,
150-65, 172-79, 181-85, 187-92, 194-96,
198-203, 205, 208-16, 218-20, 223, 225-28
civil, 29-30, 69, 144-45
of annihilation, 62
preventing, 99
prosecution of, 25
righteous, 120, 123, 125, 135
rights of, 4
spiritual, 32
waterboarding, 4
Wesleyanism, 14, 96
Whigs, 138
witness, 70, 114
World Trade Center attacks, 90, 170, 193
World War I, 4, 13-14, 106, 191-92
World War II, 7, 13, 18, 106, 134, 147, 187, 190
worship, 75
Yugoslav Wars, 36
Zealot party, 54

Scripture Index